1968

be

N

# AFRICA IN THE MODERN WORLD

*Contributors:*

Rt. Hon. Lord Hailey

Harry R. Rudin

Derwent Whittlesey

Georges Balandier

E. Franklin Frazier

W. Arthur Lewis

David E. Apter

Kenneth Robinson

John A. Noon

Robert D. Baum

George W. Carpenter

Eduardo Mondlane

Leonard H. Samuels

Melville J. Herskovits

Vernon McKay

Hans J. Morgenthau

# Africa
# in the Modern World

*Edited by* Calvin W. Stillman

THE UNIVERSITY OF CHICAGO PRESS

CHICAGO & LONDON

THE HARRIS FOUNDATION LECTURES at the University of Chicago have been made possible through the generosity of the heirs of Norman Wait Harris and Emma Gale Harris, who donated to the University a fund to be known as "The Norman Wait Harris Memorial Foundation" on January 27, 1923. The letter of gift contains the following statement:

*The purpose of the foundation shall be the promotion of a better understanding on the part of American citizens of the other peoples of the world, thus establishing a basis for improved international relations and a more enlightened world-order. The aim shall always be to give accurate information, not to propagate opinion.*

Annual Institutes have been held at the University of Chicago since the summer of 1924. The lectures contained in this volume were delivered at the Twenty-ninth Institute, November 25–29, 1953.

*Library of Congress Catalog Card Number: 55-5147*

THE UNIVERSITY OF CHICAGO PRESS, CHICAGO & LONDON
The University of Toronto Press, Toronto 5, Canada

# PREFACE

THIS volume is a product of the Twenty-ninth Institute of the Norman Wait Harris Memorial Foundation at the University of Chicago. This Foundation has as its purpose "the promotion of a better understanding on the part of American citizens of the other peoples of the world, thus establishing a basis for improved international relations and a more enlightened world-order. The aim shall always be to give accurate information, not to propagate opinion."

The Twenty-ninth Institute was held at the University of Chicago, November 25–29, 1953. Delays in publishing the proceedings of any conference are frustrating. This has been particularly true in view of the rapidity of change in African affairs. Delay has permitted us to add extra chapters, however; and in one or two cases authors have been able to send in revised manuscripts, as will be evident from the dates mentioned in their texts. The original date line for this volume was Taboga, January, 1954.

About five years ago public interest in the United States turned to Africa. The reason is plain: after the long series of losses in Asia, Americans as members of the Western world wondered if the Asian experience might be repeated anywhere else. There was only one place left; it was the continent of Africa.

The number of scholars interested in Africa was small, indeed, when the spotlight of public curiosity called them to the center of the stage. Of the small band, fewer still were mature scholars whose interest and research in African matters extended back two or three decades. Since questions somehow inevitably elicit answers, the shortage of reliable informants was filled by a host of willing substitutes—travelers, novelists, reformers; anyone eager publishers could find. It took a year or two for the academic world to rise to this challenge and to mobilize its resources better to provide answers to current questions concerning African affairs. In the last two or three years there has been a sizable number of serious and scholarly conferences dealing with Africa. Of these, this volume is a product of one.

This volume has been edited with the objective of setting forth ideas: the insights and the working concepts of persons who have been professionally concerned with African affairs. No attempt has been made to make the volume an encyclopedia of information about Africa; the volume cannot claim to be composed of stop-press news. Other volumes are appearing planned on comparable academic standards. Of those which have recently come to hand, two form very useful complementary sources.[1]

The task of fitting Africa into four days of discussions set the framework for this presentation. Two simplifying assumptions were made: one, to concentrate upon Africa south of the Sahara, without officially excluding the Mediterranean littoral; the other, to fix attention upon problems of policy in Africa which might become matters for American concern. This can best be rephrased as the question, "What are the emerging social forces in Africa which may require the United States to make policy decisions?"

Africa is a large subject; large subjects require large frames of reference. The first group of papers in this volume are contributions from men who deal with Africa as a unit, each from his special point of vantage. First of all is the lecture presented by Lord Hailey in opening the Institute, telling of Africa as it appears to a man who has devoted his life to colonial administration on two continents. Next, Professor Rudin of Yale University presents the historical context of contemporary African problems and draws some conclusions regarding the future. For the natural environment and an understanding of the strictures it places upon human habitation, we turn to the chapter by Derwent Whittlesey, a Harvard geographer interested in Africa for many years.

1. C. Grove Haines (ed.), *Africa Today* (Baltimore: Johns Hopkins Press, 1955); William O. Brown (ed.), "Contemporary Africa: Trends and Issues," *Annals of the American Academy of Political and Social Science*, Vol. CCXCVIII (March, 1955).

# PREFACE

Still dealing with the continent as a whole, three social scientists apply the logic of their disciplines to Africa in the chapters immediately following. Georges Balandier is a sociologist of France; E. Franklin Frazier is a sociologist of the United States; and W. A. Lewis is an economist—one of the precious few qualified to write on African subjects.

In Part II each chapter deals with one type of policy problem in Africa. Each type of problem is discussed in the context of one political complex—that in which it is best to be seen. There has been no attempt to tell the story of every political unit in Africa. There has been a serious attempt to present a discussion of every major problem type which has emerged in the process of establishing and administering policy in Africa.

Reading this section of the volume should underscore the differences which exist in Africa—differences in peoples, in colonial policies, in free governments, and in political stability. In view of these differences, many an expert will deny the possibility of dealing with Africa as a whole in any context whatsoever. But Africa must be dealt with as a whole, for that is the form in which questions are asked.

Part III of the volume deals with policy regarding Africa. The first chapter is a summing-up by Melville Herskovits, based upon the nine-month tour of the continent from which he had just returned. Next, Vernon McKay writes of Africa as it poses problems for non-African powers. Finally, Hans Morgenthau points up the issues for citizens of the United States.

At the very close of the conference the dean of the American experts on Africa, Dr. Emory Ross, made this comment:

> North America, western Europe, and Africa together can still *do* something in and with Africa. We of the West need encounter with Africans no 247-meeting stalemate of rancor and fruitless talk such as we have recorded in a single negotiation with Russia.
>
> Can we never learn from long and clear experience that preventing a human explosion and fire by acts of human understanding, justice, and mutual profit is more productive than "containing" and "cold-fighting" fires after they break out? With Africans, I am convinced, no blazing fires need ever flare if the West will use its gumption now.

Planning the conference which lies behind this volume was the work of several persons. Credit for the initiative goes to

# PREFACE

Bert F. Hoselitz, executive secretary of the Norman Wait Harris Memorial Foundation. No phase of this project would have been completed without Professor Hoselitz' encouragement and co-operation. Professor Quincy Wright, chairman of the Harris Foundation Committee, provided vital encouragement.

Particular assistance in planning agenda was received from Melville Herskovits, Edwin Munger, and Mrs. Ruth C. Sloan. Executive details were handled by Elaine Mehlman, Elizabeth Sterenberg, and Beverly King.

The all-important silent partner in this entire project, the contributor of the analytical approach toward Africa upon which the presentation has been based, was my wife. She it was who first suggested our trip to Africa in 1951 and who then observed that the coming locus of trouble would be East Africa, the meeting place of social forces from South and from West Africa.

CALVIN W. STILLMAN

# TABLE OF CONTENTS

## PART I. DEFINITION

## PART II. ANALYSIS

## PART III. CONCLUSIONS

# TABLE OF CONTENTS

## APPENDIX

## INDEX

*PART I*
DEFINITION

# SPOTLIGHT ON AFRICA

### The Right Honorable Lord Hailey
*Royal Institute of International Affairs*

THE title chosen for this paper is both apposite and ar-
resting. There can be no question that Africa stands
very prominently in the limelight today. I recall, indeed, that a recent pamphlet of the Foreign Policy Association
said that "yesterday the interest of America was in Asia, but
today it is in Africa." That is perhaps only partly true so far as
Asia is concerned, for Asia obviously does not intend to be
relegated to the back shelf of dead and past interests. I am
reminded of an oriental proverb which says that, if one can
inveigle one's friend into a quagmire up to his knees, it is
one's own fault if he does not go in up to the neck; and there
are those just now in Asia who seem to have taken this simple
lesson to heart. But it is nonetheless true that Africa is now
becoming one of the principal interests of America, if one may
judge by the attention given to it by the press. I may say at
once that I do not cavil at the extent of this interest. One is
of course aware that, in dealing with the public journals, one
has often to blow a little froth off the top of the flagon before
settling down to taste the beverage within it, but that does not
mean that the beverage may not be quite sound when one gets
down to it. My purpose, as I must repeat, is not to discourage
this interest; far from it. I welcome it; but I want to take the
opportunity of considering the means of turning it to the best
account for the benefit of the people most concerned, the many
peoples of Africa.

I am bound, however, to begin with a confession. I have had
some difficulty in deciding for myself the reason why there
should have been at this particular time so wide a stirring of
interest in Africa and its affairs. African developments of the
last few years have not had the same dramatic interest for the
world as, for instance, the transfer of power from British to

Indian hands in 1947 or the surrender by Holland of its control over Indonesia. The recovery of its independence by Abyssinia and the loss by Italy of its territories in North Africa were incidents of the second World War which have been overshadowed by weighty issues created by the war in other parts of the world. The racial tension in the Union of South Africa now seems, it is true, to be reaching a new stage of acerbation, but the tension itself is not new. It is the continuation of a story which began when the Transvaal and the Orange Free State were still independent republics; and, if the discords have now become more obvious, it is because the music itself has become louder, not because its theme has changed. The Mau Mau developments in Kenya have, I admit, an unpleasant novelty, but they are restricted in scale; they have not been shared by the other tribes which comprise practically four-fifths of the African peoples of Kenya. Lastly, I doubt if there is anything so dramatic in the recent federation of the two Rhodesias and Nyasaland as to warrant a new world interest in African affairs.

There are of course those who would at once dismiss a suggestion that the explanation is to be found in any such analysis of recent events. They point to more fundamental causes. In the pamphlet of the Foreign Policy Association which I have just quoted, the authors attribute our present interest in Africa to the fact that it is now standing on the brink of entry into the world of free and independent people. Africa, they say, is the last stronghold of empire, and everyone can now see clearly the writing on the wall that foretells that empire is at an end. That is a very interesting dramatization of the position, and it is one which for obvious reasons finds an answering chord in America. It is no matter whether I wholly indorse those reasons; but I agree that none of us in Great Britain doubts that we shall see a progressive attainment of self-government in the present colonial territories of Africa. Yet it is as well that we should look at the matter with some sense of proportion. Not all Africa is today under the control of colonial powers. Egypt, Abyssinia, the Union of South Africa, and Liberia are already independent. If the former Italian territories in North Africa are not yet free from tutelage, they are at all events not subject to any one colonial power. The Anglo-Egyptian Sudan is just about to decide what use it will make of the independence accorded to it. Of the great French territories, Algeria at all events cannot be thinking of its future in terms of emancipation. The eight million Africans of Algeria may be seeking a new orientation of their relation with the million French inhabitants, but they are likely to continue to regard themselves as an integral part of France, not as a colony under its control. Be that as it may, the countries of Africa which are already independent have a total population of fifty million people.

There is another point. Does not the statement that Africa is on the brink of emancipation overestimate also the speed with which the remaining colonial peoples may expect the dawn of their political liberties? Not all the African peoples have made the social and economic advance that has secured for the Gold Coast so large a measure of self-government. Not all the colonial powers have the same philosophy of rule as Great Britain. We may use what terminology we choose to describe the British response to the upsurge among the peoples which have in the past been under its control; we may say that the result has been due to the exhibition by the British of a spirit of liberalism; we may discount it as only an unwelcome concession to expediency; we may even see in it just an acknowledgment of the loss of the strength which once built up an empire. The fact remains that, whatever the reasons may have been, the noncolonial section of the Commonwealth does today constitute a society of politically independent peoples, and there is no reason to doubt that we shall see others of the British African colonies associate themselves with it as equally free and independent members. But other powers will not necessarily follow the same lines. Some of them at all events will continue to see the future of their colonies not in the attainment of independence but in a process of integration with the metropolitan country. That of course may be viewed as a form of escape from colonial status, though I fancy that Africans will be slow to agree that this form of union will carry independence for them. There is, they will feel, a dynamic about the European which will mean his practical retention of the mastery in the integrated unit of government.

One is only independent, they may say, when one can develop one's social and political institutions in accordance with the inherent characteristics of one's own people.

However that may be, it seems clear that French policy does not envisage extending to the French dependencies a future of self-government in the sense of potential independence. It points instead to wide devolution of administrative and legislative powers, subject, however, to a continuing incorporation in the political organization of the French Union. The limits which will in that case be imposed on the powers of the dependency to deal with its own status and with its internal developments still remain to be seen. It is clear enough that there will be a liberal measure of representation in the metropolitan legislature, thereby extending the existing practice of representation, but this will be subject of course to the maintenance of a complete preponderance of purely metropolitan representation. That is not, I suggest, merely a proof of the reluctance on the part of the French to abandon the ascendancy and the powers which have been secured by a long period of colonial administration; it is rather a demonstration of the firm faith of the French in the paramount value of maintaining French institutions and French culture. The strongest opponents of the maintenance of a colonial status must recognize the genuine character of this belief; the position is almost as though a sincere Christian hesitated to contemplate the return of his flock to paganism before they had been fortified in the Christian ethic.

The Belgian ideal for the future has been less clearly formulated. At the moment all attention is concentrated on improving the standards of living of the African population and on training them to take their part in agricultural and still more in industrial life. Regarding their access to the world of industry in particular, the current policy sets no horizons; if they can make the grade, whether in the lower, the middle, or the highest ranks, by all means let them make it. The Belgians seem to me to have gone much further in this direction than either the British or the French, or, I need not say, the people of the Union of South Africa. On the other hand, so far as my own observation goes, there is little tendency to encourage African aspirations toward political self-government. Even the Belgian colonist—and there are now an increasing number of them, though they are not encouraged to engage in taking up land as settlers—is not given representation in a legislature on the British model. It is apparently held that to give him such representation would invite the native also to claim similar privileges, and this must be avoided at all costs. The Belgians, it seems to me, are a very practical people, and certainly they seem to avoid the complications of political idealism. It must be realized further that they have a type of population to deal with which still reflects in some ways its former isolation in the vast woodlands of the Congo; and the Belgians rightly concentrate at the moment on the essentials of economic and industrial advance.

In this summary survey of the political practice of the colonial powers there remains to consider the Portuguese policy. It is true to say that, from the British or Belgian point of view, the Portuguese dependencies are relatively undeveloped. I think it is true also to say that, in the past, their administration did not attract the best type of personality, though this is now showing a great improvement. But, so far as concerns the future of their dependencies, it seems clear that the current gospel is one of integration in a Portuguese union, not of self-government of the British type; I mean the type of self-government that points to the possibility of independence. If at this stage the Portuguese have any formulated policy, it is in the avoidance of a color bar by the creation of a culture bar. All persons of whatever racial origin who reach a certain standard of education and manner of living are to be treated as equal in political and juridical status. That appears to me to be a very reasonable doctrine as a means of determining the access of a primitive people to participation in the administrative or political organization of their country; and it will hold good so long as the standard of culture to be attained is fixed on fair grounds and is honorably maintained in practice. One does not need to look very far around in order to realize that a provision of this kind, designed to define access to the exercise of political rights, can be grievously abused by those who for any reason seek to refuse the right to exercise these privileges.

In saying all this, I do not wish to suggest that we are not

[ 7 ]

witnessing a material change in the outlook of colonial powers on the future of their African colonies. That we are doing so is obvious. But it seems to me that this change is in itself only the reaction to what is a fact of more general significance, namely, that the African himself has for the first time begun to stand forth as a personality in the world. Up to a few years ago, as I see it, we were looking on a drama in which all the speaking parts were taken by European powers. Today the African has come in person onto the stage, and he not only has a speaking part but takes an effective share in the action of the play. Let me take a few instances which will illustrate this development. In the Union of South Africa it is no doubt the Indian who has taken the lead in the appeal to the United Nations to support his demand for political rights. But there are less than a half-million Indians in the Union, as compared with two and three-quarter million Europeans and seven and three-quarter million Bantu. It is not the Indian protest that has impelled the present government of the Union to take its recent crucial action in regard to racial segregation. It is the realization of the modern development of manufacturing industry in the Union and of the general advance in the standard of living of the two and a half million Africans who form part of the white economy that has created a situation where the African must be relegated once for all into the political background if he is not to acquire a position from which he can bargain with the white population for his political and social rights.

It is, again, the new capacity for combined action among the Africans that has constrained the Europeans of the Rhodesias to accept what they claim to be (and what we in Great Britain hope will prove to be) a working partnership with Africans in the control of affairs in the new Central African Federation. Once more, it is the emergence of an African middle class in the Gold Coast, educated, politically minded, and relatively well to do, that has resulted in securing for this territory an advanced measure of self-rule under a parliamentary form of government. I will only take one more example where so many are available: For more years than most of us can remember, the position of Egypt in regard to the Suez Canal has been viewed as a matter for international debate and decision. Who would have imagined only a few years ago that, at the moment when the powers were discussing the road along which Egypt should be guided, an Egyptian would take charge and insist on pursuing his own course, regardless of results? Let us make no doubt of the significance of those facts. They show the African in a new role of self-assertion.

All this has at times been described as the outcome of that natural and inescapable phenomenon, the spirit of nationalism. But this explanation only goes part of the way. "Nationalism" seems hardly the word to apply to the impulse which inspires the Africans of those countries in which the European, though in a minority, may nevertheless occupy at present a predominant part. If a country of this class is to gain an independent status, the African might well prefer to see this delayed until he is better equipped to compete with the European in the political field. Not only is this so, but there can be little reality of national consciousness among the collection of tribal communities which the accident of history has in so many cases joined together under a single government and where the only common tie is the unity of alien control. The position can perhaps be better described in terms of the desire of the African to demonstrate his own individuality against the European. His individuality is so different from that of the European that he is ready to claim not only freedom of European control but the right to adopt in the molding of his own future only those European institutions which may suit his own circumstances. Those who have a close working knowledge of Africa can justly object that the outlook I am attributing to the African cannot properly be said to be that of the great mass of uneducated and often primitive people who comprise the major part of the population. That is quite true. But Africa is now producing, even in the most unlikely quarters, men who seem to be able to exert leadership among the people. These may differ widely from the traditional leaders, the chiefs, the titled councilors, the tribal headmen of the past; but, as more than one instance has shown, they are able to acquire a popular following which enables them to put the older traditional authorities on one side. That is a process which is bound to grow. And Asia affords us many proofs, as some of us have seen with our own eyes, which reveal the dynamic command which can be acquired by these new leaders in the older communities of the world.

It is in considerations such as these that I find the real ground for the interest which we are bound to feel in Africa today. I do not forget that there are other potent grounds, though of a different order. In a world in which the free peoples are, alas, still obliged to devote so much of their resources to preparing their defense against possible aggression, it is important to note the extent of the contribution Africa can make to the cause of those who are defending liberty and world order. That contribution consists not only in the provision of strategic bases, as, for example, the ports and air bases on the coasts of North Africa, but in the provision of strategic materials. The list is well known: one-fifth of the world's copper and tin, nearly one-fourth of the manganese, more than one-half of the gold, almost all the industrial diamonds, and a considerable part of the uranium. But I need not prolong the list, nor need I dilate on the potential value of the market which might be provided by an Africa in which a substantial improvement in the standards of living would be followed by a demand for the more highly industrialized products of the world.

These points arise in a field of action which is already well charted, and I do not doubt that the major interests concerned, whether they be capital seeking investment or governments looking for material for their defense effort, are fully conscious of the possibilities which Africa presents. Let me therefore return to matters which, if they are less ponderable, should certainly not be of less concern here. I prefer to think that for the reader the basic interest in Africa lies today in the obligations which have been created for us by the developments which I have just been discussing. If there was in the past a time when the civilized world could be content to take only a spectator's interest in a drama such as that which is now being unfolded in Africa, that time no longer exists. I do not say that the circumstances demand a great moral crusade of the scale of that which inspired the movement for the emancipation of slaves in the early years of the last century—the first of the great ethical movements as distinguished from the great religious movements in the history of the world. Further, I doubt whether the circumstances demand any organized effort to intervene in the course of developments in Africa. But I suggest that the civilized world has a definite obligation in two directions—one arising in the field of knowledge and of study; the other, in a field which demands action of a more direct kind.

Take the first of these obligations. I have suggested that the African, as he gains in political stature, will seek to mold his social and political institutions on lines which will not be purely European but which will reflect the influence of the inherent characteristics of his own people. If so, it seems incumbent on us to acquaint ourselves with so much of the background of African life as will enable us to comprehend the character of the adjustments which he will have to make. I do not suggest that we must all become anthropologists, though anthropology can provide a valuable academic discipline. But there are things which we should comprehend, such as the institutions in which he has expressed his social life, the incentives which regulate his economic activity, and the codes which control his social conduct, for it is only by this knowledge that we can appreciate the figure which he will make as a citizen of the new world into which he is now moving. Here, I suggest, is the justification for those studies of African life on which the American universities are now embarking with the assistance of the great foundations which have already done so much for the education of the American in world affairs.

Next let me take the obligations which arise not in the field of study and comprehension but in that of co-operative action. I have myself frequently ventured to advance the proposition that, if we can adequately improve the standard of living of any backward people, we need not trouble overmuch to seek to arrange their political future, for they will see to that for themselves. If that appears to be an overconfident or an undue simplification, let us remember that this is precisely what has already happened in India; and the principle will, I myself believe, hold good in time for Africa. There was a period when I, like some others, felt obliged to remind the more doctrinaire students of British colonial policy that they had for too long devoted their attention to the political development of the African peoples instead of concentrating on their more urgent economic needs. I myself incurred some disfavor among my more politically minded friends by suggesting that a time might come when our colonial peoples would complain that, when they had asked for bread, we had merely given them a vote. Today I think that the balance has been to some extent readjusted. On every side I see proof that greater attention is now being paid to schemes of material and educational development which should result in raising the general standard of living. I hope that we may find time here to discuss the five-year or ten-year projects of development that are being financed by most of the colonial powers, as, for instance, the very considerable colonial development and welfare funds provided by Great Britain, the large provision made by France through the funds known appropriately enough by the name of FIDES, or the sums placed at the disposal of the Belgian Congo by the Belgian government out of the accumulated credits due from the Allies for supplies bought from the colony during the war. Above all, I hope that we shall find occasion to note the liberality with which America has, in various ways and through different international agencies, contributed so much technical and financial assistance in this work.

I do not suggest that the standard of living among the inhabitants of Africa is the lowest in the world. Far from it. There are, as all who have seen the facts at firsthand are well aware, parts of Asia where the standard of living is very much lower and where far less is being done for the economic or educational advancement of the people. That may be true also of parts of South America, but of this I cannot speak with firsthand knowledge. There can be no question at all that a very great deal has been done during the last half-century to lay in Africa the foundation for an improvement in the standards of living of its population, as, for example, in the introduction of law and order, the diffusion of the more elementary type of education, or the means of controlling the more devastating of the epidemic diseases. But the measure of what has been done only reveals the immensity of the task that still remains. The Western world is now recognizing its obligation to give assistance to all backward and underdeveloped peoples. Its reasons may not always be altruistic, and there may at least be that element of self-interest which comes from the recognition that lasting peace can be found only in a more balanced world—a world which has gone some way to level up the vast discrepancies in the standard of life of its various peoples. But history has given us a very special obligation toward Africa, and I pray that, when in some far future the scroll of the world's story is unrolled, it will bear witness that we in our generation have done our best to make Africa forget the wrongs done to it by our forefathers.

# THE HISTORY OF EUROPEAN RELATIONS
## WITH AFRICA

HARRY R. RUDIN
*Yale University*

THE significance of African problems for Europeans can be seen only in the perspective of a long history—a history during which African affairs have been inseparably connected with developments in other parts of the world. It may appear that I am making a difficult problem more difficult by this approach, but through such an approach we can arrive at that measure of understanding of our present-day relations with Africa which is essential if intelligence and good will are to fulfil their vocation in our time. Europe's relations with Africa are only a part of Europe's relations with other lands beyond the seas. There is an interdependence between these relations that should not be overlooked, because the ebb and flow of European interests in other parts of the world are intimately connected with the ebb and flow of European interests in Africa. From this relationship we shall obtain a better understanding of Europe and Africa than can be had from any study, however detailed, of the direct relations that exist between colonies and metropolitan powers in Europe.

It was the large interest of Europeans in the Far East five centuries ago that led to the voyages that discovered North and South America and made people aware of Africa. In the belief that distant Cathay was of greater importance than the New World they had discovered in the West, explorers continued their quest for a northwest or a northeast passage that would bring to Europe the treasures of the East. In the same way explorers felt themselves obstructed by the continent of Africa lying athwart a convenient route to the Far East. They probed their cautious way along the impenetrable coast in search of the opening that would offer a quick and easy passage to the fabulous lands of the Orient. Getting around Africa was more impor-

tant than the establishment of factories for business on its un-
friendly coasts. And it was not until near the end of the fif-
teenth century that the Cape was rounded and a route was found
for bringing rich cargoes of silk, tea, and spices from the East
to the markets of Europe. It was not really until the seventeenth century that Europeans showed any serious interest in
establishing themselves on the African coasts for the wealth
that Africa possessed. The attraction of the Orient was too
dazzling to permit that sooner. When the Dutch established
themselves in 1652 at the Cape of Good Hope, it was for the
purpose of having the opportunity to get fresh water and vegetables for the men who would otherwise suffer from scurvy on
the long east-bound voyages.

While Africa thus served travelers to the East by offering
them fresh food and opportunities for rest, Africa was also of
service to the Europeans who had extensive sugar and tobacco
plantations in the New World. The need of cheap labor for
American plantations was great; meeting the need became a
rich business in which Europeans vied with one another in a
warm and profitable rivalry. The slave trade got its real start
in the sixteenth century and became a major reason for the establishment of factories by Europeans from many countries
along the west coast of Africa in the seventeenth century. The
trade paid off. From its returns we are told that Liverpool grew
from village into city and that England obtained much of the
capital that proved to be of such advantage during the industrial revolution. The supply of cheap African labor was a boon
to the businessmen of the age of mercantilism in their efforts to
develop the wealth of their American plantation colonies at as
little cost as possible. The trade went on for two and a half centuries, during which it has been estimated that fifteen million
slaves were taken from West Africa by the Christians of Europe.
Moslems engaged in a similar traffic on the east coast.

For Englishmen this trade in human beings came to an end
in 1807, when humanitarianism triumphed over it after a long
and difficult struggle. There is some poetic justice in the fact
that Englishmen, who had made so great a business out of the
trade, should take the lead in its abolition and in persuading

other European countries to do the same in the course of the nineteenth century. In 1834 Englishmen abolished the very institution of slavery in the Empire, setting thereby an example of a relatively peaceful solution that their kinsmen in the United States were not able to follow.

This extinction of slavery and of the slave trade removed what had been Europe's greatest economic interest in Africa. By comparison, other trade was unimportant. The end of slavery was accompanied by something like a revival of interest in Africa as a base of operations for getting at the wealth of the Far East. This renewal of interest can be seen in the efforts of Napoleon to conquer Egypt and to dig a canal at Suez in order to get at the wealth of India, which the French had lost to the English in 1763. This French move had its counterpart in Britain's permanent conquest of South Africa, which was taken from the Dutch along with Ceylon in 1814–15 to assure English control of a water route to the Far East, particularly to India, where Englishmen were deeply involved in the military persuasion of Indians to accept British control.

French ambitions in Egypt were not checked by Napoleon's defeat. In the 1830's, while the conquest of Algeria was taking place in the western Mediterannean, the French gave their support to Mehemet Ali's plans to free Egypt from Turkish rule and to establish a large empire in the Near East. The English failed to block the French conquest of Algeria; but they succeeded in thwarting the ambitions of Mehemet Ali in Syria and blasted whatever hopes the French had entertained in his regard. French interest in Egypt and in that route to the Far East remained, however, and assumed tangible form in 1855, when the concession for the Suez Canal was obtained. Despite opposition from England, the canal was completed and opened to traffic in 1869. Disraeli's purchase of canal shares from the bankrupt khedive in 1875, the British occupation of Egypt in 1882, and the French recognition in 1904 of special British rights in Egypt removed the century-old fears that England had of the French in this part of the world.

European interest in Africa was greatly intensified as a result of the industrial revolution. Led by England, European countries became industrialized and experienced what must be regarded as the most far-reaching revolution in Europe's history. This change was essentially a decision to use power and machinery for the manufacture of articles that were to be traded for the food and the resources required by the appetites of men and machines. Farming was virtually abandoned as the number of acres devoted to the production of grains declined. People left the countryside for the factories, where their rapidly growing numbers expanded villages into towns and cities. With their machines men turned out vast quantities of manufactured articles which were exported in ever increasing amounts to pay for the food and raw materials being imported in larger amounts. Lands overseas expanded the production of food and of raw materials to pay for rising imports of manufactured goods. Thus, as markets and sources of supply were found in distant parts of the world, the national economies of Europe became internationalized.

The industrial revolution and the commercial expansion that accompanied it gave Europe the greatest economic security it had ever had. The gloomy predictions of Malthus that had greeted the opening of the nineteenth century were fortunately to be unfulfilled. On the contrary, Europe's population doubled in the century at the same time that the per capita consumption of wheat, cotton, iron, wool, sugar, etc., mounted. The famines that had occurred about every ten years for several centuries of European history now virtually disappeared. So natural was the flow of manufactured articles out of Europe and of food into Europe that governments found it possible to abandon the mercantilist regulations that had operated for many generations and gave men a taste of that economic freedom which Adam Smith had argued for in his *Wealth of Nations*.

This period of economic security became the greatest era of emancipation in European history by making possible the realization of dreams men had thought about earlier. This was when slaves and serfs were set free, when the minds of men were liberated from ignorance by mass education, when science and philosophy struck their mightiest blows at superstition, and when man entertained his boldest thoughts of himself and of his

universe. This was the period when legal tolerance was granted
to Jew and to Catholic; this was the period when the extension
of the franchise occurred on a scale to permit our saying that
democracy had come to Europe. Here we have the greatest
spiritual achievements of Europe's history, those freedoms
whose full return is today every intelligent man's desire.

We need to understand how these things came to be. The
great sense of economic security that existed in Europe is certainly to be ascribed to the successfully operating international
economic order that had come into being. Tariffs and other obstacles to trade declined and thus made the resources of the
world available to the peoples of Europe and the manufactured
goods of Europe available to peoples throughout the world.
Where political oppression or economic distress existed in
Europe—and there were such places—it was possible for people
to migrate, and in large numbers, to those areas of the world
which needed cheap labor. The United States was just beginning to exploit a continent's undeveloped resources and needed
help. The result was that thirty-six million people left Europe
for the United States between 1820 and 1930. The total migration from Europe in that period amounted to sixty-six million,
the largest mass movement of peoples in history. Never had the
world seen such a time as this, when national borders were so
little obstructive of the free movement of goods and of peoples.
This was the age when men traveled most freely, perhaps the
age of most successful internationalism. This was a time when
the world had an internationalism without the organization; in
our day we have the organizations without the internationalism.

There was a short period in the middle of the nineteenth century when it was believed that colonies cost so much as to justi-
fy their abandonment. Englishmen who had rid themselves of
the mercantilist state with its complex regulations believed that
colonies could be set free without loss to the mother-country,
since the principle of self-interest would bind former colonies by
natural commercial bonds to England. The dominant industrial power without any serious competitor, England could afford to think in these terms and to let policies be influenced by
them. Similar thoughts about the removal of restrictions on

trade and of the unjustifiable costs of colonies affected the commercial and colonial thinking of other European countries also.

In his speculations about industrialism and the factory system, Karl Marx had predicted the coming of a time when factories would produce more goods than could be consumed. His solution for such a crisis was that the state establish control over the instruments of production and of distribution. A crisis did come in the 1870's, by which time Englishmen had lost their monopoly of the industrial technique and found themselves in serious competition with countries on the continent of Europe. The glut of goods that could find no market was very serious. To protect themselves from the dumping of goods from abroad in their domestic markets, countries on the Continent began to adopt tariff measures. While the home market was thus protected, the problem of marketing surplus goods still remained. That problem was not to be solved by state control of the means of production and distribution but rather by a further expansion of markets overseas. Improvements in transportation and in communication contributed greatly to this expansion.

It was during this economic crisis in the 1870's and 1880's that men turned their thoughts to Africa as well as to other parts of the world. Trade had been increasing along the coasts of Africa, and competition had become more intense as more Europeans crowded into the ports to get rid of surplus goods. To protect the overseas market, Europeans found it necessary to proclaim their occupation of territories in Africa and elsewhere.

Fortunately for those with this economic problem to solve, Africa was becoming known to the peoples of Europe through the exploring activities of a large number of venturesome men who had crossed Africa from east and west during the preceding generation or two. It is difficult for us to realize today that men a hundred years ago did not know about the snows of Kilimanjaro, about Victoria Falls, or about the sources of the Nile and of the Congo. Today Kilimanjaro is a backdrop for romance-laden Hollywood films, and "western" pictures are finding a rival in those of African background. Accumulating knowledge of the interior of Africa in the sixties and seventies inclined people to believe that part of a solution for the problem of surplus goods might be found here. There was a rush to stake out claims in Africa, with the result that a great continent was partitioned within the space of a decade. Native chiefs were given their first and most costly lessons in penmanship when they were taught to affix their shaky $X$'s to treaties which, as they later found out, deprived them of much of their lands and resources. To be sure, the knowledge of the interior was not detailed enough to permit the fixing of final borders among the various claims. Boundaries had to be written in the heavens by means of latitude and longitude, until earth-bound men could discover the landmarks normally employed for such purposes.

Africa became a part of that broad internationalization of the European economy which was the base of much of Europe's prosperity and much also of Europe's finest culture. A similar expansion took place into other parts of the world. While this territorial expansion of Europe overseas is more dramatic than the commercial expansion, it should not be forgotten that a simultaneously growing commerce contributed more to the economic security of Europe than did the seizure of territories. And it is worth pointing out in this connection that the successful quest for markets postponed, for over a generation or more, the adoption of the policies that Marx had recommended for the problem of overproduction. It is of interest that Marxist parties attacked this overseas expansion; possibly, I would suggest, because they saw dimly in it an obstacle delaying the realization of their program.

Although on the face of it the rivalry of big European powers in overseas areas was frequent and intense, it should be noted that such rivalry did not lead to open war, even though war appeared very near now and then. In a very real sense, this imperialist rivalry made for peace in Europe. I am not saying that the building of empires made for peace in those regions where European states extended their control. Europeans did not come into Africa for the sole purpose of helping Africans. Those who came in were primarily interested in African markets and resources; to that end wars were fought when hostile Africans barred the way and had to be subdued. Forced labor was another unhappy result, a practice now strongly condemned although not altogether abandoned. Christian imperialism was not all evil either, and that fact should be obvious to anybody who knows what the conditions were in Africa before the white man came. It is contrary to fact to regard Africa as a paradise into which the white man brought evil as a serpent in the guise of trader or missionary. Europeans brought both good and evil, to remind one of the first short speech in English given by that German-speaking Hanoverian, King George I, when he sought to comfort anxious Englishmen: "I haf come for your goots."

When I say that imperialism in Africa and elsewhere made for peace in Europe, I have in mind the fact that European governments found it possible to establish friendly relations with one another for short periods on the basis of exchanging territory or of recognizing claims to territory that belonged to unconsidered third and innocent parties in Africa and in Asia. I have in mind the very large number of agreements made by European powers between 1880 and 1915—agreements that relaxed tensions and established friendships: the Anglo-Japanese Alliance of 1902–5, which sacrificed Korea; the Anglo-French Entente of 1904, which placed Egypt and Morocco eventually under Great Britain and France, respectively; the Russian Entente of 1907 with England in terms that disregarded the interests of Persia; and the many agreements of Italy with other powers in Europe for the purpose of enabling Italy to acquire possession of territory in North Africa. Many other agreements could be mentioned, for the list is a long one. No one can question the fact that the disappearance of unoccupied lands or of loosely held lands in our day has rendered more difficult the efforts of statesmen to maintain friendly relations between their countries, although the Hoare-Laval Pact of 1935, the Munich Accord of 1938, and the Yalta Agreement of 1945 indicate that the practice has not been wholly discarded in recent times.

What needs stressing in this perspective account of a phase of European history is that the territorial and commercial expansion of Europe overseas enabled Europeans to keep the peace for one generation longer, to enjoy a longer prosperity, to maintain their democratic institutions, and to have a growing and fairly well-satisfied population in their expanding cities. The Marxist contention that the only beneficiaries of this expansion were a small group of capitalists is not true, for all classes of Europe benefited. The prosperity and the liberties of Europe rested heavily on this broad international economic base, of which Africa was a significant part. It is important to realize that Europe in the nineteenth century found that the solution of its major problems lay outside Europe, far beyond its borders; that this kind of economic internationalism has done for Europe more than has been accomplished by any other ism. What happens when countries are forced to find solutions for their major problems within narrow national borders and inadequate resources is painfully clear in what has happened to Europe since the first World War. The successfully operating internationalism of the nineteenth century made democracy possible; the economic nationalism of Europe since 1920 has made totalitarianism a necessity.

Since this internationalism before 1914 was not embodied in abiding international institutions that would insure its continuation, it had a serious weakness. This dependence of European countries—their large urban populations, their prosperity, their security, even their democratic institutions—on faraway places made them particularly vulnerable. They were made aware of this fact in the 1890's, when the writings of an American naval officer, Captain A. T. Mahan, stressed the critical importance of naval power in history. European statesmen now were made to realize how much their lands depended upon these tenuous lifelines of empire that stretched over vast marine distances. Hence the rapid growth of navies, the changing size of which may be taken as a measure of the deepening sense of dependence on commerce and empire for the prosperity and security European countries enjoyed. Only because Germany was dependent upon its trade and its colonies was it possible for the naval blockade of the first World War to bring Germans to their knees in defeat and surrender. This evidence of the fateful dependence of large populations upon lands far outside their borders was recognized by the League of Nations Covenant, where

Article XVI provided for the imposition of economic sanctions against any member of the League resorting to war contrary to its covenanted obligations. This article may well be regarded as a kind of charter for the international economic anarchy that has prevailed in the world since 1920, because it has prevented the restoration of that internationalism that had proved so successful prior to 1914. Contrary to popular impression, economic internationalism died with the first World War; it might be nearer the truth to say that the war hastened its death in view of prewar signs of ill economic health. It is well to recall that the greatest restrictions of modern times on the free movement of goods and of peoples have come in an era that regarded itself as international merely because it had an organization like the League of Nations. It is not far wide of truth to say that the League's buildings at Geneva were a tomb of a dead internationalism rather than the sheltering home of a living one.

Let us see what happened since 1920. For generations European commerce had not faced such overwhelming difficulties. By becoming involved in two world wars in our century, the great powers of Europe, that had traded their manufactured articles for the food and raw materials produced elsewhere in the world, broke that vital connection by rendering themselves incapable of fulfilling ordinary commercial contracts. This disruption of trade was hard on those who had come to rely upon European states for certain manufactured goods; as a result of two wars' proving the inadvisability of depending upon Europe, many countries decided either to produce their own manufactures or to turn to producers more dependable than the warring Europeans. As a consequence, Europe has found it nearly impossible to re-establish those lifelines of trade that brought in essential food and other materials. In addition, the imposition of many kinds of trade and currency restrictions, the rising tariffs and quota systems, the lack of credit, the inflationary trends—all these have co-operated to make it difficult for Europe to get the supplies that kept its growing populations at the height of prosperity in the nineteenth century. If not famine, at least want has returned to Europe.

I stated above that it had been possible for peoples in Europe to move to other lands if political or economic conditions made life intolerable at home, and that the United States cared for thirty-six million people during the last century. In our present "international" era the New World has ceased to be the asylum it had been for three centuries for those dissatisfied with their lot in Europe. Unable to solve their problems at home and unable to move large masses of surplus population into areas that once begged for cheap labor, discontented people must now remain at home. There their grievances become the nuclei of new political programs or make them susceptible to the persuasions of Communist or other totalitarian solutions. The effects of all this have been seen in the growth of Nazi, Fascist, and Communist ideologies and in the armed political parties organized to seize power.

While trade was languishing and while unemployed peoples could not migrate, there took place a further contraction of the international economic base, viewed territorially. Dependent areas have sought and have obtained greater independence of ruling European states. Extra-territorial rights have disappeared in many parts of the world; China has rid itself of the so-called "unequal treaties." Europeans have been ousted or have moved out of some parts of the world—Indonesia, India, Burma, Ceylon. The freedom these peoples have won is now the goal sought by the peoples of Indochina and of Malaya. In the race struggles of South Africa, in the violences of the Mau Mau in Kenya, in the demands of Africans in the Gold Coast and in Nigeria, in Tunis and Morocco, one can see the actual or threatened continued contraction of colonial empires. Even foreign capital is feared because it may mean foreign control. The states that have only recently achieved their independence are almost daily challenging the powers of the West to grant similar independence to native populations in various parts of Africa.

This diminution of the economic base of European life comes at a time when Europeans find themselves in greater need than ever of the colonies that remain in their control. Since masses of people cannot migrate as they did in the nineteenth century, whites have been going in larger numbers to Africa, but not, be it said, in a number approaching that of migrants to North and

South America before 1914. Portugal, no longer finding Brazil a haven for surplus population, has a plan for settling five hundred thousand people over a period of fifteen years in its African overseas territories. When one bears in mind that the greatest tension between Africans and Europeans exists where the latter settle in large numbers, it is very likely that serious trouble may develop in those parts of Africa where Portuguese settlers make their future homes. While supplying homes for more white immigrants during the past generation, Africa is finding it more difficult to provide adequate lands for its own people because of the increase in population and because of the decrease of suitable land through soil erosion and exhaustion.

Recent efforts to produce food in Africa indicate another aspect of Europe's interest in African lands. I refer to the hopes that rose a few years ago when it seemed likely that new drugs had eliminated sleeping sickness and made it possible for the British to raise cattle in Africa and thus to obtain the meat no longer available in Argentina because of the shortage of dollars. One might also refer to the unsuccessful British experiment with raising chickens in West Africa. The groundnut scheme in East Africa was an attempt to produce needed vegetable oils within the sterling area.

Scientific invention and the new weapons of war have still further increased the dependence of Western countries upon Africa. The demand for some critical minerals seems incapable of being satisfied. Africa is becoming more and more the land where they are being sought, other areas having become unavailable because of nationalism and its hope for complete independence.

This rising demand for minerals has a significance beyond that held by palm oil, ivory, precious woods, and other natural products that attracted traders into Africa in the late nineteenth century. Uranium is required in the manufacture of atomic weapons, and Africa, so far as one can tell who is not privy to military secrets, is the greatest source of this indispensable element. Modern industry requires alloys for the hardening of steel. When Russia a few years ago placed a ban on the export of chrome and manganese, the United States turned, among other places, to Africa for the solution of a suddenly difficult problem. For the manufacture of heat-resistant steels required in jet planes, columbium and cobalt are essential, and here also the West must turn to Africa. The United States no longer possesses adequate reserves of copper and of lead and has had to turn to Africa for the supplementary quantities required. The depletion of high-grade iron-ore reserves in the United States during the second World War has made it necessary for our country to turn to Liberia for iron ore. Vanadium and bauxite are other essential minerals. The location of these many critical minerals in African colonies enables the metropolitan powers to use them directly for their own immediate needs or to turn them into much-needed dollars by special arrangements with the United States, where high prices are offered for them.

As one analyzes these simple facts, it becomes clear that Africa in a variety of ways has become an essential prop in the security system of the West, which has already established its main strategic line across North Africa, from Casablanca to Suez—a line that must be held if Europe should be overrun by the Communist armies of Russia.

Adding up the various ways in which Africa is of help to the West in the solution of economic and security problems, one quickly sees that the loss of Africa would be a prime calamity. Africa is not to be envied because its peoples' labor, land, and resources are so much needed. The study of history shows more than once that those people who are essential to another people's security are exposed to many dangers. A nation deeply concerned about its own security is not inclined to be sensitive toward the need of others for security. That Western security rests today upon a definite disruption and dislocation of African life does not appear to cause much concern. There is no telling to what lengths a nation's demand for security will drive it. We have seen what Italy did to Ethiopia in the 1930's in the effort to solve serious economic problems that could not be solved within Italy's narrow borders; and we have also seen Hitler's effort to acquire living space at the expense of peoples in Europe. Japan's efforts to solve its difficult problems led to the attempt to establish a large empire in Asia. Whereas in the nineteenth century it was possible for a time through trade and migration to solve internal problems, that possibility has vanished with the intense nationalistic policies that have become typical of an age which thinks of itself as international. Since it is a fact that the solution of most serious domestic problems has to be found beyond the borders of a particular state, the question for the twentieth century is whether the solution is to come in the relatively peaceful manner of the nineteenth century or in the aggressive wars countries are forced to wage beyond their borders.

Just as our need has increased for what Africa can do for our economic and military security, Africans very naturally become alarmed, and with some measure of right, because they sense that our security depends in part upon their insecurity. We have recognized the existence of these fears by assurances stated and restated—in the Fourteen Points, in the League of Nations Covenant and in the League's arrangements for mandates, in the Atlantic Charter, and, finally, in the provisions of the United Nations Charter. The latter are far-reaching, not only with regard to trust territories, but particularly with regard to non-self-governing territories. Article 73 of the Charter deserves rereading:

Members of the United Nations which have or assume responsibilities for the administration of territories whose peoples have not yet attained a full measure of self-government recognize the principle that the interests of the inhabitants of these territories are paramount, and accept as a sacred trust the obligation to promote to the utmost, within the system of international peace and security established by the present Charter, the well-being of the inhabitants of these territories, and, to this end:

*a.* to ensure, with due respect for the culture of the peoples concerned, their political, economic, social, and educational advancement, their just treatment, and their protection against abuses;

*b.* to develop self-government, to take due account of the political aspirations of the peoples, and to assist them in the progressive development of their free political institutions, according to the particular circumstances of each territory and its peoples and their varying stages of advancement;

*c.* to further international peace and security;

*d.* to promote constructive measures of development, to encourage research, and to cooperate with one another and, when and where appropriate, with specialized international bodies with a view to the practical achievement of the social, economic, and scientific purposes set forth in this Article; and

*e.* to transmit regularly to the Secretary-General for information purposes, subject to such limitation as security and constitutional considerations may require, statistical and other information of a technical nature relating to economic, social, and educational conditions in the territories for which they are respectively responsible other than those territories to which Chapters XII [International Trusteeship System] and XIII [The Trusteeship Council] apply.

These promises have not been kept, for the signers of the Charter have made it generally clear that their own interests are paramount rather than those of the Africans. A strict adherence to the principle that there should be no intervention in the internal affairs of other countries has prevented action by the United Nations in behalf of Africans who feel that their interests have been disregarded. That the North Atlantic Treaty Organization could place Tunisia and Morocco within the defense perimeter of the Atlantic Alliance without consulting the peoples of those two areas is regarded, to put it mildly, as serious inattention to their interests. Perhaps the most alarming development has been the United Nations creation of the independent state of Israel, an act which, in effect, told eight hundred and fifty thousand Arabs to make room in their country for persecuted Europeans whom no Western power desired to assist by the offer of its own territory for asylum. There is no telling when natives in Africa or elsewhere may be similarly commanded to yield their land to other Europeans.

Thus it happens that people with grievances adopt measures of violence to solve their problems, convinced that the United Nations is unwilling or unable to act in their behalf. It has been interesting to compare, so far as material has been made available, the activities of the Mau Mau in Kenya with the underground activities of the Serbs in Austria-Hungary and in the Balkans prior to 1914. These nationalists, who sought the union of all Serbs in one territory, had their very secret society of which the members pledged themselves in somber quasi-religious ceremony to carry out any orders issuing from above, no matter how desperate or brutal they were. Each oath-taking member agreed to forfeit his own life if he failed, consciously or unconsciously, to carry out the solemn obligations of his vows. There are other such secret societies of desperate men in European history, enough to indicate that the Mau Mau pattern is no historical novelty.

Africans who feel themselves aggrieved or threatened have recourse to Russia for help, not because they like communism but rather because they feel an affinity for the enemy of their enemy. Communist Russia is ready to extend a helping hand because of the conviction that imperialism is capitalism's last bulwark, the elimination of which will result in the rescue of the victims of capitalist exploitation and in the collapse of the West. Russia has made clear its interest in liberating all exploited peoples from the control of the West. Without needing any Communist ideology to support their policies, the countries of the West have made it clear in two world wars in our time that Germany and Italy had first to be defeated and driven out of Africa before their misrule could be brought to an end. In like fashion, Japan was deprived of its empire. All this shows that the wars of the twentieth century involve empires in a very direct way. The West has already made it clear that one of its aims is the liberation of the satellite states and other peoples from Communist oppression. The future of Africa is at stake in the current struggle between East and West. One shudders to think what may happen to the West if we are found wanting and eventually divert the affections of the Africans to Russia, thus depriving ourselves of labor and resources that we sorely need.

So much is Africa involved in the present ideological conflict that it is not hard to see that the struggle between East and West could finally be settled in Africa. At stake for the West is far more than the profits of a favored few, for upon the friendship and support of Africans depend the prosperity, the security, and even the democratic institutions of the West. Today Africa carries much of the burden that was borne by the larger colonial world in the nineteenth century. Metropolitan European powers and the United States must realize now that the Africans are desperately needed on our side and that everything should be done to give them a vested interest in our victory over Russia. The hope must be held out to them that the promises of the Atlantic Charter and of the United Nations Charter are binding upon us and that we have every intention of living up to them. I do not advocate the immediate granting of independence. Such a policy is full of danger, especially when one recalls that the countries liberated in eastern Europe at the end of the first World War have lost the independence they won because international economic policies rendered impossible the maintenance of an independent existence. Broad economic arrangements like those that operated so successfully in the latter part of the nineteenth century are needed if independent countries are to have the international base on which freedom can rest.

At a critical time like this in the world's affairs one principle must guide our thinking and inspire our policies. History has underscored the principle often. It is this: If, for any reason whatsoever, men of intelligence and good will decide that a problem cannot be solved, solutions must be found by unintelligent and malevolent men. It would be tragic both for us and for Africans if communism should win in the present struggle because intelligence and good will defaulted.

# RESOURCES AND REGIONS OF AFRICA

DERWENT WHITTLESEY
*Harvard University*

TO THE geographer the continent of Africa falls into two unequal parts, separated by the barrier of the Sahara—a broad belt compounded of sparsely scattered desert plants and wastes where no vegetation grows (Fig. 1). Northward a narrow coastland faces Europe and belongs to the Mediterranean world. Southward lies the Africa that is the subject of this paper. The great mass of the continent turns inward upon itself in the form of saucer-like basins, half of them plateaus. Its coastline, shorter in ratio to its area than that of any other continent, has few harbors and is nearly everywhere either a desert or a thicket of trees. Except in the far south, where nature's defenses were most easily broken into, the coastland was penetrated and the interior opened to the outside world only a half-century ago.

It is natural that, to the general public of far-off America, Africa should long have been a vague composite picture of stampeding herds of big game and densely forested jungles through which flow romantic rivers—Nile, Congo, Zambezi. That world is understood to be inhabited by pygmies and also by the tallest men on earth.

## AFRICA, CONTINENT OF SURPRISES

Such persisting glimmers from the Dark Continent are reflections of actualities. All those marvels are to be found in Africa, although not in any one place. Once they are sorted out and distributed to their rightful locales, they are seen in a clearer light. But, even then, Africa remains the continent of the unexpected and the contradictory, forever presenting surprises to people whose homeland is North America or Europe. Some once-dumbfounding facts have ceased to astonish but remain as curiosities. The fabulous animals that overstrained the credulity of a preceding generation can now be seen in the zoo, and photographs have made bizarre tribal markings familiar to readers of travel books and magazines as well as to anthropologists. Other equally startling facts remain sources of misunderstanding, because they cannot be transferred for inspection to other continents. Reports of these facts contradict the experience of outsiders, who may refuse to believe what they hear or may fail to grasp the meaning of what they read.

Now that Africa has suddenly moved into the spotlight of public interest, those who wish to inform themselves about that strange continent are confused by the paradoxes they encounter and may, regrettably, lose interest. Those who are obligated to deal with African affairs without firsthand knowledge can make serious mistakes in spite of the best intentions, as in the attempt to produce peanut oil on a large scale at the end of World War II.

Confusing contradictions and anomalies appear in every aspect of African geography; their range and character are readily illustrated from the resources of the continent, as a half-dozen examples will show.

1. The solid stands of huge trees in the middle of Africa (Fig. 1, big bush) are thought by many to indicate fertile soil, but in fact the soil is notably inferior, being leached of plant foods by the incessant rains.

2. Between the streams in both big bush and small bush (Fig. 1), wherever the slope is gentle, the soil is hard to work, and after two or three years it gives out and has to be allowed to rest, generally for several years.

3. Soils of the very high uplands (above 5,000 feet) are likely to be more productive than those lower down. At any elevation the choicest cropland lies on slopes, many of them steep. Fields in such locations are subject to serious erosion.

4. The total area of cropland is greatly exceeded by land good only for grazing animals, but immense tracts otherwise suited to cattle are useless because of the tsetse fly. Wherever possible, cattle are kept in large numbers, because they are prized as evidence of wealth. Numbers alone count, and the range is overtaxed by small, ill-nourished creatures that give little or no milk

and are slaughtered for meat on only the rarest festal occasions.

5. Africa is very rich in minerals, but nearly everything mined is exported to other continents. While Europe and North America are thereby enriched, Africa is being impoverished.

6. Africa ranks first among the continents in potential water power, but most of it lies secluded in the hot, wet forest of the central region, and no attempt to use it as a foundation for large-scale manufacturing is in prospect.

7. Five major river systems crisscross the continent, but they

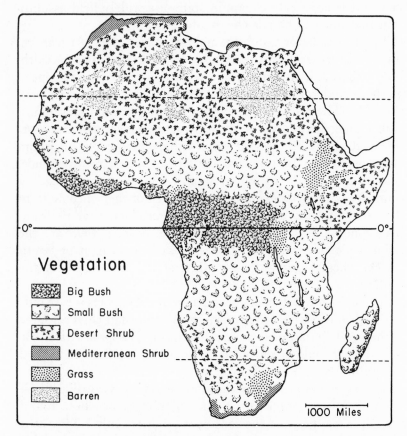

Vegetation

- Big Bush
- Small Bush
- Desert Shrub
- Mediterranean Shrub
- Grass
- Barren

1000 Miles

FIG. 1.—Vegetation regions of Africa. The three principal sorts of natural vegetation depicted here are so closely related to other aspects of the natural environment—climate, surface configuration, soils, water supplies, and native animal life—that they provide a key to the distribution of the continent's resources, except for minerals. They also indicate broadly the possibilities and limitations of land use.

fail to lay the interior open to navigation. Many streams rage in flood at one season only to lie in pools and trickles in sandy beds at another. Those that flow full of water throughout the year are interrupted by numerous falls and rapids.

8. Manpower is usually considered the leading resource of Africa. This was undeniable when slaves were the chief export of the continent. It is debatable today, although almost every employer takes it for granted. Nowadays the labor is used within Africa, but it is always insufficient and generally inefficient. Hence it is not really cheap, in spite of a widely held assumption that low pay equals cheap labor.

The contradictory and anomalous character of African resources is further illustrated by details about its mineral wealth. Everywhere the important deposits are extracted by European methods under European management. Africans furnish only the labor. The continent's share in the world output of all minerals is an estimated 9.2 per cent by value. This is a modest portion and might be thought too low by most people, to whom minerals are the best known of African products (diamonds, gold, and uranium spring to mind). Indeed, several leading countries within Africa do derive so much of their income from the extraction and exportation of mine products that their entire economy is based on this resource. Among them are the Belgian Congo, the two Rhodesias, and the Union of South Africa. These together cover much of the area south of the Equator.

Such a degree of dependence upon mineral exports is rare outside Africa. Most countries of the world find their chief resource in their soil. In nations where minerals do rival products of the soil, they include some of those on which modern industrial society has been built.

African contributions of those minerals are very slight.[1] Of the all-important mineral fuels, no petroleum has been found (except in Egypt), and the continent produces only 1.3 per cent of the world's coal. Of the key industrial metals, Africa yields

1. The percentages that follow are composites of selected years prior, during, and since World War II. Many are derived from William Van Royan and Oliver Bowles, *The Mineral Resources of the World* (New York: Prentice-Hall, Inc., 1952).

only 2 per cent of the iron and 1.5 per cent of the bauxite (the ore of aluminum). Prospects for the chemical industry are even dimmer; besides the small amount of coal, there is only salt, produced solely for the food market and amounting to only 1.5 per cent of the world's supply.

In contrast to its weak position in minerals needed to set up an industrial society, Africa leads the world by a spectacular margin in certain minerals that are precious and in some that are rare. A part of that output—chiefly gold, diamonds, and platinum—finds its way into luxury items, but the larger share takes a place in more prosaic wares. Several, such as cobalt and fluorspar, are never seen by the general public, because they are hidden in familiar products like steel or because they vanish in the process of manufacture.

Africa is almost exclusive as the world's diamond producer, with just under 98 per cent (by weight) of the total output. Eighty-five per cent is used in cutting tools and abrasives, the remaining 15 per cent being sold as gems. The first important uranium mine was in Africa, and it remained the sole source of radium for a generation. Even with the greatly increased output of uranium ore required for nuclear fission, and consequent production in other continents, the original African mine was producing 60 per cent of the total in 1942, the latest year for which figures are available. The immense waste piles from the gold mines of the Union of South Africa have since been found to contain uranium, and systematic reworking of tailings has just now been undertaken. Placer gold brought to market on the heads of porters has become negligible compared to vein mining by European methods. For a time the African output of gold exceeded that of all the rest of the world, and, in spite of recent increases elsewhere, it still stands at 38.5 per cent of the total.

Of several other items Africa is a substantial producer, notably of certain critical minerals used in the smelting of iron to make steel of different properties: columbium, 100 per cent; cobalt, 74 per cent; chromite, 27 per cent; manganese, 20 per cent; vanadium, 12.5 per cent; and fluorspar, 0.5 per cent. The three leading nonferrous metal contributions are copper, 18 per

cent; platinum, 16 per cent; and tin, 15 per cent. The list of outstanding products includes also asbestos, with 16 per cent, and
graphite, with 8.5 per cent of the world tonnage.

The deficiency of Africa in fuel may someday be partially offset by energy from other sources. Thanks to large streams with
many falls and rapids, the continent is estimated to have 40 per
cent of the world's potential water power. Fissionable minerals
may in the future be used locally. However, at least three-
quarters of the potential water power and all the uranium mined
up to the present are confined to the African Center, where the
market is tiny and no large increase in demand seems likely in
any predictable future.

The mineral wealth of Africa, important as it is to today's
economic structure, cannot become a permanent foundation for
a prosperous future. Rather, it must be viewed as a scaffolding
that can aid now in building up a sound and durable edifice for
the future. The money brought in by mineral products through
extraction at the mine, transportation to a port, and sale to a
distant country will continue to flow only until the mines are
exhausted. In some cases the end is in sight. Several of the early
copper mines are already abandoned after three or four decades
of digging. The cost of gold procured on the Rand is increasing
with depth of the workings and threatens closure of mines there.
To be sure, many locations have prospects of a long life, and
new deposits remain to be discovered. But in the end all will
be exhausted.

The long-term future welfare of Africa depends in part upon
utilizing the current proceeds from the mines to develop lasting
resources, such as water-power and agricultural potentials, to
improve access to the interior and between the different regions
by building railroads, motor roads, and airfields, and to con-
solidate trade and manufacturing in the most advantageous
urban centers. No other continent is faced with so many acute
problems that must be solved before a satisfactory, permanent
way of life can be achieved. The present surplus from the mines,
if sagaciously applied, can help to guarantee a stable outlook
for the continent as a whole.

# RESOURCES AND REGIONS OF AFRICA

## AFRICA AND THE LAND

In spite of the current emphasis on minerals and mineral production in Africa, the ultimate welfare of the continent depends upon the land as a source of food, clothing, and shelter. A number of African countries have little or no mineral wealth and so have always had to build their economic life wholly or mainly on the combined resources of soil, water, climate, and slope which provide the natural environment for tilling crops and grazing livestock. Until Europeans came, this was subsistence agriculture, and a large fraction of the crops raised and livestock reared is still consumed by the groups that produce them.

Markets in the growing African cities and overseas have stimulated some commercial farming and ranching, but its total value does not equal that of African mineral production. In value of commercial agriculture, Africa ranks last among the continents. Prospects for increase are not bright. In some African countries there is unused land in the hands of governments, corporations, and individuals. But not all of it can be used for commercial crops and livestock. Some does not have the needed qualities, and a good deal will be allocated to farmers producing only subsistence. Of the land in commercial farms, too much is deteriorating under present unwise management. Improved methods will rehabilitate a part of it, but some is passing permanently out of use.

In the long run the amount of new land available for commercial agriculture will be limited by the needs for its own subsistence of the rapidly growing population. For the African tribesman the land has always been the prime source of food, clothing, and shelter. A very large fraction of all that the soil yields is consumed by the farmer and his ramified family. The yield is low. As population increases, the soil is overtaxed, and the yield falls lower.

The state of the land varies greatly with natural conditions, with density of population, with tribal practices, and with policy of the responsible European or local governments. Hence the land as a resource can best be understood if we look at it region by region.

Climate and land forms interact upon each other and upon soil, slope, and drainage to create distinct natural regions, roughly suggested by the vegetation (Fig. 1). Human societies modify these natural subdivisions where it is desirable, if they can, and at the same time adapt themselves to conditions that are beyond their control. Before the advent of Europeans,

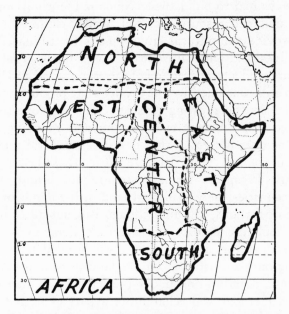

FIG. 2.—The geographic realms of Africa. The outstanding subdivisions of human geography in Africa are the five regions shown here. They have become differentiated through utilization of natural resources and adaptation to earth conditions by many generations of Africans, modified in recent centuries and particularly during the last fifty or seventy-five years by Europeans and Asians.

African man appears to have altered his habitat rather little. Europeans have imported tools and technology that have accelerated change. They have also oriented the continent toward the outside world. Today people familiar with Africa speak of the West, the Center, and East, and the South (Fig. 2). These are primary regional divisions so distinct that a brief consideration of their separate characters should clear away much of the confusion that comes from assuming Africa to be alike everywhere,

Of the four regions south of the Sahara that are widely recognized by people familiar with Africa, the most neatly outlined is the West (cf. Figs. 1 and 2). It backs up to the Sahara barrier, makes occasional contact with the nearer oases and nomads, and serves as the southern terminus for desert crossings by air and motorbus. It faces the ocean.

The bands that stripe the vegetation map denote zones of natural plant cover: big bush (solid stands of tall evergreen trees), small bush (low trees in clumps or scattered over grassland), pure grassland, and the sparse shrubs of the desert. Other maps of critical natural conditions would show much the same striping: from south to north, increasing fertility of soil, increasing seasonal range in temperature, and, most important, decreasing length of the rainy season from copious rain all year round along the south coast to rare and unreliable showers in the desert. Nearly all of the West of Africa is a lowland plain, although part of its eastern limit is marked by a mountain range.

Settlement by Africans has fitted into the pronounced east-west grain of the region. In the north the Sudan, where rains are brief and natural vegetation is grassland dotted here and there with clumps or scatterings of low trees, the Moslem way of life filtered in from the adjacent desert and also along the belt of open, grassy country that crosses the entire breadth of the continent. The cities could be anywhere in the Near East, with walls pierced by defensive gates and inclosing garden land as well as compounds. When Europeans conquered this extension of Islam into the "Land of the Blacks," they built their business and administrative towns near the existing cities.

In contrast to the north, the people of the wooded south are divided into many tribes, some of whom have accepted the Christian religion. They wear the dress that has been embraced generally in Africa—shirt and shorts for the men, bright print dresses for the women.

The European innovations were slight until the end of the nineteenth century, when the combined barriers of the coastline were first effectively penetrated. The surf is the highest on earth and has piled a bar beach with navigable openings—and those shallow—only at the mouths of the Niger and at four points along the west end of the region. Surfboats were and still are the chief means of handling sea-borne trade, although long, high piers are used in the worst season to avoid the gauntlet of the surf itself. At great cost eight harbors have been built during the last twenty-five years to accommodate ocean vessels. Once through the surf, other hazards remain. Shallow lagoons lie between beach and mainland, and their shores are fringed with mangrove trees, whose interlacing roots form a continuous palisade against landings from boats. Except at the west end of the region the mainland shore originally supported a dense forest of tall trees. Everywhere the hot, humid climate harbors flies, mosquitoes, bacilli, and worms that can transmit to man and beast a long list of tropical diseases. The coast of the West of Africa was called the "white man's grave" until the danger of these diseases was reduced by sanitary measures introduced when finally their etiology was worked out.

Once the coast was made accessible and habitable, rails were built inland from each port, one, or rarely two, to a colony. Later on, motor roads began to penetrate the interior, and some of them make contact between the holdings of different nations. There is also some local air travel, as well as intercontinental services.

As elsewhere in Africa, minerals have been an item of export from the first, as the name "Gold Coast" and the British gold guinea prove. Gold is still produced, but other minerals are now far more important. They include chromite, manganese, tin, iron, and bauxite; the output of most of them is increasing. The mining companies and the supervision are European; the labor, African.

The products of farm and range outrank minerals in the West of Africa. Originally the whole continent was poor in crop plants, but the food supply was greatly enlarged by introductions from the American and Asian tropics, mainly after A.D. 1400. The West of Africa is populous, thanks to staple cereals and root crops suited to local varieties of climate and soil and to tree crops. The oil palm has long been encouraged by the simple expedient of cutting back competing growth and thus creating rough but modestly productive orchards.

Palm oil is one indigenous vegetable product that has become an export under the stimulus of European trading firms. Other tree crops, likewise grown by individual farmers in response to a cash market, are kola nuts, coffee, and cacao. The West of Africa is the leading producer of cacao in the world. The beans are collected at roadside warehouses, where each lot is inspected by government experts to maintain standard quality and sent by the buyers to the coast for shipment.

Tree crops can yield a profit only if the trees remain on the land for a number of years. The grower is thereby tied to one spot, and two significant consequences are appearing. He can no longer shift his food-producing fields every few years and must discover ways to keep his land under cultivation for longer periods. By remaining on the same land during the productive life of his trees, he associates that particular piece of ground with himself. In other words, he substitutes the concept of individual ownership for the communal holding of land generally practiced by African tribes. Cash crops include some annuals. In the drier north peanuts and cotton have become leading exports.

Cotton textiles were woven and dyed in the West of Africa long before Europeans appeared there. Hides and skins were tanned and turned into leather goods. These handicrafts and also work in brass and copper and in ivory are still carried on, but imported cloths, hardware, and gewgaws are supplanting them in local favor.

The West of Africa has been in contact with Europeans longer than any other of the four regions south of the Sahara, but no part of it has been considered suited to permanent European habitation. In consequence the African society, although modified through novel uses of its resources, has been able to maintain exclusive occupation of the land while increasing its output. From the Gold Coast, an early and increasing source of wealth and long under British tutelage, has sprung a demand for local government which the metropole is putting into operation at a rate that astonishes everybody. It is a rate which meets with skepticism in adjacent French colonies and with resentment from European settlers in the South and the East of Africa. The budding local government will not view its natural and human resources in quite the same way as did the British government overseas in London. Just what changes will occur cannot at this time be predicted.

In the vast Center of Africa the zones of vegetation, soils, and climate already met in the West of Africa continue eastward and are duplicated on the south side of the Equator in inverse order (cf. Figs. 1 and 2). Except for a narrow coastal strip, the whole area is set off from the Atlantic Ocean by the steep face of a plateau, but it is not much above 1,500 feet high, except in the south. There it rises to some 4,000 feet above the sea, with a few patches standing between 5,000 and 6,000 feet.

The coastline is favored with more harbors and less surf than that of the West of Africa, but the stiff climb and dense forest hamper ingress, while only the highest levels rise above the continuous heat and humidity that overspread all lowlands in low latitudes.

The inner zone of the African Center (i.e., the part lying along the Equator) is covered with big bush (Fig. 1)—a solid stand of tall trees that gives way abruptly to a tangle of smaller trees (small bush), many of them thorny, or to tree-dotted grassland. Remote districts of the deep forest are peopled scantily by primitive tribes who live mainly by hunting. More generally, small patches of forest trees are girdled to make way for crude plantings. These are abandoned to jungle after two or three seasons. The produce is carried to the farm village, perhaps to await a motor truck that will take it to some railway or port town of the region. Cash crops include palm oil, cotton, coffee, and plantains (green bananas cooked to provide a staple food). European firms operate a few large-scale plantations, and some forest trees are felled for cabinet wood.

The Congo River and its tributaries have been the traditional means of access to the forest. At Stanleyville, the metropolis of the middle Congo, the main stream is majestically broad, but the town is there because just above are rapids which compel portage, now and for many years handled by a short railroad. From this point a road has recently been run eastward through the big bush, lined in places by the useful oil palm. This and the few other roads are interrupted by broad rivers, which must be crossed by ferries—platforms on dugouts poled by men from a near-by village. Painstaking road maintenance in the hot, wet climate can never be relaxed.

All around the inner Congo lies country where less rain falls and small bush is the natural vegetation. The trees are too small and gnarled to yield more than firewood and frames for huts. Where the soil is productive, the population is moderately dense, although far less so than in the West of Africa. Extensive expanses of almost flat land grow no crop or none better than millet in two seasons out of five or more.

The conspicuous product of the African Center is minerals—gold in the northeast; tin in the east; copper and cobalt, uranium, zinc, and vanadium in the southeast; industrial diamonds in the southwest. The copper deposits of the Congo-Zambezi watershed are among the richest on earth. Mining began just before World War I, the ore being scooped up from surface pits. Later workings have been driven beneath the surface. Roan Antelope Mine is a fair sample. The smelter is erected on the ore body, which is a kind of no-man's land, except where roads and rails serve the pit mouths. Alongside the ore body hundreds of small houses have been built by the company on a treeless slope for the African miners and their families. They are more commodious than the usual habitation built by Africans for themselves. On the opposite flank of the ore body stands the European quarter, also built by the company, with a neat business center, and bungalows and dormitories shaded by trees and vines. The European recreation center completes the picture of European social life. Some mines have elaborate recreational facilities for the African workers as well. Coal was once used to furnish power for the copper mines, but its remoteness (nearly 400 miles to the south) and inadequate rail transport are causing it to be replaced with electric power generated at waterfalls of the region.

The copper-mining district has become a magnet drawing

railroads from all the ports around the part of Africa that lies south of the Equator. They are the first spokes in a wheel pattern that puts the far inland African Center in contact with the outside world. Motor roads are few but are being extended. Major airways cross this region in linking Africa to Europe and the Americas. Every urban center has a field equipped to handle local air traffic. Leopoldville has become the hub of both the intercontinental and the internal air routes.

The African Center was the last of the four regions to be subjected to development, and neither the French nor the Portuguese governments have pushed their operations beyond the initial stages. The Belgian Congo, in sharp contrast, is being combed for mineral and agricultural resources. Plantations are permitted where there is land to spare. If European ventures require more labor than can be had locally, the companies are required to build housing for immigrant workers' families and to provide hospitals, schools, churches, and recreational facilities. Young people are taught trades, chiefly skilled crafts, and encouraged to live like Europeans. By these means the natural and human resources are being fused into an economic structure that so far seems to have given general satisfaction. University education has only just been made available to Africans, and no political opportunities are offered them. The Belgian metropole intends to keep executive authority in its own hands. In the British segment of the African Center, mining is conducted much as in the adjacent Congo, but European farming produces livestock and grain rather than plantation crops, and the economic and political life of both Europeans and Africans is only loosely supervised by the metropole. This district is now being given still more local autonomy, in a federation with districts that belong geographically to the South and the East of Africa.

### THE SOUTH OF AFRICA

The southern tip of Africa extends into the middle latitudes— that is, into climates undeniably suitable for Europeans to live and work in (cf. Figs. 1 and 2). The southeast coast resembles the Carolinas, and the southwest coast is much like California. Highlands ranging from 4,000 to 6,000 feet project almost to the northern boundary of the Union of South Africa and offset the decreasing latitude with bracing weather not unlike that of New Mexico. The political boundary itself is drawn where a broad belt of desert and lowland river valleys breaks the continuity of favorable climates. To the north of these interruptions other highlands rise to form outliers climatically almost as well fitted for European habitation as the Union itself. If they are included, the region of the South of Africa extends nearly to the Zambezi River.

By every standard, the South is the most highly developed part of Africa. It has large and active cities, some of which are busy ports. The coast has several natural harbors which have been improved to serve ships of all classes. Access to the interior is burdened by no barriers except that somewhat stiff climb to the plateau. On the highland cities have grown into imposing centers resembling European counterparts, except Johannesburg, the metropolis of the region, to which many skyscrapers have given the appearance of a North American city. It is the rail and road hub of the one real network of surface transportation on the continent and the terminus of the intercontinental airways that link Africa to Europe and the Americas.

The population in the South having European antecedents exceeds two and a half million. From the nature of its climate alone, most of this country might have become, like Australia, the exclusive home of a people transferred from Europe. Unlike Australia, it is an extension of a low-latitude continent peopled mainly by non-Europeans, and the twelve million Africans form an indispensable part of the population.

A great many inhabit their tribal lands, generally in the lower, drier, and more rugged districts. The rest live permanently or intermittently on European farms, at European mines, or near European cities. In all these places they perform all manual labor and domestic service. Together they constitute a human resource on which the prosperity of the South of Africa at present is based and to which its future is indissolubly linked.

A small number of Africans have been able to demonstrate skill in crafts, and some are making places for themselves in business and professions within the African society. Their participation above the level of manual labor is restricted by laws of long standing.

Both Europeans and Africans have to reckon with three hundred thousand people of Asian antecedents. They are mainly small traders and skilled craftsmen. A few large operators compete with Europeans in retail trade and real estate, while the many small fry hopelessly outclass Africans in petty trading in all sorts of merchandise. Resentment toward this rapidly growing segment of the population has been one cause of recent outbursts of violence.

Turning from human to natural resources calls attention to an economy that is based primarily on the output of mines, although agricultural production is not far behind, and manufacturing is growing. This was not so in the older settlements, where the Dutch farmers became known from their vocation as Boers. But for some seventy years minerals have occupied a prime position in affairs of the South African provinces and in Southern Rhodesia, the last-named having been settled primarily as a mining community.

There, as in the African Center, all the minerals for which the country is known at large are exported. Diamonds were formerly dug primarily for gem stones in open pits, of which the "Big Hole" at Kimberley is a famous relic. For many years diamond mining has been underground, and the output is throttled down to the market demand for gem stones. Less romantic and less valuable, but more useful, is the by-product yield of industrial diamonds for abrasives and cutting tools. In output of such diamonds the South of Africa ranks far below the Center and even the West, as percentages (in carats) of world production make plain:

|        | Per Cent |
|--------|----------|
| Center | 73.3 |
| West | 16.8 |
| East | Very little |
| South | 7.2 |

Gold is the leading mineral of the South in every sense— value, labor employed, private and public interest, and service as the bulwark of the local economy. Mines range from shallow pits worked by one man, through every grade in depth and size, to the almost continuous string of huge operations in very deep mines along the foot of the Rand, a ridge more than 60 miles long. At midcentury the South contributed 34.5 per cent of the world supply of gold, and the Rand produced all but 2 per cent of this impressive total. Increasing costs of very deep mining threaten its paramount position. Since the end of World War II, some Rand operations have shut down, while promising mines have been opened 160 miles farther south. Back on the Rand the extensive gold tailings are beginning to be reworked for the uranium they contain.

Additional minerals exported in large amounts are chromite, asbestos, and tungsten. Besides these, most other metals are mined in some quantity in the South of Africa. Nearly all output of metals can be used best in parts of the world where manufacturing is already well established, meaning chiefly Europe and North America. In thus losing the use of its mineral resources, the South is similar to the West and Center.

The South of Africa is exceptional in possessing coal of high quality, and it is coming into use as the source of power for manufacturing. Some of it is converted into coke at steel mills of modest size, preferably located on iron deposits and close to the limestone needed for the processing. The resource of coal and iron promises to keep the South technologically ahead of the other regions of the continent, all of which lack this foundation of industrial society.

Also this region, while based mainly on mineral resources, far outdistances the other three in utilizing its agricultural resources. Much of the country is too dry to yield crops and must remain range for livestock. But extensive areas are suited to growing cereals, chiefly corn (maize—called "mealies" in the South of Africa, where it is the staple of the native diet). Specialized crops that can afford the cost of transportation to the European market are grown where nature favors. Such are wine near Cape Town, fruits produced in ten or a dozen widely scattered locations, and tobacco. Some of these specialized districts are irrigated because they are subject to recurring drought.

Nearly all the high upland ("high veld" in local parlance) is in European farms operated by the owners with the labor of

Africans, who generally live with their families in the vicinity of the farmhouse. Farm implements that would be considered out of date in North America, and even in Europe, are in universal use. The typical plow is pulled by eight yokes of oxen and takes two men.

Many areas have been set aside as native reserves. They range from Bechuanaland (larger than Texas) to small tracts unequal to supporting a subtribe. Africans complain that the Europeans have taken all the best land. It is painfully apparent that the reserves are less prosperous and suffer more acutely from soil erosion than the European districts, even when holdings of both races share identical natural conditions. It is also true that many reserves are in rugged or dry areas or at low elevations where the climate has discouraged European settlement.

A specific grievance asserts that the Europeans have taken the productive clay soil and have left the Africans with infertile sandlands. Reserves can be found that are bounded by the contact line between these two soil types. In such places the red, heavier soil owned by Europeans bears a thick stand of native trees, if it is not already yielding ample crops or pasture. The yellow, light soil of the reserve is incontestably sandy. Trees that once made up its natural vegetation have been cut except on rugged or rocky land to make way for crops or pasture. But crops are low in yield and quality, and livestock finds poor pickings, whether turned into stubble during the dry season or onto the bunch grass that grows sparsely on fallow land.

History supplies an explanation for this antithesis. Before the advent of Europeans, African farmers grew crops only on the light, sandy soils that could be worked with their primitive hand tools. Farming operations used the land lightly, and the soil was given plenty of time to recuperate after each period of use. Pioneering Europeans found the heavier, clay soils unoccupied except for intermittent grazing by native cattle, and they took up such land for their farms. It could readily be worked with the animal-drawn implements brought from Europe, and their large holdings provided for woodland as well as cropland.

Unspecialized European.estates yield a balanced output of

grain and livestock and if well managed remain prosperous year after year. In contrast, land in most of the native reserves is being overworked, whatever the soil, climate, and surface. Once the ground is laid bare of vegetation by plowing or overgrazing, torrential rains may cut the surface into gullies that can reduce a field to a wasteland in a few seasons. And every year the pressure of population on the land increases because the death rate has rapidly declined since the Europeans stopped slave-trading and tribal wars and introduced medical service and sanitation. Fewer deaths have not been offset by fewer births.

Allocation of land between African and European farmers threatens to be the thorniest of all questions arising from natural resources. The South of Africa is the only region in which Europeans comprise more than a tiny fraction of the population. The Africans occupy a subordinate position, politically, socially, and economically. They have lost the land as well as the mineral resources, and the Europeans are in general accord that Africans must not be allowed to regain control. They differ among themselves in their views as to whether the country should continue its practice of collaboration between the races or adopt the policy of "apartheid," which means regional segregation. It is hard for an objective observer to see how the resources of land and minerals can be developed without the participation of the human resource of all races living in the region.

## THE EAST OF AFRICA

The East of Africa is the most diverse of the four regions south of the Sahara (cf. Figs. 1 and 2). It includes not only the highest highlands of the continent but also extensive coastal lowlands and river basins not more than 1,200 or 1,500 feet above the sea. Its vegetation, soil, and climate are correspondingly varied and patchy. The traveler is frequently reminded of both the South and the Center by natural environment and by modes of human living. To picture the region adequately would require division into its several subregions. Instead, the following sketch touches on traits of different districts intended to serve as typical or recurrent samples of the character and the resources of the whole area.

It is unlike any of the other regions in that no very rich mineral deposits have ever been found. Its livelihood therefore depends mainly upon its fields and ranges, with some production from its treelands. Having no mines of first consequence, it is the poorest of the four regions in its relations to the outside world. Much of the land is used for subsistence, but there are districts of European farms and also districts where Africans produce crops or livestock to be sold for export. Because of poverty in natural resources, the spots where population is dense are labor reservoirs for mines and plantations in both the Center and the South.

Nowhere are contrasts in land use more striking, whether for livestock or crops. The highland's higher patches rule out the tsetse fly and therefore permit cattle. Because these beasts are cherished by Africans mainly as a sign of wealth, there are too many, and a good many men and women spend their lives as herders. In dry districts or seasons the heavily stocked range is left without a spear of grass or a leaf of bush, and growing gullies are fast degrading much land to uselessness. Only a few Africans depend on their cattle for food; and those who do, consume milk and blood rather than meat. The quality and condition of the cattle on overstocked tribal lands contrast sharply with the stock reared on lush pastures of European ranches and dairy farms.

Cultivation by Africans for subsistence is destroying the soil in many places, just as in the South of Africa. Because the African and European landholdings are often intermingled, there is a sharp contrast between well-grassed European range and denuded and eroded pasture of African reserves. In some reserves steps to control erosion have been introduced by European administrators. This has been easiest where a tree crop induces fixed abodes and where fertile land for growing the family's food is at hand. Such is the case on the lava soils of Mount Elgon's foothills, where bananas and coffee are cash crops, and on coffee-planted slopes of the volcanoes Meru and Kilimanjaro.

In Abyssinia, alone in Africa south of the Sahara, the Africans themselves ages ago worked out a system of plowing with cattle that minimizes soil wash on pronounced slopes. The steepest are left in grass, and the neatly bordered holdings bring out the special advantage of much of the Abyssinian highland in being surfaced with lava soil that can be planted year after year without resting. In other parts of the East African upland, opened to farming during the past half-century, steep slopes have been cleared of forest and planted to crops. Whether they will stand repeated cultivation as do the soils of Abyssinia is not yet known.

Some cash crops are grown in the East of Africa on plantations owned and operated by Europeans. Sisal, tea, coffee, and sugar cane are plantation crops grown in several districts.

Occupying much more land than the plantations are the fields and orchards where Africans grow crops for sale. The oldest of them are the coffee plantings of Abyssinia, where native trees have been encouraged to spread under selected shade trees. However ancient the groves, the marketing is handled in modern motor trucks.

Slightly different, because it stems directly from European administrators, is production of Africa's one indigenous cereal —millet—in the Sudan. Wells and ponds have provided water for men and their livestock, making it possible for farmers to move into an area formerly uninhabitable. The main cash crop (millet) is extensively planted, and the auction at the chief collecting points has become big business. The railway carries the crop to consumers throughout northeastern Africa.

The extensive Gezirah cotton district of the Sudan required a large outlay of European capital for irrigation works on the Nile River, and the ginneries are correspondingly large. Their output of both fiber and oil is marketed in Europe.

In a district on the Nile-Congo watershed, 1,500 miles from a seaport, a different organization of the business has been worked out by the European administration. Cotton grows well without irrigation, but it is too remote to pay the cost of shipment to the market overseas. Tribesmen are encouraged to grow as many acres as they can handle and to take it to a nearby market on their heads, where they sell it to an agency that bags it and moves it by motor truck to an up-to-date local cotton mill. There it is made into coarse cloth, and the cottonseed oil is extracted for sale to the local people, who can use the money they have made in growing the raw material to buy clothing and food at a price free from heavy transport charges.

Transport is a key to the future of the East of Africa, because so much of the country lies high above the sea or remote from it. Surface lines are costly to build and to maintain. The different highland units are separated from each other by differences in altitude as well as by distance and mountain or canyon barriers. Surface lines are costly to build and to maintain, and air traffic has become commonplace.

Political insurgence is seeking satisfaction nearly everywhere but differently in the several physical and political units that make up the region. The status of the moment ranges widely: Abyssinia, independent; Eritrea, autonomous within Abyssinia; the northern Sudan, looking forward to some sort of federation with Egypt; Uganda, where the leading African tribe is being prevented by European authority from dominating the lesser tribes; and Kenya, in the grip of violence between Africans and Europeans that amounts to guerrilla warfare.

### A KEY TO CONTRADICTIONS

The political issues that have thrust Africa into the spotlight of public interest, like much else in the continent, appear contradictory. In both the West and the East of Africa some colonies are experimenting with autonomy that may lead quickly to independence. In other parts of the East violence has been raging, and in the Union of South Africa the government has adopted a position that reverses the trend toward African political emancipation. Contrasts to both extremes appear in the Center, where steps are leading to federation of British colonies officially committed to reciprocity between all races and where the Belgian Congo appears to be a model of relations between African colony and metropolitan authority, running smoothly in the groove that until recently was accepted throughout the continent.

Some of the ferment appears to have arisen from accelerated movement within the continent and to the outside world. For European passengers, for mail, and for some freight, the air is the sovereign route. One or more airports in each of the four regions can accommodate planes of all types. Minor fields serve practically every urban center. The long-used navigable lakes and rivers continue to carry both powered ships, introduced from abroad, and native boats ranging from dugouts to sailing vessels. Railways handle much freight and many African passengers, and a few are being extended. The highway has lately become an effective competitor of the railway. Much freight reaches its market by motor truck. Passenger vehicles move along all principal roads and in the cities already create traffic jams and parking difficulties. Many Africans move by the busses which ply between chief towns or which take laborers to distant places where they can find work. Those who do not have bus fare make their way by using the roads as footpaths, resting where water is available. In lion country they may pass the nights in crude shelters built among the branches of trees. Sometimes it seems that all of Africa is forever on the move. Circulation of ideas is an unavoidable partner of the circulation of people.

However far afield their migrations, most Africans return to their tribal homeland for a season or for a year or two and, at last, to die. Minerals, important as they are to the position of Africa in world economy, concern Africans chiefly as mines where jobs may be had, and the alienation of mineral resources to European firms causes no trouble apart from strikes such as may occur in any large-scale industry. In contrast, the attachment between the tribe and its land is shared by all the members of the group. Underlying this sentiment is the hard fact that the land is the ultimate natural resource of the continent.

Where farmland has been alienated to Europeans in such amounts that the rising population feels the retribution that comes from overtaxing their remaining acres, a bitter issue arises. This is epitomized in the Mau Mau troubles in Kenya, where the beautiful and productive high upland between the Indian Ocean and Lake Victoria is divided between African and European farmers. The settlers purchased their holdings in good faith from Africans who in equal good faith supposed they were only leasing the land. Holdings of the two races are interspersed and lie at the city limit of Nairobi, the capital of the country. Since 1952 members of the African tribe most concerned have resorted to assassination in an effort to dislodge the Europeans. Here the basic African resources of land and manpower have been combined with violence to lay bare the raw edges of change that elsewhere in Africa has taken peaceful and often progressive forms.

# SOCIAL CHANGES AND SOCIAL PROBLEMS IN NEGRO AFRICA

GEORGES BALANDIER

*International Research Office on Social Implications of Technological Change*

## I

THE decade starting immediately after the second World War has been, for Negro Africa, a period of particularly rapid acceleration of the processes of economic, political, and sociocultural change. It has seen this important group of territories cast off its character as a "marginal" continent and break down finally the obstacles which, in varying degrees, isolated the African peoples until the end of the nineteenth century. Africa, for so long made up of self-contained units, is making itself felt in a wider area of relations in the world order. There are no longer any Negro-African societies not affected, at least indirectly, by influences generating important changes. Sociological research which confines itself only to study of the most traditional Negro communities cannot ignore such a state of affairs without grave risks. In my earlier studies of the colonial problem I pointed out that societies experiencing only a tenuous contact with the outside are still affected by it in diverse ways. A recent article on the weakening of the process of integration in the case of ethnic groups of North Dahomey shows the importance of such a point of view.[1]

Signs of such accelerated changes are many; I shall select those which seem most revealing because of their intensity. The most significant characteristic of the present African population picture is the rhythm of the process of urbanization, as shown in Table 1.

Such transformations create new civilizations and social dif-

---

1. P. Mercier, "L'Affaiblissement des processus d'intégration dans des sociétés en changement," *Bull. Inst. Franç. d'Afrique noire*, Vol. XVI, Nos. 1–2 (January–April, 1954).

ferentiation of a modern character. They also have important political consequences when they alter the numerical ratio of Africans to Europeans. In the territories of West and Central Africa, where relatively few Europeans were present until the last decade,[2] the growth of cities is accompanied by an increase in the white population, which has repercussions in racial relations. From 1946 to 1951 the number of Europeans rose by 93 per cent in French West Africa and by 200 per cent in French

TABLE 1

DEVELOPMENT OF THE URBANIZATION PROCESS

| Territory | Period | Nature of the Increase | Percentage of Increase |
|---|---|---|---|
| Senegal | 1942–52 | Increase of Dakar, Saint-Louis, Rufisque, and Thiès | 100 |
| Ivory Coast | 1942–52 | Increase of Abidjan and Bouaké | 109 |
| Cameroons | 1933–52 | Increase of Douala and Yaoundé | 250 |
| French Congo | 1936–52 | Increase of Brazzaville and Pointe-Noire | 239 |
| Gold Coast | 1931–48 | Increase of the five largest cities | 98 |
| Belgian Congo | 1940–51 | Increase of the "detribalized" population (including camps) | 130 |
| Union of South Africa | 1936–51 | Increase of urban population | 10.9 |

Equatorial Africa; in the Belgian Congo, in Leopoldville alone during the single year 1952 the increase was 26 per cent.

Such changes affect the climate of relations between dominating and dominated groups in at least three ways. The increase in the European population is interpreted (or actually experienced) as making possible stronger pressure by it in its role of dominant minority. On the other hand, the economic factors (relations between employers and employed) and the political and racial factors overlap one another in a complex way in the relations between the colored and white sectors of cities. The closeness between problems of race relations and problems of class relations is especially enhanced within the urban environ-

2. E.g., before 1939, Europeans were 1 per thousand of the population in West Africa and 2 per thousand in the Belgian Congo.

ment. Finally, European communities, becoming larger and composed of normal familial groups, may now have an autonomous existence which was impossible for them before.

The second point demanding attention is the recent but accelerated character of the measures of economic development which have been under way in Negro Africa since 1944. Such an undertaking implied the improvement (or the creation) of the social overhead: the ports, the aerial communications, and the roads constitute a network which finally makes possible the export of commodities and stimulates the movement of men; the production of power (chiefly hydroelectric) is beginning to expand, along with the establishment of the first processing industries, while the search for coal and oil goes on. In addition, the predominating factor is the elaboration, since 1944, of plans of economic and social development which look to the diversification of an economy hitherto colonial in type and which favor the process of modernization.[3] As examples we may recall the Colonial and Welfare Act (1940 and 1945) for the British territories, the so-called "ten-year plan" for the French territories, and the ten-year plan presented in mid-1949 for the Belgian Congo.

Apart from social overhead, investments have been made primarily in the agricultural and mining sectors, with, moreover, very differing successes in the former. But the preservation of the "primary" characteristics of the economy has often provoked the reaction of African leaders who remain sensitive to any policy which might appear to be simply a modern version of the old *pacte coloniale*. This fact is obvious, even in the Belgian Congo, which shows rapid progress relative to the other colonial territories, where the volume of metallurgical and mechanical activities (especially the latter) appears still small considering the capacity of the country for mining and energy.

It is important to point to the increase of elite groups which have benefited from a modern education. This is true even though the effort to supply basic education has remained, throughout the African territories, very far behind the needs.

3. Cf. Jacques Richard-Molard, "Les Plans de développement en Afrique noire," *L'Afrique et l'Asie*, 1951.

As proof of this fact I offer the following statistics, which show the importance of the school population relative to the total population:[4]

|  | Per Cent |
|---|---|
| Belgian territories | 9.4 |
| English territories | 4.5 |
| Union of South Africa | 3.7 |
| French territories (including Madagascar) | 2.7 |

The full significance of these figures becomes apparent only if one recalls how the French and English dependencies, where the presence of Islam is very important, experience difficulties in competing with the Moslem schools. The Moslem elites do not enter into the present Negro-African society in the same way as the elites educated by the West, who assert, for their majority, adherence at least in principle to Christianity. The numerical data also call for an analysis explaining the manner in which the school population is divided among the different grades of instruction. The Belgian territories, which show a relatively high proportion of school people among the population, until now, on the contrary, show almost no opportunities for access to higher education. In the French dependencies, the establishment of the Institut Universitaire of Dakar and especially the fellowships to facilitate studies on the level of French specialized schools and universities has permitted the formation of an elite with an intellectual equipment on a par with that drawn from the mother-country. Though the base of primary instruction remains rather narrow, the opportunity for higher education is widening and is now posing problems of professional integration; let us add, for the record, that the distribution among the different levels of instruction was in 1952 as follows: primary, 90.5 per cent; secondary, 7.1 per cent; higher and specialized schools, 2.4 per cent.

Let us add yet one more example, that of the Gold Coast, on the basis of information furnished by the remarkable *Census of Population* (1948). It is interesting to the extent to which it shows very unequal access to the highest levels of instruction according to region (because of their unequal development)

4. Cf. J. C., "Chronique étrangère," *Zaïre*, VIII, No. 5 (May, 1954), 522.

and according to whether the surroundings are rural or urban.[5] Entrance into "Standard VII," which corresponds to schooling of ten years, and after that to higher education, is in fact achieved by 1 per cent of the rural population. One notes that the coastal region, known as the Colony, happens to have 1.6 per cent, while the Northern Territories have 0.13 per cent. In the eleven cities which have a population above 10,000 inhabitants, by contrast, the percentages at the same educational level constitute an average of 6.2. Surely this is not surprising; one must, however, emphasize the coincidence which exists between urbanization, modernization, economic expansion, and intellectual development which always has characterized the city in all places and in all periods of history.

The rise of educated elites, even if their number remains limited, involves difficult problems both in their relationships with the dominant European minority, which is afraid to let itself be supplanted, and in their relationships with the native societies still profoundly influenced by tradition. Their participation in local administrations, in the direction of enterprises of some importance, and in the "liberal" professions remains very far behind the employment demands of such a social category. This is witnessed by the fact that some students who have come to Europe, mistrustful of the possibilities that will be open to them in Africa, give up seeking employment in their native countries or returning there for some time. Political and racial factors partly explain such a situation for most of the African territories. In a recent study I stressed three kinds of difficulties that arise in the relations of the educated elite:[6] "The lack of preparation for granting to members of this elite the superior status which is due them; the difficulty of integrating them into the structure of various professions, especially at a level which appears dangerous to the Europeans occupying inferior positions; the resistance to mixed marriages, which have justifiably

5. J. Boyon, "La Gold-Coast: De la colonisation à l'autonomie" (unpublished thesis, Institut d'Études Politiques, Paris, 1954).

6. Georges Balandier, "The Socioeconomic and Cultural Expression of Race Relationships in West and Central Africa" (unpublished paper submitted at the Honolulu Conference on Race Relations in World Perspective, summer, 1954).

increased with the widening of the African elite." In a very schematic but significant way, one could say that the expansion of this social category necessarily transforms, or will transform, the nature of established relations with the European minorities and that of the relations existing between "modernists" and "traditionalists" within the native society.

## II

After this discussion of some of the major phenomena which bear witness to the intensity of the changes affecting Negro-African societies, I now examine in a detailed (but necessarily theoretical) way the principal categories of social changes. In so doing, I will stress the new processes of differentiation which have generally entailed the breakdown of the old equilibriums and the loss of efficacy of the old systems of compensation.

1. The most apparent fact is clearly that of the changes which have come about in the "techniques of space management,"[7] of exploitation and circulation of wealth. The transition is taking place in a society whose economy is open, has become sensitive to the vicissitudes of the exterior market, and has permitted an accumulation of capital inconceivable within a traditional framework, from a society with a closed economy, characterized by its limited extent and the strict control exercised over the production and circulation of goods. The rigorous principles governing the purchase and sale of brides exhibits the limits of this primitive economic control. This is a process of transformation from an agricultural society with a loosely knit population and a decentralized administration to a society in the process of industrialization, in which this process together with the centralization of power by the colonizer favors the rapid growth of an urban population; from a society limited in its relations with the exterior world to one in which the methods and the frequency of communications are being multiplied and accelerated.

Similar transformations are overtaking Negro-African societies in two fields which used to be sources of equilibrium: the

7. This expression (*"techniques d'aménagement de l'espace"*) is borrowed from the French geographer, P. Gourou.

factors assuring the permanence of custom, of tradition, which stress the virtue of conformity, and the techniques contributing to the security of groups and of individuals. The market economy and the necessity of having recourse to wage employment involve a redistribution of the population in terms of commercial routes and centers of production (a redistribution which may be spontaneous or brought about by direct or indirect constraint), a circulation of men and of wealth, a coming-into-contact with strange elements quite as much as a trying-out of radically new behavior. These relationships take on added importance, and monetary needs, constantly increasing, multiply the number of individuals who must participate in the activities of the "modern" sector. Social types appear—planters, merchants, and tradesmen, wage-earners making up a labor force of exceptional mobility—who represent an equal number of homes for, or conveyors of, the modern spirit. In an uninterrupted way, and at an accelerated pace, relations with things (the soil, in particular) and with men are transformed. One can, by observing the societies of South and Central Africa, which are the most disorganized, judge to what degree these changes are making ready for a real social mutation.

Such a transformation alters the old power relations and the traditional status system. As often pointed out, in societies which were once hierarchical, rank and power no longer coincide (barring an adaptation of the "chief" to new economic conditions), and in societies which one might describe as exhibiting "egalitarian tendencies" (e.g., the Fang of the Cameroons and Gabon) possibilities for personal advantages develop at the same time as magic observances called forth by jealousy or the refusal of inequality. Customary honors and positions of importance are explained by reference to a precise social system, based on the sacred character of the chief or the elder; the new political relations reveal the determining and brutal role of the economic conditions introduced by the colonial power. Any authority exercised over an individual tends to lead to the use of this individual as a producer of wealth; in such a case the relations between different generations, between sexes, and between unequal elements of the same group are distorted. Every exploitation of one of the channels of the circulation of wealth tends to become a continual accumulation of goods and of capital, which is then put to a usurious use. The deterioration of the system of exchange of women (and of commodities of high value which are treated in an analogous fashion to women) can be explained as a result of this double tendency.

The question which arises now is to know in what measure the new social strata foreshadow *classes*, in the sense in which we understand them in our industrial societies. One must note, in this connection, that the process of their formation is very different from that which took place, in Europe, for example, following the industrial revolution. It is linked to an economic development conditioned by intervention from the outside (that of a metropolitan power) and gives birth to social categories which, whatever their mutual power relations, are *all* inferior with respect to the dominant foreign elite.[8] During the initial period this group, which one might call the "economic elite," or economically advanced portion of the population, can be formed only by means of collaboration with the foreign elite. This explains why these new forces have often appeared on the fringe of the traditional authorities who generally constitute centers of resistance to foreign domination. Thus we have observed in Central Africa the rise of former "slaves" simultaneously with the downfall of traditional chiefs. But, in a second phase, the economic elites discover a limit to their rise and experience the colonial situation as an obstacle to their expansion; antagonism follows co-operation, and they find themselves again among those parts of the population who feel themselves oppressed by the foreign elite. The associations of native African planters, in East and West Africa, often appear as originators of organized opposition to the foreign elite.

Tensions between unequal elements of a Negro-African society are lessened according as the antagonism to the foreign elite

8. [In the French original the dominant foreign minority is called *société coloniale* and is opposed to the native-governed majority called *société colonisée*. These terms are explained further in the author's "La Situation coloniale: Approche théorique," *Cahiers internationaux de sociologie*, Vol. XI (1951). In order to avoid misunderstanding, the term *société coloniale* has been translated as "foreign elite" and the term *société colonisée* as "native society."—EDITOR.]

is enhanced. That limit, already noted, to the expansion of the new social strata entails, consequently, a limit to the development of relations involving open conflict between individuals of unequal status. The colonizing power has created a situation involving profound social changes, but the control which it exercises imposes an upper limit to these processes; there is here a fundamental contradiction which explains the more or less obvious state of crisis of the most "advanced" Negro societies. In addition to this observation of capital importance, it is fitting to stress that the maintenance (even at a low level) of the familial economies and the persistence of certain traditional relations between individuals of unequal economic status also contribute to the weakening of the antagonisms. I have drawn attention to this double action, at the time of my sociological study of the Brazzaville Negroes, in the midst of a very transformed environment. I wrote: "This analysis leads us to conclude that the relative persistence of traditional relations [common ethnic and kinship ties] and the opposition unified to a certain degree against the foreign elite contribute, in addition to the shallowness of the economic structures, to counteracting the formation of those radically incompatible groups which are the social classes."[9] These considerations invite caution and suggest the necessity of an approach adapted to a new type of situation. As concerns the definitions of social strata, this approach, though no less specific than that based on the concept of classes, must first be made more precise.

2. Nearly all the societies of Negro Africa, even most of those which have become converted to Islam, have only oral traditions. Their material signs and symbols have not developed to a systematization of current usage. They are, according to the terminology of the Anglo-Saxon anthropologists, nonliterate. Colonization has brought them writing and some of the knowledge transmitted thereby; it has imposed on them techniques of administration of men and of goods which demand recourse to writing. Such a cultural change is of great consequence; it

9. Georges Balandier, *Sociologie des Brazzavilles noires* (to be published in "Collection de la Fondation Nationale des Sciences Politiques" [Paris: Armand Colin]). The expression "radically incompatible" groups is derived from Georges Gurvitch.

entails a new organization of thought and imposes the knowledge of the literate man or of the clerk. Systematic studies
could show, and evaluate, the nature and extent of the transformations which have come about with regard to knowledge
accumulated since the introduction of this new technique. In a
work devoted partly to the Fang of Gabon, I noted the changes
which are due to the introduction of writing: The idea of power
—from the example of the "orders" or regulations emanating
from the administration—tends to associate itself with the use
of writing; recourse to the written word becomes established as
a "means designed to bring about innovations in custom," "as
a substitute for the former rules of evidence," and as a possibility of bringing in the idea of the authority of past judicial decisions. Finally, the different attempts at social reconstruction
have shown the role of a "rudimentary bureaucracy" foreign to
that introduced by the colonial administration. These are only
brief indications, however, which suggest to what degree research oriented along these lines could bring new insights.

The place which the literate native, or person with "advanced education," tends to take is nevertheless likely to create
antagonisms. In a traditional environment the conflicts of more
or less immediate concern have to do with competition for
power; in an urban environment they take on the aspect of tensions between newly differentiated groups. Monica Hunter, in
her study of the Pondo of South Africa, has stressed the gulf
existing between the educated and the noneducated groups.[10]
I, too, in my *Sociologie des Brazzavilles noires*, emphasized the
reality of this gap caused by the acquisition of modern education:

The gulf exists and is apparent at different levels; it is accompanied by the
fact that this social stratum [the group with "advanced education"] is conscious of forming a superior group apart, aspiring to the highest incomes, but
having responsibilities and duties tied to the leadership role which it tries
to assert. One must likewise note the appearance of a *morale* peculiar to this
group . . . a certain spirit, which one could call bourgeois, tends to establish
itself and to reinforce the consciousness that this group has of itself.[11]

I will show elsewhere how the relations maintained with the
other different strata of the native society and with the foreign
elite are particularly ambiguous.

10. *Reaction to Conquest* (London, 1936).          11. *Op. cit.*

3. Finally, among the most active processes of differentiation, careful attention must be given to the evangelizing of the colonizers. It involves the degradation of the traditional religious foundations and the establishment of serious inconsistencies (the most notable of which is the impossibility of being at the same time Christian and polygamous). It also involves what has been called by some the expansion of "imported differences," such as those which arise between Christians and pagans or between Christians of different denominations. Thus, a Negro essayist of Central Africa, J. R. Ayouné, harshly blames the religious confusion on the colonizer and goes so far as to demand that the latter intervene to re-create the lost unity. He condemns "a state of affairs which only has the effect of creating a lamentable confusion in moral development" and adds: "The Negro of Africa, whoever he may be, has a rudiment of religion; to take it away from him and substitute atheism or a confusion of imported religious doctrines is a sure way to make of him an alienated person; he must choose one of them and it is up to the colonizer to find it."[12] This quotation is very revealing, but it does not sufficiently express the depth of the transformation which is going on. Christianity has tried above all to gain an influence over those social groups which are lowest within the traditional society—the "slaves," the women, the children— and has brought into the open some latent conflicts. It has also, in a completely involuntary way, begun the political education of the African by bringing him a knowledge likely to nourish his protest, while condemning the contradiction which exists between the teaching of the colonizer and the situation which he creates alongside of it.[13] Without any doubt its importance in the interplay of the conflicts between groups is considerable.

## III

In reviewing these different processes, we must state precisely the way in which antagonisms between individuals and groups are actually expressed. I can do it only in a general form,

12. J. R. Ayouné, "Occidentalisme et africanisme," in *Renaissances*, special number, October, 1944.

13. Cf. Georges Balandier, "Messianismes et nationalismes en Afrique noire," *Cahiers internationaux de sociologie*, XIV (1953), 41–65.

but I will take care to refer constantly to the results of my own investigations in Central Africa.

1. The colonial situation involves not only intervention and the introduction of new techniques and cultural models, the appearance of new processes of social differentiation; it entails, with respect to that dominant minority which is the "foreign elite," a reorientation of the social structure. In overturning the traditional equilibriums, it lets come to the surface some of the very antagonisms repressed in order to maintain these equilibriums. This is particularly apparent in the relations between sexes and between generations; the relative emancipation of women and young men, who were traditionally dominated by means of the economic, political, and cultural conditions brought about by the colonizer, appears to be one of the most widespread changes. It is accomplished by utilizing the opportunities which the foreign elite can present (help of the religious missions, the role of the school, and flight to the wage-earning sector and the cities) and consequently arouses the reactions of the individuals most interested in maintaining the traditional order. Thus I have observed in the Fang country, in Gabon, the development of a veritable antifeminism which attributes to the fact that women "have become wrongheaded" all the alleged disorders and especially the decline in fertility of the men and the soil.

I have mentioned how the introduction of new techniques of exploitation of wealth and the market economy has transformed the political relations; however, the antagonisms which could result from this are provisionally limited because they are forced to model themselves on traditional patterns—to acclimatize themselves, one might say, to the traditional environment. I verified this while studying the phenomena of social change among the Fang of Gabon and of the Cameroons. Thus, the accumulation of personal wealth "is not tolerated if a group of some importance is not present to protect it and to participate in it in return"; the formation of a rudimentary agricultural wage-earning class in the service of the important Negro planters was possible at first only with the help of certain devices, for example, keeping young workers by helping them to assemble a dowry, for the "rich" man can only with difficulty dominate directly other men from his clan.

2. The mechanism of utilization of traditional models for new purposes constitutes one of the principal characteristics of the transformations at present going on in Negro Africa. I have just briefly emphasized the operation of this among the Fang. The aims of this phenomenon can be defined in the following ways:

*a*) To serve the interest of certain social strata by means of the disorders which come to light in the traditional environment. One could cite as an example in the case of matrilineal societies the conflicts between maternal uncle and real father over the "capital" (in labor, wages, and dowry) represented by the children—conflicts which are expressed and which individuals strive to settle by invoking custom, now inadequate in the new economic context.

*b*) To favor the most indispensable adaptations while maintaining a sociological structure which continues to be significant and familiar for the majority of individuals—those who experience the upheavals and cling all the more closely to the tradition which they feel the more threatened. This aspect remains the most apparent in the interior of the Negro towns. It is a question of a "tactic" of adaptation simultaneously with a reaction to the downfall of the sociocultural structures. With respect to the research at Brazzaville, I indicated concerning the first point: "The form has been maintained, favoring thus the adherence of the noneducated majority which continues mistrustful of the radically new organizations, but the contents have been transformed; in this way is brought about the transition to social models better adapted to the situations which arise in the urban environment." It is no less true that this is a "recasting" resulting in new political relations within the native society and at the same time a hostile reaction to the ascendancy of the foreign elite.

*c*) To protect, by means of the cultural time lag existing between colonized and colonizer, the countermeasures to the domination exercised by the latter. In fact, there is here a "strategic" utilization of cultural diversity and at the same time the manifestation of a need explained by the limits which the colonizer imposes on all reorganization of a "modern" type. Thus the most dynamic attempts are those which operate under cover of a cultural screen which deceives or inhibits the dominant foreign minority. For example, in the Negro Brazzavilles the politico-religious organizations, formed on traditional patterns, continue to represent a preponderant political force which reduces the field of action of the modern parties but above all can act more efficaciously than the latter. A study of the current nativistic movements in South and Central Africa reveals that these movements, which appear at first glance to be a return to religious organizations and behavior of a traditional type, really have a modern content as nationalistic reactions or social protest movements.[14]

3. Finally, we must point out the ambiguity which fundamentally governs the relations existing among the strata emerging within the native society and those existing between the latter and the foreign elite. I demonstrated this in my publications on Central Africa, for example, by showing "the freedom of movement permitted by the time lag between traditional laws and the law appropriate to the urban environment" and in revealing "how behavior regarding women and feminine emancipation varies greatly for the same individual according to the social strata to which he successively belongs," by showing in the case of the Fang of Gabon how recourse to custom takes a different direction (and often contradictory in spite of the apparent unanimity) according to whether it is the "young Fang" or the "old Fang" who are involved. Behavior toward the dominant European minority is likewise of an equivocal nature; the degree of collaboration remains a function of the advantages provisionally expected from it. It is precarious, or adapted to circumstance. Thus the so-called "educated natives" attach themselves to the foreign elite to the extent to which they do not succeed in asserting their authority within the traditional environment from which they come and to the extent to which they find themselves "compromised" because of their education and the uses to which they put this education.

I have been able to adduce only general information—the

14. *Ibid.*

observation of processes and conflicts which are among the most apparent. It is certain that important variations occur in different situations. Negro-African societies do not all have the same capacity for internal resistance; they are not all subject to the same kind of economic, political, and cultural pressure from the European powers. This explains why the problems which they pose do not all manifest themselves in the same order of priority. For certain of them (in Central Africa, for example) the problems of internal reorganization are the most urgent; for others, less affected internally by colonial contact, demands for autonomy predominate. But one must not believe that it is a question here of two series of separate phenomena, for the native societies advance toward internal reconstruction, and those manifesting a need for greater autonomy will necessarily be closely linked.

# THE IMPACT OF COLONIALISM ON AFRICAN SOCIAL FORMS AND PERSONALITY

## E. FRANKLIN FRAZIER

*Howard University*

IN A book published not many years ago, Toynbee made the
prediction that future historians would say that "the great
event of the twentieth century was the impact of the Western civilization upon all the other living societies of the world of
that day. They will say of this impact that it was so powerful
and so pervasive that it turned the lives of all its victims upside
down and inside out—affecting the behavior, outlook, feelings,
and beliefs of individual men, women, and children in an intimate way, touching chords in human souls that are not touched
by mere external material forces—however ponderous and ter-
rifying."[1]

Whether or not future events will confirm Toynbee's prediction, there can be no question of the correctness of his own brief
but vivid description of the profound effects of the impact of
Western civilization on non-European peoples. Of the non-
European peoples who have been influenced by Western civilization, none reveals more strikingly the changes described by
Toynbee than the peoples of Africa. It is with the changes which
have occurred in Africa that this paper is concerned. An attempt will be made to define in a systematic fashion the sociological problems which have resulted from colonialism or the various types of economic exploitation and systems of social control
through which African peoples have experienced the impact of
Western civilization. These problems are sociological in the
broad meaning of the term, inasmuch as the impact of the West
has, in Toynbee's words, "turned their lives upside down and
inside out"; that is, it has destroyed the social forms in which

1. Arnold J. Toynbee, *Civilization on Trial* (New York: Oxford University Press,
1948), p. 214.

the traditional "behavior, outlook, feelings, and beliefs of individual men and women" were shaped and had meaning.

## I

Before attempting to characterize the nature of the sociological problems resulting from the impact of colonialism on the social organization and personality of African peoples, it is necessary to consider the changes in the physical milieu within which the drama of a new social life is developing as well as the consequences of the demographic changes which have resulted from European contact and control. In the vast territory south of the Sahara the original form of settlement consisted of agglomerations of family groups that cultivated in common the soil from which they drew their subsistence.[2] Between these family groups and the land they cultivated there has always existed a sacred bond. The religious character of this relationship is revealed in the major role of the priest, who served as mediator between his clansmen and the gods of the earth.

The size of these agglomerations of family groups has varied considerably, ranging from what might be called mere hamlets to villages or rural communities. The size as well as the stability of these rural communities have been affected by needs for defense against invasions, the type of agriculture in which the families were engaged, and the necessity to seek new lands to cultivate or for their flocks to graze. In the spatial patterns formed by the agglomeration of families is often revealed a past nomadic existence, as, for example, in the starlike arrangements of the huts among the Peuls in West Africa or the circular arrangement of the Hottentot kraals in South Africa. Even when conquest and the development of political structures have created large settlements, the relation between the family groups and the soil has retained its traditional sacred character.

The colonization of Africa was carried out principally through the conquest of the native peoples, who maintained a fierce opposition to European domination until after the first World

2. Max Sorre, *Les Fondements de la géographie humaine* (Paris: Librairie Armand Colin, 1952), III, 76 ff. For West Africa see Henri Labouret, *Paysans d'Afrique Occidentale* (Paris: Gallimard, 1941).

War.[3] Force was not utilized, however, simply to establish European control. It was used to suppress the slave trade carried on by the Arabs, which had disrupted African society and depopulated the country. Force was also employed to suppress native wars and establish peace and security among African peoples. In fact, it is generally agreed that one of the main beneficial results of European control has been the establishment of peace and security in Africa. At the same time, the establishment of European control brought about a dislocation of the native populations, which has had more far-reaching consequences than native wars and the slave trade. It has radically changed the physical basis of life for large sections of the native population.

The dislocation of native peoples has resulted from industrialization and urbanization, which are often closely tied up. There has been an industrialization of agriculture through the development of plantations, as, for example, the rubber and palm-oil plantations in the British and French Cameroons. Included in the same category are the large-scale schemes for commercial crops, as, for example, cacao farming on the Gold Coast. Although originally cacao farming was carried on by small farmowners, large plantations with tenants have gradually come into existence. In cacao farming on the Gold Coast as well as in the growing of groundnuts in Senegal much of the labor is performed by seasonal workers who are drawn from the interior. The influence of industrialization on the dislocation of native populations is even more striking wherever mining has been introduced in Africa. Similar consequences have followed the introduction of the timber industry in the Belgian Congo, Kenya, and Nigeria.

The urbanization of the native population through the growth of industrial centers and the development of commerce and transportation have brought into existence large concentrations of native populations, numbering in some cases more than a hundred thousand individuals.[4] The changes in the

3. See Sir Harry H. Johnson, *A History of the Colonization of Africa by Alien Races* (Cambridge: University Press, 1913), *passim;* see also Jacques Richard-Molard, *Afrique Occidentale française* (Paris: Éditions Berger-Levault, 1952), pp. 145–46.

4. See, e.g., Jean-Paul Lebeuf, "Centres urbains d'Afrique Équatoriale française," *Africa*, XXIII (October, 1953), 285–97.

physical basis of life arising from the concentration of native peoples about mines and industrial centers and in cities are reflected in the new types of housing to which they must adjust. The traditional African hut and its place in a pattern of village life represented an adaptation not only to climatic and physical conditions but to a way of life as well. When houses were first erected in the mining camps to provide for the shelter of African workers, they were built without regard for the traditional culture and social needs of the occupants. But, in order to preserve a healthy, happy, and regular supply of labor, there has been a growing disposition on the part of Europeans to build houses for their native workers to conform to the traditional habitations of natives in addition to improvements in regard to hygiene, sanitation, and arrangements for familial relationships.[5] Moreover, in planning the conditions of physical existence, increasing attention is being paid to the location of housing in relation to gardens and the agricultural resources surrounding the new settlements. On the other hand, in the new cities which have sprung up in Africa there is still need for planning in order to provide the physical conditions necessary for social life. For example, a recent survey of the housing in an African city with a native population of forty-five thousand revealed that many natives slept in the streets and that those who slept in houses were often crowded in rooms with four persons.[6] There were inadequate provisions for sanitation, which has become a problem where the creation of quasi-urban and urban areas has introduced a new physical basis of social life.

The changes in the physical basis of social life which have resulted from European contact and control have been accompanied by demographic changes which have affected the traditional culture and the social organization of native life. Since the beginning of European contacts, natives have been drawn from their native villages to perform services for the whites. In leaving their traditional way of life, they have not acted as free

5. E. Deleeuw, "L'Agglomeration indigène de la 'geomines' conditions materielles—œuvres sociales," *Comptes rendus du Congrès scientifique* (Elizabethville, 1950, 13–19 Août), Vol. VI, *Comité-Special du Katanga* (Bruxelles, n.d.), p. 119.

6. K. A. Busia, *Report on a Social Survey of Sekondi-Takoradi* (London: H.M. Stationery Office, 1950); see also Ellen Hellman, *Rooiyard: A Sociological Study of an Urban Native Slum Yard* (Cape Town: Oxford University Press, 1948).

agents choosing a new way of life.[7] It has been pointed out, for example, that, when the demands were first made for native labor in the mines of the Belgian Congo, the natives were fearful of accepting employment.[8] In fact, when the natives have left their villages, they have done so because of the forceful measures employed by Europeans to secure native laborers. They were forced to become laborers because of the scarcity of land resulting from the alienation of their lands by Europeans,[9] or they were forced to become laborers in order to pay taxes imposed by Europeans. Then systems of forced labor were established in the various colonies to secure a large and regular supply of labor. It was not until 1930 that the majority of the colonial powers agreed in the Geneva Convention on Forced Labor to eliminate compulsory labor.

Under a system of voluntary recruitment of labor as well as under the now disavowed system of forced labor, the recuitment of natives for work in mining, in timber, and in the cities has affected the age and sex distribution of the native population in villages. It has always been the young men who have left the villages to seek wages, or sometimes adventure, in the mining camps and the freer life of the cities. Consequently, it has been the old men and women and children who have been left behind to carry on the traditional life of the villages. This prosaic demographic change has been dramatized in the case of South Africa in the opera, *Lost in the Stars*, where the opening chorus sings: "These are the valleys of old men and old women, of mothers and children."

Among the natives in the rural areas of South Africa there are 86.4 males for every 100 females, and nearly a half of the population is under sixteen years of age.[10] Studies have revealed

7. John A. Noon, *Labor Problems of Africa* (Philadelphia: University of Pennsylvania Press, 1944), p. 5.

8. L. Mottoulle, "Contribution à l'historique des recrutements et emplois de la M.O.I. dans les Territoires du Comité-Special du Katanga," *Comptes rendus du Congrès scientifique*, VI (1950), 18.

9. Noon, *op. cit.*, p. 5. See Raymond Leslie Buell, *The Native Problem in Africa* (New York: Macmillan Co., 1928), for compulsory labor in the various colonies. See also Lord Olivier, *The Anatomy of African Misery* (London: Hogarth Press, 1927), *passim*.

10. Ellen Hellman (ed.), *Handbook of Race Relations in South Africa* (New York: Oxford University Press, 1949), pp. 14–19.

COLONIALISM AND SOCIAL FORMS AND PERSONALITY

the same type of demographic selection in other parts of Africa where the impact of European civilization has been experienced. In the villages of Gabon in French Equatorial Africa, where the age and sex distribution of the native population shows striking abnormalities as the result of labor recruiting over a long period, there is deficiency or total absence of young men.[11] A recent survey of Ashanti in the Gold Coast showed that there was a deficiency of both men and women between the ages of twenty-five and thirty-five, but the deficiency was greater among the men.[12] In fact, in recent years women in Africa have begun to migrate to the cities, and this is having its influence on the problems arising from urbanization.

Nevertheless, there continues to exist a large excess of males both in the native settlements about mining and timber enterprises and in the cities themselves. For example, in the urban areas of South Africa, the native male population is more than double the number of females, and 85 per cent of the males are of working age.[13] Not only are the native populations in the cities predominantly male; they are heterogeneous in that they are composed of representatives of many tribal origins. The survey of Sekondi-Takoradi, Gold Coast, revealed that there were sixty-one tribal divisions represented in the native population, not including Europeans and other foreigners.[14] Although there was some tendency for the different tribes to predominate in certain quarters, on the whole representatives of the various tribes were found in all parts of the city. The urban centers of French Equatorial Africa likewise show considerable tribal and racial heterogeneity.[15] For example, in Fort-Lamy, with a population of approximately forty thousand people, four-fifths of whom are Mohammedans, and in Bangui, which probably attained a population of one hundred thousand in 1953, the native population is composed of representatives from all over West Africa and the Belgian Congo.

11. Georges Balandier and J.-Cl. Pauvert, *Les Villages gabonais* ("Mémoires de l'Institut d'Études Centrafricaines" [Brazzaville, 1952]), pp. 16–27.

12. M. Fortes, *The Ashanti Social Survey: A "Preliminary Report"* ("Human Problems in British Central Africa," Vol. VI [New York: Oxford University Press, 1948]), p. 8.

13. Hellman, *op. cit.*

14. Busia, *op. cit.*, pp. 3–4.     15. Lebeuf, *op. cit.*

The vitality and the growth of the native populations under the new conditions of life are subjects to which much attention is being given. We are not concerned with this phase of the demography of Africa except so far as the growth or decline of African peoples affects the new social forms which have come into existence as the result of European contact or as the health and the vitality of the native peoples influence their response to the demands of a new type of social life.

## II

Let us examine, then, against the background of the changes in the physical bases of social life and demographic changes sketched above some of the more important results of the impact of European contacts on the social organization of African life. The impact of European civilization on the African family must be considered first because of the importance of the family in the entire organization of African life. The importance of the family has been indicated by the large amount of study which has been devoted to analysis of the effects of European contacts and control in its organization and functioning under changing conditions. In fact, the study of the family provides the most fruitful approach to study of detribalization.[16] Dislocations in any part of the native social structure are reflected in the family, while the disruption of the family system affects the entire social structure. In a recent comprehensive survey of African marriage and family life it is pointed out that "the family is the most significant feature of African society," and the family is described as the "central institution."[17] In this study the nature of marriage and the family in African society is described as follows:

> The family itself, in Africa as in other parts of the world where people get their subsistence from direct production through the cooperation of kinsmen, is often differently constituted from the grouping to which the name is given in Western society—the unit consisting of two parents with their children which some anthropologists call the elementary family. The feature

16. Eileen Jensen Krige, "Changing Conditions in Marital and Parental Duties among Urbanized Natives," *Africa*, IX (January, 1936), 1–23.

17. Arthur Phillips (ed.), *Survey of African Marriage and Family Life* (New York: Oxford University Press, 1953), p. ix.

of African marriage which is perhaps most widely known to the general public is that of polygamy—the legal marriage of one man to two or more women concurrently is permitted. In fact this rule is only one aspect of a system where cooperation in tilling the fields and herding the cattle is provided by a group of people bound by the obligations of kinship and marriage and not by the relationship of wage earner to employer. The larger the cooperating group, the greater the possibilities of wealth and of defense against enemies, and the more children are born to any group, the greater its hopes of expansion in the future. Legitimate children are secured by marriage in due form, and the importance of securing legitimate descendants accounts for the most characteristic features of African marriage law. Women have their own share, an important one, in the division of labour, and both the wealth of the group and its hopes of progeny are greater in proportion to the number of wives.[18]

This description makes it understandable why it is in the family that the disintegration of African society resulting from European contact is most apparent. The disintegration of the traditional family is shown first in "the diminishing importance of the collective or group aspect of marriage."[19] Marriage is becoming an arrangement between individuals in which the prospective husband, instead of his kinsmen, provides the bride price (*lobola*), which is so important in cementing family groups. Thus the weakening of the authority of the kinsmen results in the decay of the bonds which hold the traditional society together.

In the rural areas the economic factor is largely responsible for the emergence of individual needs and wishes in opposition to the traditional solidarity of kinsmen because of the need for money to pay taxes. Generally the only way that cash can be obtained to pay taxes is for the young men to seek work in the industrial establishments of Europeans. The introduction of money into the economy has tended further to secularize the customary bride price and weaken the sacred bonds of kinship and the obligations associated with it.[20] As the men become wage-earners, they want to pay the bride price in cash rather than in cattle. Then, in those parts of Africa where the young

18. *Ibid.*, p. 1.

19. *Ibid.*, p. xvii.

20. Cf. Richard C. Thurnwald, *Black and White in East Africa* (London: George Routledge & Sons, 1935), pp. 108 ff.

men owe their fathers-in-law certain customary services, they are offering goods and money in the place of these services.

The economic and social forces which have been responsible for the destruction of the traditional African family in the rural areas become even more destructive in the urban areas. It might be said that the new social forms which are coming into existence are due to urbanization or a new way of life.[21] In the mobile life of the city, where contacts tend to be impersonal, the traditions respecting marriage not only become unsuited to the new social environment but may become an obstacle to marriage. This has been true of the Bantu marriage negotiations in the cities of South Africa.[22] Then, since the urbanized native often maintains contacts with the rural natives and may secure a wife from among them, conflicts are likely to arise. Sometimes there are conflicts between the girl's parents and the prospective husband over the bride price, which the completely detribalized native may reject on principle.[23] Moreover, since the urbanized native population is drawn from many different tribes, there is no agreement in regard to marriage customs. A sample survey of 333 families in Sekondi-Takoradi showed that 30.6 per cent of the marriages were intertribal.[24] Conflicts often arise in intertribal marriages because of cultural differences, as, for example, the differences in the laws of patrilineal and matrilineal tribes respecting inheritance.

In the urban environment the traditional definitions of the roles of husband and wife in marital and familial relations lose their force, and there is much confusion concerning the responsibilities and duties of the partners in marriage. Any attempt to establish a polygamous family in the city is rendered impossible because of the character of housing in the city. Then, too, polygamy is generally not countenanced by the municipal authorities, and the wife may complain to the authorities if her husband brings a second wife into the house.[25] Among African tribes it is customary for the wife to cook and work for her

21. See Louis Wirth, "Urbanism as a Way of Life," *American Journal of Sociology*, XLIV (July, 1938), 1–24.

22. Krige, *op. cit.*, pp. 17–18.

23. *Ibid.*, p. 13.

24. Busia, *op. cit.*, p. 29.

25. Phillips (ed.), *op. cit.*, p. 29.

mother-in-law before establishing her own house.[26] This means that the native wife in the city must leave her husband and return to his mother in the village. In traditional African society the wife has a status inferior to her husband, but in the city, where the wife becomes a wage-earner, she is likely to revolt against an inferior status. The responsibility of the husband in regard to his wife takes on a new character when the traditional division of labor no longer exists. It may happen that, as in the case of the matrilineal Akan society in the Gold Coast, both husband and wife have to share their income with maternal kin.[27]

Similar problems arise in regard to the relations of children with their parents. In the cities the parents are unable to exercise the same supervision and enforce the same discipline as in rural areas. In the villages the father arranged the marriages of his sons, and his authority could be enforced because he provided his sons with the bride price. On the other hand, in the city, where the son is able through his own labor to secure the bride price, he may not accept his father's choice of a mate and may insist upon marrying the woman whom he selects. In fact, the city provides many opportunities for young men and women to meet and choose their marriage partners.

The confusions and disorder in the relations of men and women in the city result sometimes from the fact that the traditional family mores are not applicable to urban life. For example, in South Africa it has been observed that many young men cannot marry because of the expense of helping to support their sisters' illegitimate children.[28] The confusion and disorder in the relations of the sexes result in desertion, adultery, divorce, illegitimacy, and the neglect of children. There is much concubinage in the cities, and the unions which men and women form are very unstable. Even when regular marriages are entered into according either to traditional forms or to the new Christian and civil forms, there may be adultery, since polygamous practices have not been abandoned entirely. Moreover,

26. Krige, *op. cit.*, pp. 18–19.

27. Phillips (ed.), *op. cit.*, p. 151.

28. Krige, *op. cit.*, p. 20.

marriages—civil as well as religious—in the city involve expenses which generally cannot be borne by the partners.[29] Consequently, it happens that many couples may live together in a stable association over a long period without marriage. As the result of such unions, as well as the less stable unions, there is much illegitimacy. In the case of illegitimacy resulting from less stable unions, the father may assume responsibility for the children because of the traditional attitude toward children. In the city, on the other hand, wives and children are not considered the source of wealth and prestige as in the rural areas. Therefore, illegitimate children may swell the ranks of juvenile delinquents, who are becoming a problem as the result of the destruction of the traditional African family.[30]

The changes in the structure and functioning of the African family which have been described thus far are attributable partly to the influence of Christian missionaries and European administration. It is necessary to consider more specifically, though in a summary manner, the impact of Christianity and European administration on the traditional African family. Christian missionaries have condemned ancestor worship as a superstitious practice. The abandonment of this practice has affected the social solidarity which it created and maintained. Christian missionaries have also condemned polygamy, and, when natives were received into the Christian church, it has been on the condition that they had abandoned the practice of polygamy. Christian opposition to polygamy has doubtless had some influence, but changing economic conditions have been more effective on the system of plural marriages. The condemnation by the missionaries of premarital sex relations has not prevented the continuation of such practices, which may have certain beneficial results. Christian marriage in some parts of Africa has been a stabilizing force for some favored elements in a changing society, but it has also introduced conflicts in moral ideals and required accommodations on the part of the masses.

29. *Ibid.*, pp. 15–16.

30. Busia, *op. cit.*, chap. vii on juvenile delinquency in Sekondi-Takoradi. See also J. D. Rheinhallt Jones, "Social and Economic Condition of the Urban Native," in I. Schapera (ed.), *Western Civilization and the Natives of South Africa* (London: George Routledge & Sons, 1934), p. 189.

On the whole, Christian teachings have supported equality between the sexes and have thus given moral support to women who are escaping from their traditional subordination to their husbands. It was probably due to a recognition on the part of the various Christians of the above facts that at the La Zoute Conference in Belgium, in 1926, there was a "change in emphasis by all missions from outright condemnation to general sympathy toward African custom" and that missions were recommended to condemn "evil customs," not to condemn customs not incompatible with Christianity, and to purify and use African customs which have a valuable substance, though some features of them are "evil."[31]

It is more difficult to make a general statement regarding the influence which various European administrations have had on the traditional African family. This is not due, as it might appear on the surface, to whether the colonial administrations have been committed to a policy of assimilation or parallel development. For, as one student of African problems has stated, "in a sense every African administration must contain elements of both principles, and it is sometimes misleading to set them in opposition to one another as competing principles of governments."[32] As regards marriage and domestic relations, every administration has had to take account of the traditional practices and the indigenous system of African law. It has been mainly in respect to monogamous marriage that European statutory law has influenced marital relations.[33] There has been a general recognition of customary laws except where they were opposed to public order and what was regarded as "natural morality." But, where it has been necessary to recognize polygamous marriage and the obligations involved in it, polygamy has not been regarded as opposed to "natural morality." As the result of the undermining of the economic and cultural basis of the institution of the bride price, it has been necessary for native administrations to introduce statutory regulations of this

31. Phillips (ed.), *op. cit.*, pp. 371-72.

32. Edgar H. Brookes, "Native Administration in South Africa," in Schapera (ed.), *Western Civilization and the Natives of South Africa*, p. 241. For a similar point of view see Robert Delavignette, *Service africain* (Paris: Gallimard, 1946), pp. 87-90.

33. Phillips (ed.), *op. cit.*, Part II, "Marriage Laws in Africa," pp. 176 ff.

important institution. Native administrations have also had to deal with divorce, and here customary law has also been recognized. Although native administrations have been opposed to the marriage of immature persons, they have been reluctant to interfere with native practices. On the other hand, European authorities have been less tolerant of child marriages. It is impossible to enumerate here the multiplicity of problems which native administrations have faced in dealing with the problems of domestic relations which have arisen as the result of European contact and control. It might be stated that, even where the greatest efforts have been made to bring about an accommodation between customary practices and new regulations, the very existence of statutory law has tended to affect traditional relations and to accentuate individualism in the new African societies.

Since, as we have seen, African marriage and family life were based upon economic co-operation among members of the same kinship group, the disorganization of the traditional African family has affected the organization of labor in the African villages. The most obvious effect of family disorganization appears in the fact that the migration of men to mining and industrial centers and cities has placed the burden of agricultural production upon women and boys.[34] This has generally resulted in decreased production, since, with the disorganization of the traditional family system, the absent man's kinsmen do not feel the obligation to aid his wife. The less obvious but nonetheless important effects of the decay of the traditional family system on the organization of labor come to light when one studies the relation of the family to the economic life of the village.[35] In the African village the household is the economic unit within which the husband with his wives and children co-operate in gaining a living from the soil. The husband, who acts as the head of the household, may plant a garden for his wives and provide them with a granary. There is a division of labor based upon sex

34. I. Schapera, *Married Life in an African Tribe* (New York: Sheridan House, 1941), p. 132.

35. See, e.g., Audrey T. Richards, *Land, Labour, and Diet in Northern Rhodesia* (New York: Oxford University Press, 1939), pp. 383–86.

within the household as well as in the village. Sometimes men and women form separate groups to carry out the division of labor between the sexes. The village is a larger economic unit under the direction of a headman whose authority rests upon kinship ties. There are organized forms of labor outside the kinship group which include the work of slaves (who really live as members of the household), the temporary service which women especially render to householders at harvesting time, and the communal forms of labor known as working bees.

European contact has tended everywhere to destroy the traditional organization of labor. For example, in South Africa, where the plow has been introduced, it has meant that men have assumed the role in agricultural production formerly played by the women with the hoes.[36] Thus, men who, as the result of European control, have "lost their old occupation of fighting" have begun to play an important part in agriculture. One result of the introduction of the plow with male labor has been an increase in agricultural production. On the other hand, in some areas of Africa, as the result of European contact, the drive behind agricultural production, which was associated with beliefs in the authority of the chiefs, has been weakened.[37] The manner in which European contact and control has affected the organization of production is shown in the case of the institution of cattle-keeping.[38] The difference between the European and the native attitude toward cattle-keeping has been well summed up as follows: "To Europeans cattle keeping is an economic activity, primarily concerned with profit and loss in terms of money. The Ngoni . . . keep cattle chiefly for purposes other than purely economic ones."[39] Among the Ngoni in Northern Rhodesia, the ownership of cattle was formerly a mark of an aristocratic rank. Since with the introduction of money anyone can buy cattle, wealth and rank have become dissociated, with the result that the ownership of cattle does not carry with it the

36. I. Schapera, "Present Day Life in the Native Reserves," in *Western Civilization and the Natives of South Africa*, pp. 41–42.

37. Richards, *op. cit.*, p. 403.

38. Margaret Read, *Native Standards of Living and African Culture Change*, supplement to *Africa*, XI, No. 3 (1938), 25 ff.

39. *Ibid.*, p. 25.

power to command labor. As a consequence, not only has the entire web of social relationships involving definite social obligations been disrupted but the production of food has suffered.

In studying the effects of European contacts on the organization of labor and agricultural production, it is necessary to consider the important consequences of European land policies in Africa. Some passing attention has been given to the fact that these policies have changed the physical bases of African society. Here we are concerned primarily with the manner in which land policies have affected the social organization of the native's life.

"There is no matter in which colonial policy expresses itself so conspicuously," wrote Lord Hailey, "as in the use which administrations make of their powers in regard to land, and certainly there is no question which has influenced more critically the attitude of Africans towards the governing powers."[40] The truthfulness of this observation is indicated by the notoriety given to facts concerning the alienation of native land all over Africa and the favorable reception which the Bantu agitator receives, for example, when he states: "When the white man first came to you, he had the Bible and you the land; but now you have the Bible and he has the land."[41] The land policies of the European powers have been based upon the theory that the European had a right which transcended the claim of the natives to occupy and exploit the resources of Africa. Backed by their governments, European settlers and European companies that were in need of land proceeded to take the land from the natives. The extent to which native land was alienated and the form of the alienation have been determined both by whether or not the land was suitable for European settlement and the natural resources of the land. If the land was suitable for European settlement, not only was the land alienated but the native population was expelled and placed in reserves. In South Africa, for example, where the Europeans constitute only one-fifth of the population, they control seven-eighths of the land, while the

40. *An African Survey* (New York: Oxford University Press, 1938), p. 712.

41. D. D. T. Jabavu, "Bantu Grievanc̈es," in Schapera (ed.), *Western Civilization and the Natives of South Africa*, p. 288.

natives, who constitute four-fifths of the population, have only one-eighth of the land for themselves.[42] Likewise, in the highlands of East Africa, especially in Kenya, native lands have been alienated not only for European concessions but for European settlement. On the other hand, in those areas of tropical Africa where European settlement on a large scale was not feasible, the alienation of native land has been restricted to concessions for the exploiting of the natural resources.

The alienation of the natives' land has had a profound effect upon the traditional organization of African society. Land hunger has become the major problem, social as well as economic, for the natives in many parts of Africa. In the Union of South Africa, where native landownership is restricted to the native reserves, the natives are crowded within a small area which can no longer support the native population. The policy of placing the natives on reserves was inaugurated and is continued solely in the interest of the European population. For example, in Kenya, where war has broken out recently between the natives and the Europeans, the latter have even pushed the natives off the reserves when gold was discovered or additional land was desired for exploitation. The very act of alienating the natives' land is in conflict with the African's concept of land, which was based on communal ownership. The distinction which Europeans have made between individually owned land and unused communally owned land which has become state or crown land was never accepted by the Africans.[43] The alienation of land has restricted the traditional economic activities of the African, such as hunting, collecting fruits, and grazing, and upset the system of customary practices which were associated with cattle-keeping. These economic activities were a part of a system of social relationships and were supported by certain value systems which have been destroyed by the alienation of the natives' land. As the result of the congested conditions in the native reserves, the natives have been forced to work on European farms, where they are kept in debt and subject to a type of con-

42. H. A. Wieschhoff, *Colonial Policies in Africa* (Philadelphia: University of Pennsylvania Press, 1949), p. 49.

43. *Ibid.*, p. 58.

trol legally supported by the pass laws, which make their condition hardly better than slavery. In order to escape these conditions, natives migrate to the towns and cities, where they hope to find a more attractive means of livelihood.

The African who goes to work in European mines and industries carries with him his traditional ideas and attitudes toward labor as well as whatever skills and talents he may possess. Labor for the African was a collective, familial, or communal undertaking and had for its end the subsistence of the group, and the value of labor was estimated in terms of the products distributed by the chief.[44] Moreover, the techniques utilized in work were involved in rites and prayers, which reveal the religious conceptions associated with labor. Magical practices were also involved in labor, while the rhythm characteristic of African labor was an emotional expression of its social character. These traditional ideas and attitudes are opposed generally to the situation which the native encounters when he arrives at the mines or in the towns.[45] Only under exceptional circumstances, as in West Africa, when the native goes to work at a new craft, he may be absorbed in the guilds which have taken the place of the lineage organizations associated with the traditional crafts.[46]

But the great mass of natives who go to work in European industries are placed under the supervision of unsympathetic Europeans and assigned to tasks which have no meaning from the standpoint of their traditional view of labor. Consequently, there is much complaint about the laziness and inefficiency of the native worker. The apathy and lack of energy on the part of the native are due partly to malnutrition. But the main reason for the so-called laziness and lack of efficiency on the part of the urbanized native is the absence of incentives, this fact being due to social conditions.[47] Of primary importance is the

44. J.-Cl. Pauvert, "La Notion de travail en Afrique noire," in *Le Travail africain* (Paris: Présence africaine, Éditions du Seuil, n.d.), pp. 98 ff.

45. J. Clyde Mitchell, *A Note on the Urbanization of Africans on the Copperbelt* ("Human Problems in British Central Africa," Vol. XII [New York: Oxford University Press, 1951]), pp. 20–27.

46. Peter Lloyd, "Craft Organization in Yoruba Towns," *Africa*, XXIII (January, 1953), 30–44.

47. See Boris Gussman, "Industrial Efficiency and the Urban African," *Africa*, XXIII (April, 1953), 135–44; see also Noon, *op. cit.*, pp. 14–22.

fact that the social evaluation of his work and the co-operation of his kinsmen which provided incentives in his traditional culture are absent. Then, when he goes to work in European industry, he is housed as though he were a work animal or a machine. There is little opportunity for a normal family and community life to provide a social milieu in which new incentives can take root and grow. The monetary rewards which are the chief inducement to work have little real meaning for the native under the conditions in which he works. There are restrictions placed upon the amount of money which he can earn, and he is excluded from competition with the European. As a consequence he has little concern for either efficiency or productivity and continues to regard the traditional way of life with kinsmen as the only secure form of existence.

Nevertheless, as the traditional tribal organization is being dissolved in the urban environment, new types of associations are growing to meet the needs of a new way of life.[48] In meeting the new needs of the urban environment, there is a tendency for the native to associate himself with those of the same ethnic origin as himself. For example, this has been revealed in a study of two native centers in Brazzaville, one of which was a veritable melting pot, containing more than sixty ethnic groups from French Equatorial Africa alone.[49] Spontaneous associations for cameraderie, for mutual assistance in securing a lodging or employment at better wages, or for recreation were based upon affiliation with the same ethnic group and the same community of origin. Moreover, the ties of family, though weakened, still operated as a basis of association. They provided the basis of a privileged class as well as the basis for economic co-operation between the rural community and the town.

The formally organized tribal associations which are coming into existence in various parts of Africa represent a transition

48. Hellman (*op. cit.*, p. 110) takes as her standard of detribalization the following criteria: "permanent residence in an area other than that of the chief to whom a man would normally pay allegiance; complete severance of the relationship to the chief; and independence of rural relatives both for support during periods of unemployment and ill-health or for the performance of ceremonies connected with the major crises of life."

49. Georges Balandier, "Approche sociologique des 'Brazzavilles noires': Étude préliminaire," *Africa*, XXII (January, 1952), 23–34.

from tribal life to the urban way of life. At the same time they may offer an obstacle to the development of civic responsibilities because of their tribal or ethnic exclusiveness.[50] They play an important role in the political life of the cities, where natives enjoy political rights. But generally these tribal associations have many functions, including mutual aid, the promotion of education, and the keeping-alive of tribal loyalties. They may undertake some of the functions of labor unions, but drastic restrictions are placed upon such activities by the administrators of native affairs.

The organization of African workers into unions only became important during World War II, and this development has been restricted to West Africa and the Union of South Africa. Labor unions have sprung up in French West Africa during recent years. In Nigeria about 16 per cent of the natives employed in European enterprises are members of unions.[51] A similar development has occurred in other West African colonies. The organization of African labor in East Africa has only begun on a small scale. In the Union of South Africa, where African workers have not been permitted to join white unions, it was not until 1943 that native labor unions were accorded legal recognition.[52] Because of the occupational color bar, the opposition of white workers, and the general policy of maintaining the native on a low standard of living, the native unions have had little influence on the working conditions and standard of living of the African workers.

There are other types of organization which have come into existence in the urban environment, designed to serve the new needs of the African and to give him a new orientation toward life. First among these organizations are the schools, which are changing the entire intellectual outlook of the African. The education of the natives was begun by the missionaries, but economic, social, and political developments within the colonies as well as in the outside world have required the colonial powers

50. Busia, *op. cit.*, pp. 73–76.

51. Noon, *op. cit.*, pp. 32–34.

52. Hellman (ed.), *op. cit.*, pp. 163 ff.

to give state aid to existing schools and to set up schools.[53] Many problems have been involved in the education of the African: the place of the vernacular in his education; the necessity of industrial and agricultural education as opposed to literary education; education in new ways of health and hygiene; and the education of women.[54] It is primarily in the school that the processes of culture change are occurring today. The school provides the African with his most important contacts with European civilization and introduces him to the new ways of satisfying his aspirations. But it is also in the schools that the conflicts of culture occur.[55]

We come, finally, to the new religious associations which have been brought into existence as the result of European contact and control. Many of these new associations are branches of the established Christian churches and, therefore, are helping to spread European culture. But there are other new religious associations, the independent African churches, which represent a rejection not only of the political domination of the European but, in a way, of European values.[56] The separate churches have much in common with religious movements of the messianic character among suppressed people in other parts of the world. At the same time these movements are tied up with nationalis-

53. For latest statistics on education of the African see *Public Expenditure on Education: A Preliminary Statistical Report Prepared by Department of Social Sciences, Statistical Division, UNESCO, 3d January, 1953* (Paris, 1953).

54. R. F. Alfred Hoernle, "Native Education at the Cross-Roads in South Africa," *Africa*, XI (October, 1938), 389–411; "Textbooks for African Schools: A Preliminary Memorandum by the Council," *Africa*, I (January, 1928), 13–20; Clement M. Doke, "Vernacular Textbooks in South African Native Schools," *Africa*, VIII (April, 1935), 183–207; William H. Laughton, "The Teaching of African Language in Schools: A Note on the Position in Kenya," *Africa*, III (April, 1930), 137–45; H. Labouret, "L'Éducation des masses en Afrique Occidentale française," *Africa*, VIII (January, 1935), 98–102; F. R. Irvine, "The Teaching of Agriculture in West Africa," *Africa*, V (October, 1932), 464–73; Mary Blacklock, "Co-operation in Health Education," *Africa*, IV (April, 1931), 202–8; and Eveline R. G. King, *On Educating Girls in Northern Rhodesia* ("Human Problems in British Central Africa," Vol. X [New York: Oxford University Press, 1950]), pp. 65–74.

55. See F. Musgrove, "A Uganda Secondary School as a Field of Culture Change," *Africa*, XXII (July, 1952), 234–49, and "Education and the Culture Concept," *ibid.*, XXIII (April, 1953), 110–26.

56. See Bengt G. M. Sundkler, *Bantu Prophets in South Africa* (London: Lutterworth Press, 1948), and see comments on the same by J. A. Barnes, *African Separatist Churches* ("Human Problems in British Central Africa," Vol. IX [New York: Oxford University Press, 1950]), pp. 26–30.

tic movements in Africa.[57] These movements are significant not only for the changes which are occurring in African social forms but for the changes in the African personality, to which we now turn.

## III

Here we are interested in the changes which are occurring in the personality of the African as the result of culture changes and the emergence of a new social organization. Although we cannot accept Malinowski's opposition to the study and analysis of the historical processes in studying culture changes, we agree with his statement that the ethnographer could not "accomplish the task of sorting out a westernized African into his component parts without destroying the one thing in him that matters—his personality" and that "the educated African is a new type of human being, endowed with abilities and energies, with advantages and handicaps, with problems and visions, which neither his European neighbor nor his 'blanket' brother are heirs to."[58] Thus the personality which the African has acquired as the result of social changes should be regarded as one aspect of an organic process involving an interaction between changes in the personality and changes in culture of the group.[59]

The first important effect of the changes resulting from European contact on the African's personality seems to be the development of an individualism that was unknown in traditional African society.[60] As we have seen, in the traditional African society the native was enmeshed in a web of social relationships, implying obligations and providing security, which left little room for the assertion of himself as an individual. "African

57. See Georges Balandier, "Messianismes et nationalismes en Afrique noire," *Cahiers internationaux de sociologie,* XIV (1953), 41–65.

58. Bronislaw Malinowski, *The Dynamics of Culture Change* (New Haven: Yale University Press, 1949), p. 25. For a criticism of the theories set forth in this book see Max Gluckman, *Malinowski's Sociological Theories* (Cape Town: Rhodes-Livingstone Institute [Oxford University Press], 1949).

59. Ellsworth Faris, *The Nature of Human Nature* (New York: McGraw-Hill Book Co., 1937), "Culture and Personality among the Forest Bantu," pp. 278–88.

60. *Ibid.,* p. 288.

society," writes Westerman, "is characterized by the prevalence of the idea of community." He adds:

> The individual recedes before the group. The whole existence from birth to death is organically embodied in a series of associations, and life appears to have its full value only in these close ties. Though there is in them a well-ordered gradation between persons who command and who obey, yet the prevailing feeling is that of equality. Class distinctions as we know them are absent or but feebly developed. They may be of greater weight in countries where there is a marked distinction between a ruling group and a subject people, but usually within a social unit the consciousness of a strong sense of solidarity is predominant. The group imposes duties on the individual but it also grants privileges; it takes from its members much of their personal responsibility and offers them its protection.[61]

The economic factor favors the development of individualism from the first contacts that the native has with European industry. When he goes to work on a European farm or at the mines, "he receives wages as an individual; he pays tax as an individual; . . . if he marries he finds the necessary cattle out of his own earnings instead of relying upon the obligations of his clansmen or kinsmen to contribute."[62] Conversion to Christianity has tended to reinforce and provide a moral and religious basis for the individualism that has resulted from European contact. The very act of becoming a Christian has generally meant an assertion of his individuality in opposition to group pressure. For, as Westerman has pointed out, "conversion is a personal matter, an affair between man and God. A man may draw his family with him, but for them as for him it is a personal step. When a person living in pagan surroundings adopts Christianity he often loses the protection or even membership of his group and has to stand by himself."[63]

As the African has been compelled "to stand by himself" in economic and social relations, he has been compelled to adopt a rational attitude toward the world. This does not mean that he has escaped from the influence of his traditional world domi-

61. Diedrich Westerman, *The African Today and Tomorrow* (New York: Oxford University Press, 1949), p. 65.

62. Edwin W. Smith, *Knowing the African* (London: Lutterworth Press, 1946), p. 65; see also L. P. Mair, *An African People in the Twentieth Century* (London: George Routledge & Sons, 1934), pp. 275 ff.

63. Diedrich Westerman, *Africa and Christianity* (New York: Oxford University Press, 1937), p. 102.

nated by magical and religious beliefs and rituals. An observer has noted the absence of economic sense among East Africans.[64] This is attributed, however, not only to their present lack of opportunities for acquiring Western economic values but also to the absence of markets in their traditional culture. The necessity for Africans, freed from their traditional culture, to adopt a rational attitude toward the world has led to much confusion and contradiction in their behavior. It has raised questions concerning their intellectual capacities. Gradually the traditional ideas concerning the intellectual capacities of the so-called primitive peoples, which were given a classical formulation by Herbert Spencer, have been discarded.[65] Moreover, if the more recent notions concerning the mystical and prelogical mentality of preliterate peoples have any meaning, they can be understood only in relation to the culture of a people. It is probably true, as a sociologist has remarked, that "there was probably quite as much magic in the Rome of Augustus Caesar as now on the Congo."[66] Because of the manner in which culture and personality are intimately related, there are many difficulties that stand in the way of studying the personality of non-European peoples.[67] In view of the difficulties involved in applying the various intelligence tests to non-European peoples, it has been proposed that tests be developed to determine the different types and qualities of intelligence rather than quantitative differences.[68] Whatever may be the outcome of the tests concerning qualitative differences between Africans and Europeans, the personality of the African is being developed along the lines of the European personality. In those parts of Africa where European settlement will remain negligible, the new personality of the African is being created as the result of the fact that he per-

64. Elisabeth Hoyt, "Economic Sense and the East African: Impressions of a Visiting American Economist," *Africa*, XXII (April, 1952), 165–72.

65. See Faris, *op. cit.*, "The Mental Capacity of Preliterates," p. 262.

66. *Ibid.*, p. 283.

67. See Ralph Linton, *The Cultural Background of Personality* (New York: D. Appleton–Century Crofts Co., 1945), pp. 126 ff.

68. See S. F. Nadel, "The Application of Intelligence Tests in the Anthropological Field," in F. C. Bartlett, M. Ginsberg, E. J. Lindgren, and R. H. Thouless (eds.), *The Study of Society* (London: Kegan Paul, Trench, Trubner & Co., 1939), pp. 184–98.

forms all the technical functions of an industrial society. Moreover, in the schools he is acquiring the ideas and values of European civilization. The development of large university colleges in the Gold Coast and in Nigeria, where African graduates of English universities are serving as professors, is indicative of the processes by which a new African personality is being created.

The importance of education in changing the personality of the African derives largely from the fact that the African regards education as the chief means of acquiring European culture. Whatever may be the attitude of the African toward European rule, he places a high value upon European civilization. His leaders resist any attempt to set up a system of African education which is different from European education. Although education cannot wipe out all traces of the ancestral cultural heritage, nevertheless, in the new social situation in which the African finds himself, the traditional culture loses its meaning.[69] The students who come from many different tribal backgrounds are integrated into the patterns of organized behavior which exist in the school. Even when they form new and spontaneous associations within the social framework of the school, the traditional distinctions and values tend to fade and lose their force. The substitution of Christian beliefs and practices for traditional religious ideas may not create the conflict that might be expected, since the attribution of sickness and misfortune to God differs little from his beliefs concerning similar behavior on the part of pagan gods and spirits.

In the school the African acquires new needs and new aspirations. The mere routine of living at school accustoms him to new needs in regard to food and clothing and health. Moreover, the acquisition of literary and mechanical skills is seen as a new need in relation to the world which is coming into existence about him. In comparing the world from which he has come with the new world about him, he aspires to play a role in the new world. He may decide to become a mechanic or a clerk or to subject himself to a longer discipline and become a doctor or

69. See Musgrove, "A Uganda Secondary School as a Field of Culture Change," *op. cit.*, pp. 234–49.

a lawyer. Each advance opens up a larger world of opportunities to which he may aspire. It is in this manner that new values become effective in the lives of the Africans and that they acquire a fresh conception of themselves.

Nevertheless, there are culture conflicts involved in the acquisition of European culture which affect his personal orientation toward the world. It has been found that African students sometimes have difficulty in understanding and accepting the Western idea of natural causation and that the idea of causation in terms of the human will or personal activities was preferred.[70] Conflicts may also arise from the Christian teachings. These conflicts are often related to their new conception of themselves as the result of European contacts. Under the old tribal system the African thought of himself as a member of a group that was bound together by kinship and communal ties. As the old tribal life is breaking up, he is beginning to think of himself in a broader and more abstract sense. He thinks of himself as a black man as opposed to the white man who exercises control over his life. Therefore, he may become suspicious of Christian teachings concerning humility and regard them as an instrument of control.

Out of the culture conflicts resulting from European contact come "marginal men" or cultural hybrids, so to speak. In the Union of South Africa the Cape Colored, who have come into existence as the result of race mixture, represent a marginal group. But we are interested primarily in the African who acquires European skills and ideas but still feels identified emotionally with his traditional culture. "The Christian convert," wrote Park, "in Asia or in Africa exhibits many if not most of the characteristics of the marginal man—the same instability, intensified self-consciousness, restlessness and malaise."[71] As the result of the intensified self-consciousness, the African who has acquired European culture will be very sensitive in regard to his status where the European is concerned. If he has acquired his education in European institutions, his marginal position may be accentuated. When he returns to his native country and

70. *Ibid.*, p. 247.

71. Robert E. Park, *Race and Culture* (Glencoe, Ill.: Free Press, 1950), p. 356.

becomes a member of the new African elite, he may not identify himself with the interests of the natives, though at the same time he opposes white domination.

White domination has undoubtedly had a traumatic effect upon the personality of the African. The extent and intensity of this traumatic experience have been determined by the character and extent of European contact and control. During the early days of European conquest and settlement, the traumatic effect upon his personality was obvious because of the violence employed and the systems of forced labor which were set up. But, even where a more humane system has developed and the European has taken seriously his civilizing mission, the personality of the African has suffered from the domination of the white race. Acceptance of the doctrine of Christian humility is sometimes a defense mechanism of the African in his helplessness before white domination. To the African, European civilization is not alone a different social organization and a different system of values; it is the proof of the superiority of white men over black men.[72] No teaching of racial pride or encouragement of native arts on the part of the white man can remove the implication of black inferiority.

In order to escape from the traumatic effects of white domination upon his personality, the educated African may become a leader of a nationalistic movement, or he may adopt a revolutionary ideology. African poets and thinkers may even challenge the attitude of the European toward work and production and extol the superiority of the traditional view of existence. The great masses of Africans who have been uprooted from the traditional culture sometimes seek an escape from frustration and confusion in various religious movements. Although generally these religious movements which have attracted the masses have a messianic aim, they are also of a nationalistic nature.[73] They often offer the African an escape from his hurt self-respect, from the trauma which his personality suffered from white domination, by rejecting European values and creating the hope of a new world of African values.

72. Pierre Charles, S.J., "Le Traumatisme noir," *Zaïre*, VII (May, 1953), 451–68.

73. Balandier, "Messianismes et nationalismes en Afrique noire," *op. cit.*, pp. 49 ff.

In concluding this discussion of the impact of colonialism on African social forms and personality, we should point out that no attempt has been made to relate the changes which are occurring in Africa to any specific sociological frame of reference, as, for example, Tönnies' conception of *Gemeinschaft* and *Gesellschaft* types of social organization, within which these changes might be studied. Nor has any attempt been made to indicate the intensity of these changes in different areas and in relation to such factors as transportation and communication and degrees of industrialization and urbanization. We have restricted our discussion to a systematic analysis of the *nature* of the social changes which are occurring in Africa in terms in which their significance can have relevance and meaning for social policy and social planning. It is only necessary to call attention to the "new colonial charter, "which is, in fact, a repudiation of the doctrine of colonialism, contained in Article 73 of the Charter of the United Nations. In this article there is an implied recognition of the facts presented here and a pledge on the part of the world as well as the colonial powers to recognize the primacy of the interests of the inhabitants of colonies, to carry out measures for their economic and social welfare, and to educate them for self-government. There are no guaranties that these pledges will be fulfilled by the colonial powers. But there is a general recognition that there is a growing revolt against colonialism in Africa as well as in Asia and that the colonial powers must accommodate their policies to the changes which have occurred in the lives and institutions of native peoples.

# THE ECONOMIC DEVELOPMENT OF AFRICA

*University of Manchester*

AFRICA is the continent in which cultural change is at present proceeding most rapidly. Its economic development is far from negligible. One index of this is the growth of the African population, which is thought to have doubled during the past century and to be increasing currently at a rate of around $1\frac{1}{2}$ per cent per annum. Output not only has kept up with population growth but has exceeded it. Apart from the share of output which goes to non-Africans, whether to overseas interests or to the immigrant communities, there is also clear evidence of rising African material standards in the improved housing and diets, especially of the rapidly growing urban populations, as well as in the increased ownership of clothes, bicycles, furniture, phonographs, and other personal goods. No one has tried to measure the rate of growth per capita of African real incomes, but it seems pretty clear that this rate has been rather higher than the rates of growth of India or China and rather lower than the rates of growth of western Europe or North America.

The current rates of growth of output do not satisfy the aspirations of nationalist political leaders, partly for material, partly for cultural, and partly for political reasons. On the material side they are conscious of the poverty of the great mass of Africans and of everything that goes with poverty—poor nutrition, poor housing, high infant mortality rates, and the like. A low cultural level is one of the associates of poverty; much is made in nationalist circles of African art and music, but Africans are conscious that their music is not so great an artistic achievement as that of Beethoven, that they are without a literature, that their religions are on rather a low level, and that their kinship and other social patterns, which are such a joy to the anthropologist, are too frail to withstand the fer-

[ 97 ]

ments of the twentieth century. Beyond all this, Africans want material progress because they wish to be recognized to be "as good as" other human beings in a world where the test of equality and the protection of superiority seem to be the possession of material goods. African self-respect seems to demand that Africa should catch up rapidly. The reasons here suggested may not be the driving reasons, and, if they are, they may be false, in the sense that material progress may not bring any of the things which Africans really want; however this may be, there is no doubt that the hearts of the new political leaders are set upon material progress. The old leaders, the chiefs and traditional authorities, do not all share this outlook, and, as one moves from modern towns into remoter villages, it is shared less and less by the masses of the people themselves. But this is nevertheless a challenge which Africa's rulers have to meet in all their political relations with the new African.

Since per capita national incomes in western Europe and North America increase by up to 2 per cent per annum, which means a doubling in thirty-five years, "catching up" in the material sense would imply a rate of growth of real national income of 4 per cent per annum or more, when allowance is made for population growth. No African community remotely approaches this rate of economic growth. Neither is this the only possible meaning of "catching up." That there is an increasing disparity of material standards in the world may be accepted while at the same time emphasis is put upon catching up in other spheres—in literacy, in public health, or in artistic achievement, for example. It is not possible to set a target rate of growth for African national incomes. All we can say for certain is that many people, African and non-African, would prefer the rate to be greater than it is, while others, African and non-African, sigh for a slower pace.

Apart from the obvious physical difficulties of the continent, the economic development of Africa has been held back in the past by three factors: (1) the backward techniques of its inhabitants; (2) lack of entrepreneurship; and (3) lack of capital. This list of factors could be extended both by addition and by subdivision. It forms, nevertheless, a convenient framework into which the principal African problems can be fitted, and we propose to use it for this purpose. In what follows we consider how each of these factors has inhibited the growth of material output, with a view to assessing the prospect of more rapid change in the immediate future. The discussion is confined to Africa south of the Sahara Desert.

### TECHNOLOGY

The improvement of African techniques requires research, education, and capital. We shall consider capital in a later section; in this section we consider research and education.

Research into African problems is meager when compared with research expenditures in other continents. It is arguable that Africa should spend a larger proportion of its national income on research than is spent in Europe or North America, because of its greater need, whereas in fact the proportion of the national income spent on research is trivial. Several reasons account for this, besides the poverty of the continent. One reason has been the idea, vaguely held, that European science was freely available to Africa—an idea which overestimates the ease of transplantation. The basic principles of science are freely available, but it is necessary to spend much effort in applying them to the peculiar problems of Africa before technologically useful results can be obtained. Another reason for the small expenditure on research is the greater dependence upon governments. In Europe or America much research is done by large commercial corporations and by private universities, and it is only very recently—in the case of the United Kingdom only since the first World War—that governments have begun to take a hand in organizing or paying for research. Since research was not regarded as one of the major functions of government in Europe, the European governments of Africa did not have the subject on their minds and are only slowly realizing their obligation to fill this gap. Again, a good deal of technological progress has in the past stemmed from the curiosity and experiments of private persons with some education in scientific or mechanical principles. Since Africa is only now beginning to grow an educated class, research depends all the more upon organized effort.

Research expenditures have grown rapidly in the last twenty

years, even though they are still only a tiny proportion of national income. Growth is hindered by shortage of money, by shortage of scientists, and by political boundaries. The boundaries have inhibited the proper organization of research even as between colonies of the same metropolitan power, but nowadays there is greater facility in organizing research on an intercolonial basis, and even the barriers created by the existence of several metropolitan governments are being lowered by the organization of scientific conferences on a regional and even on an all-Africa basis. The shortage of people has been of greater importance since the end of the second World War and has been due partly to the shortage of scientists in the metropolitan countries themselves. This shortage becomes steadily less acute, and research organizations should find it easier to fill their vacancies, especially if they improve their conditions of employment. As for the shortage of money, this did not exist in the immediate postwar years, and there are still one or two African colonies which have large reserves and budget surpluses. Most governments, however, are once more having to trim their budgets and would welcome outside contributions toward their research expenditures. If organizations like the United Nations or the Ford Foundation are wondering how to help this continent, they would find no better way of doing so than by helping to enlarge the facilities for research into African problems of all kinds.

Side by side with research comes the dissemination of information. The level of educational achievement is easily gauged by the proportion of the population recorded as attending school. In countries with birth and death rates such as the African, the proportion of the population under the age of fifteen is usually around 40 per cent. If all children of school age were in school, the proportion of the population attending school should be around 20–25 per cent. A United Nations study which made calculations for the year 1948 found that the percentage of the population in school in Trinidad was 20.1, in Greenland 20.2, and in the Gilbert and Ellice Islands 22.9.[1] The

1. *Non-self-governing Territories: Summaries of Information Transmitted during 1950* (New York: United Nations, 1951), Part III, p. 39.

following figures, from the same source, show how far Africa is from the ideal:

| | Per Cent | | Per Cent |
|---|---|---|---|
| Basutoland | 15.6 | Uganda | 3.9 |
| Nyasaland (1945) | 9.4 | Nigeria | 3.1 |
| Northern Rhodesia | 8.3 | French Somaliland | 2.9 |
| Belgian Congo | 8.1 | Gambia | 1.5 |
| Gold Coast | 6.5 | Sierra Leone | 1.5 |
| Swaziland | 6.4 | French Equatorial Africa | 1.4 |
| Kenya | 6.1 | French West Africa | 0.7 |
| Bechuanaland | 5.7 | British Somaliland | 0.2 |

This source does not give figures for the self-governing territories of Africa.

The deficiency of primary education is matched at all other levels—in technical education, in agricultural extension, in secondary education, and so on. If more expenditure on research is the first priority for African development, more expenditure on education is clearly the second priority. This fact has come to be recognized within the last ten years, and educational facilities of all kinds are expanding rapidly. A visitor to almost any part of Africa will find much activity in building new schools, colleges, and universities, in training teachers, and in expanding the numbers attending school.

Because of the great leeway to be made up at all levels, one of the problems which has emerged is the relative priority to be accorded to expenditure on different forms of education. Take, for example, the relative expenditures on primary, secondary, and university education. Some people believe that the first task is to get all the children into the primary schools and that, before this is done, it is unfair to spend public funds on giving secondary and university education to a privileged few. Obviously, this argument must not be taken to excess; any country needs people at secondary and university level as well as at the primary level, and even the extension of primary education itself is difficult unless there are higher institutions to train the teachers and to train those who train the teachers. All the same, there can be wide differences of emphasis: Nyasaland has proportionately three times as many children in school as Nigeria, but it has proportionately fewer children reaching university-entrance level than Nigeria has, because it has made extremely little provision for secondary education. From the point of view of supplying people for jobs, it is better to increase primary, secondary, and university education in step with one another than to concentrate nearly all the resources on trying to achieve universal primary education.

Another priority to be established is that between spending on children's education and spending on education programs for adults. In recent years much emphasis has been given to "mass education" programs for adults, emphasizing literacy, hygiene, civics, and agriculture. The agricultural extension program is usually financed from the budgetary vote for agriculture; but, from the viewpoint of economic development, it is one of the most crucial of the educational programs, and its relative neglect in Africa is one of the main reasons for the backwardness of African agriculture. Facilities for training agricultural assistants for these programs are now being expanded, subject to limitations of finance, of the shortage of persons with secondary education, and of the shortage of teachers for farm schools.

## ENTREPRENEURSHIP

An entrepreneurial class is needed for economic development because of the economies of large-scale operations. It is possible for agricultural operations to be carried on without entrepreneurs on family farms using no hired labor, and it is possible for these farms to show steadily increasing productivity if, as in Japan or the United States, large sums are spent by government on agricultural research and agricultural extension. Outside agriculture, however, in mining, manufacturing, transportation, wholesale distribution, education, and most other activities, progress requires some organization on a scale exceeding that of the individual household and is therefore dependent on the emergence of a class or classes of persons willing to organize the factors of production appropriately.

The corollary of the need for an entrepreneurial class is the need for a proletariat. That is to say, there must be a supply of people willing to support themselves by working for wages under the supervision of other persons. One of the first difficulties encountered in the development of Africa at the end of the nineteenth century was the absence of such a proletariat. Since population was sparse and land abundant, every African had rights to use of enough land to satisfy his traditional wants. New wants developed slowly, and since, in addition, Africans were reluctant to leave their villages and their traditional way of life to work as laborers in mines, on plantations, or on public works, great difficulty was encountered in recruiting an adequate supply of labor for large-scale works. In these circumstances every metropolitan government in Africa resorted to some form of compulsory labor. Chiefs were required to organize *corvée* for road or railway building or even to order young men to work for neighboring planters or mines. Large concessions of land were made to Europeans, and Africans were accorded the status of squatters and required by law to do at least a specified number of days of labor service per year. And, beyond this, taxes payable only in cash were imposed on Africans, with the expectation that this would force them to leave their farms and take paid employment from the proceeds of which to pay their taxes.

With the growth of population, the alienation of land from African ownership, and the development of new wants, it is no longer necessary to exercise force in order to get Africans to work for wages. Labor is still in short supply for wage employment over the greater part of the continent, but it is no longer possible to argue that this is because Africans are unaccustomed to wage labor or because their material needs are so low that they would not know what to do with money if they received it. All the evidence is that Africans are as materialistic and as acquisitive as other peoples. The farmer may be reluctant to move to urban employment, but the evidence is that, if he is shown some change in his agricultural habits which will certainly increase his income, he is not slow to adopt it—witness the speed with which African farmers created the enormous cacao industry of the Gold Coast, or the groundnut industry in Nigeria, or the cotton industry in Uganda. If Africans do not react to offers of money, it is not because they do not value money but because they think they can make better use of their resources in some other way.

We turn now from the need for entrepreneurship and its requisite conditions to consider who the entrepreneurs are. In Africa entrepreneurship is performed by three different groups —by private Africans, by private immigrants (European, Arab, and Indian), and by public officials. The clash among these three is Africa's greatest political problem.

As in other backward continents, the recent economic development of Africa was initiated almost exclusively by immigrant entrepreneurs. Their earliest contact was disastrous, since it was for the purpose of the slave trade, which destroyed peace and government throughout the continent. After this trade was abolished, the immigrants turned to legitimate commerce, and the great agricultural export industries of the African farmers —the cacao, oilseeds, cotton, coffee, and tobacco—are due in the first place to the courageous pioneering of early European traders. Africans had been active in mining before the Europeans came, and they still are; but the great mining industries which have played so large a part in opening up the continent are again primarily due to European initiative. It is not open to question that Africa would be a poorer continent economically if immigrant entrepreneurs had not opened it up.

African and immigrant interests have nevertheless clashed at five principal points—labor supply, trade monopolies, the color bar in employment, the supply of land, and the disposal of profits. We must look briefly at each of these topics.

For the most part (though not entirely), overt pressure to work for immigrant enterprises has been abolished. Instead, in the territories controlled by the British Colonial Office (but not elsewhere) the influence of the government is now thrown rather on the side of the employee. Trade-union organization is legalized, if not also encouraged; machinery for determining wages is set out; and conditions of recruitment and of employment are regulated. The bargaining strength of labor is still very weak, and wages are still miserably low by any standard; but at least the accusation which could safely be made thirty years ago that all African governments were anxious to keep wages as low as possible is now no longer universally true.

The trade monopolies have affected mostly the farmers and would-be African competitors. African trade, since it depends upon the prices of primary products, is subject to great fluctuations in the course of which small traders with small financial resources tend to be wiped out. Trade has accordingly tended to be concentrated in the hands of a few large firms, surrounded by a great number of smaller competitors subject to very high birth and death rates. From time to time the large firms have entered openly into cartel-type agreements to advance and protect their position, both as against their customers and also as against other competitors. These agreements have been deeply resented, and Africans have brought political pressure to bear on their governments to control the activities of the great trading firms. This is the origin of the numerous statutory marketing boards and statutory price-fixing agencies now found throughout the continent.

The color bar in employment results from a clash between the vested interests of white skilled labor and the growing number of Africans capable of doing jobs which were previously done only by white people. Originally this color bar was practiced throughout the continent by all white employers, including governments. Its purpose was then partly the maintenance of white prestige, without which it would have been impossible for so large a continent to be kept in subjection by a bare handful of white men, and partly to avoid the risk of appointing to superior positions persons whose cultural background might prove unsuitable for the job in hand. In these days, however, Africans are making their way into every kind of employment except in those countries where the white population is relatively large and where this immigrant population controls the government. In the Union of South Africa and in British Central Africa, where the reins of government are in the hands of the local settlers (but not in the Belgian Congo, where the metropolitan government retains political control), Africans are not permitted skilled employment in the mines, on the railways, or in the public service. One of the anomalies of Africa can be seen every day as the train between Northern Rhodesia and the Belgian Congo reaches the frontier; since Africans drive trains in the Congo but may not do so in Rhodesia, the African always hands over to, or takes over from, the white man at this point.

Conflict over land is again confined to territories where the white population is relatively large and has political control. In practice it is not of great importance except in Kenya and in the Union of South Africa, since in the rest of the continent there is ample land capable of development. Moreover, the conflict over land is as much a conflict over labor as it is over land. If European families in Kenya owned only as much land as their families could cultivate without hiring labor, European farming would not be a political issue. The "White Highlands" are mainly occupied by a black population, on contracts of labor tenancy. Called "squatters," these Africans are allowed to cultivate land on condition that they give a minimum number of days of labor service per year. If the rights of occupancy of these Africans were confirmed, their holdings increased to economic size, and their labor rents commuted to cash payments, the white economy of the Highlands would collapse.

Finally, African and immigrant interests clash over the disposal of the profits of the great mining concerns. A number of these concerns acquired their lands on very favorable terms, either from ignorant chiefs or from conniving metropolitan governments, and the royalties and rents which they pay for these valuable properties are a fraction only of the true economic rent. In addition, up until 1939, rates of taxation were very much lower in the African colonies than they were in the metropolis. Recently political pressure has been brought, both by Africans and also by white people settled in Africa, to tax the mines more heavily, so that a larger part of the wealth they create may remain in Africa and may be used for developing public and social services. This process has been taken furthest in the Union of South Africa, which has made an art of levying high taxes and royalties upon mining enterprises; but most other governments have also moved in the same direction.

The most important challenge to African enterprise lies in the sphere of agriculture. Most Africans are farmers, and agriculture is, will be, and should remain primarily an African activity. Currently, agriculture is the least progressive sector of the African economy; indeed, its productivity may even be falling, whereas other sectors are expanding with some vigor. It is true that, where prices are favorable, African farmers switch from growing food to growing commercial crops for export; but, even where commercial production is well developed, as in the Gold Coast, it is still the case that 50–60 per cent of African farmers are engaged in growing food. Progress in food production is associated with the use of improved varieties of plants and animals, with increased use of fertilizers, conservation of water, pesticides, new systems of rotation, mechanical equipment, and so on. None of these is proceeding at other than snail's pace on the African food farm, through deficiencies of research, of agricultural extension, and of capital. The European governments of Africa interested themselves in the beginning primarily in what could be exported—in slaves, minerals, and commercial crops. The challenge of developing the home economy has still to be met and must be met chiefly by helping the African farmer to increase his productivity. This is an awkward challenge for Europe to take up, since anything that raises the productivity of the African food farmer moves the terms of trade against Europe. If Africans can produce more on their food farms, it will require high wages to induce them to move to European mines and higher prices for commercial crops to induce them to produce for export. Nevertheless, since most Africans are farmers, raising the productivity of African farmers is a *sine qua non* of raising the African's standard of living.

Besides the entrepreneurship of private Africans and private immigrants, the development of Africa calls for intelligent entrepreneurship by governments. We may leave on one side the problem of choosing between private and public operation of business, since the issues this raises are not very different in Africa from what they are elsewhere. This still leaves a much wider range of activity for government enterprise in Africa than in Europe or America. There is the whole field of public utilities —docks, railways, telecommunications, water, electricity, and the like—which needs to be pushed ahead of development in order to stimulate development and which is therefore quite inadequately provided if left to private enterprise. More generally, there is the greater need for pioneering activity, both because of the scarcity of competent private entrepreneurs and because of the greater risk attaching to all new enterprise. One of the problems inherent in the situation of all backward countries is that they need better government than the developed countries, just because they are backward, but they get worse government, just because they are backward. Most countries in Africa have better government, in the administrative sense, because of their colonial status than they would have if they were independent; but until the end of the second World War, when most European governments embarked actively upon programs of colonial development, it could not have been said of any that it was even trying to be remotely adequate to the entrepreneurial situation in which it found itself.

We may consider separately the capital requirements of European enterprises, of African business, and of the governments of Africa.

It is not necessary in this context to elaborate on the capital requirements of European enterprises. These have access, in varying degrees, to the capital markets of their metropolitan countries and to a network of financial institutions in the colonies themselves.

African business, on the other hand, has virtually no access to external capital markets, and even the banks and other European financial institutions on the spot tend to be much more reluctant to lend to African businessmen (mainly because they doubt their commercial experience and ability) than they are to lend to Syrians, to Indians, or to Europeans. African business depends primarily on its own savings, which are small.

It is very desirable to do all that can be done to stimulate habits of thrift in Africa. Savings institutions are increasing in number, though still relatively insignificant—post-office banks, co-operative thrift societies, mortgage or building societies, insurance, and so on. All the same, the most that can be expected from these sources in the near future is very small. If African enterprise is to have more capital, it must be thought of primarily as a potential borrower. Governments are moving in the direction of providing capital for Africans—through agricultural credit societies, through industrial finance corporations, and through housing agencies—but they are rightly moving with caution, since people who have little capital of their own tend to be cavalier in treating what they borrow from others. All the same, there is no doubt that Africans could use a lot of capital productively, especially on their farms, and the sums which could usefully be provided for these purposes are large in relation to current resources.

Governments need some capital for lending to Africans through financial institutions, but they need even more for their own purposes, since it is arguable that the priority use for government funds in Africa is to provide an adequate framework of public services. We have seen on an earlier page how woefully inadequate are the facilities for education; much the same applies to every aspect of the public services—to roads, water supplies, harbors, electricity, hospitals, and the rest. The list of public projects that could usefully be executed exceeds several fold the resources available to the governments.

The African governments get money for capital formation out of taxes, grants from their metropolitan governments, loans, and grants from international agencies. The principal source is taxation, since even the loans have usually to be repaid out of taxes. The best-placed countries from this point of view are those with large, profitable mining industries; these industries were formerly rather lightly taxed, but it is now the order of the day to levy upon them rates of taxation not dissimilar to the rates levied in the metropolis. The next best placed are those which export commodities of which the price has risen several fold since the war and which withhold part of the proceeds from the farmers. The luckiest of these is the Gold Coast, in respect of cacao. The price of cacao before the war was about £30 a ton; its price at the time of writing exceeds £500 a ton. The Gold Coast farmer receives around £150 a ton, and all the rest, apart from marketing expenses, is claimed by one government agency or another—some of it to be disgorged if the world price falls below the home price, the rest to be spent on development. There is the same pattern in Uganda, except that the price of cotton has not rocketed so high as the price of cacao. Apart from the Gold Coast, Uganda, Northern Rhodesia, the Belgian Congo, and the Union of South Africa, however, African governments have only small revenues, in relation to national income, and are almost chronically short of money.

Since the second World War, their resources have been supplemented to some degree by grants from metropolitan governments toward development expenditure. Nearly every African territory has drawn up a four- or five- or ten-year plan of development expenditures by public authorities on roads, water supplies, agricultural extension, and other public services, and the contributions of metropolitan treasuries to these expenditures range from about one-third to about two-thirds of the cost. This is a new departure. Before the war colonial treasuries were expected to be self-supporting. Even now the contributions, while large in some absolute senses, are small relatively to colonial budgets and to national incomes.

Contributions from other sources have been on a much smaller scale. France diverted a considerable part of the Economic Co-operation Administration aid which was received from the United States to colonial development (more in North Africa than in Africa south of the Sahara); but, apart from this, only a negligible fraction of the foreign aid dispensed by the United States in the last ten years has been assigned to Africa, either directly or from counterpart funds. It is difficult to explain this in any but political terms, since economic aid could have been used as fruitfully in Africa as anywhere else. The European powers who rule most of Africa are unwilling to admit that they do not do for Africa all that Africa needs, and the United States is equally reluctant to offend by seeming to take too great an interest in African affairs. Meanwhile the real losers in this game of prestige and diplomacy are the Africans. Much the same applies in relations with the United Nations and its specialized agencies, including the International Bank. Africa would probably get much more aid from non-European sources if it were able to speak for itself.

However, in the immediate postwar years lack of money was hardly a significant restriction on African development, since most governments had more money than they could spend. First there was an acute shortage of materials—of steel, of cement, of water pipes, of telephone equipment, of railway locomotives, and so on. This was a world shortage, which has now largely disappeared. Then there was a shortage of qualified staff —of administrators, scientists, engineers, and teachers. This shortage remains. The British colonies, for instance, have hundreds of posts unfilled in these categories. The shortage is aggravated by national distinctions; there was, for example, a considerable flow of trained European refugees after the war, very few of whom were accepted for service in Africa, and the availability of Dutch technicians since the independence of Indonesia has also not been exploited by other metropolitan powers. Africa has also been very slow to utilize the opportunities offered by the United Nations and United States technical assistance programs. The third shortage has been of African artisans and semiskilled workers. This has affected the building industry in particular and has combined with the shortages of materials and of skilled persons to retard by as much as two or three years the commencement or completion of several projects for which the finance was available. However, all these shortages of real resources are being relieved, and most African governments are now back in their chronic condition of being handicapped by lack of financial resources.

There are very few estimates of the rate of capital formation in Africa. Up to 1945 it may be guessed that the only territories where gross capital formation exceeded 5 or 6 per cent of national income were the territories with profitable mines, namely, the Union of South Africa, the Rhodesias, and the Belgian Congo; and even in these territories the major benefit accrued to overseas shareholders and to resident Europeans. In the other territories substantial capital formation would have been possible only if there had been substantial aid from overseas or if taxation upon Africans had been substantially higher. Since 1945 the Gold Coast and Uganda have joined the list of territories with high capital formation; in the Gold Coast gross capital formation is estimated to be about 15 per cent of national income, which is probably not far short of the level in the mining territories. By contrast gross capital formation in Nigeria was estimated for 1951 at 7 per cent, which is probably typical of all the nonmining countries except the Gold Coast and Uganda. Crucial to the levels of public expenditure and of capital formation is the fact that personal taxation upon Africans is low throughout the continent, apart from the effects of the marketing schemes in the Gold Coast and Uganda.

We began by noting the high rate of economic growth which African political aspirations require. Nothing remotely approaching this rate will be achieved unless one or more of three possibilities comes to pass. First, the governments may find the political support and courage necessary for levying much higher taxes upon Africans; the political support will not be forthcoming without much closer identification between the governments and the new African political leaders. Second, new rich mines may be discovered and may be exploited in African rather than in European interests; this also requires quite a change in political outlook. Or, third, there may be substantially increased aid from abroad; but this depends upon more United States aid finding its way to Africa, either directly or through international agencies. Since none of these three is on the cards at present, we may expect African levels of living to remain low and to grow only at rates substantially below the rates of growth in America, in Europe, or in the Soviet Union. But Africa is not a continent of which it is safe to predict what will happen next.

*PART II*
ANALYSIS

# POLITICAL DEMOCRACY IN THE GOLD COAST

DAVID E. APTER

*Northwestern University*

## INTRODUCTION

IN THIS paper we shall seek to examine particular authority patterns in Gold Coast politics in terms of their integrative and instrumental foci in order to cast light on the institutionalization of parliamentary democracy. What is involved here is the identification of patterns of political norms and political structures found in social systems. The theory and methods of which this work is a consequence have been applied to a general study of Gold Coast politics carried out under a grant from the Social Science Research Council during the year 1952–53. Therefore some of the statements made in this paper will derive from conceptual premises and data not directly offered here.[1]

While this discussion is limited to the Gold Coast, the only part of British West Africa where the writer did field work, it is felt that most of the problems which emerge have immediate relevance to other parts of the area. In broad terms, the analytical aspects of British West African political problems are the same, while the substantive aspects represent differences of degree rather than kind. If this assumption is correct, then much of what has occurred in the Gold Coast has relevance for a general understanding of political change and adaptation leading to the emergence of central political institutions in British West Africa.

Although the Gold Coast Colony proper became a British colony in 1874, the effective domination by Great Britain of the territory as a whole dates from 1901.[2] On the other hand, parts

---

1. See *The Gold Coast in Transition* (Princeton, N.J.: Princeton University Press, 1955), where both the thesis offered here and the methodological premises are more fully developed.

2. The last campaign by the British occurred in 1911 in the Northern Territories.

[ 115 ]

of the coast have been in contact with the West for over five hundred years. It is an area which derives its main income from cacao, with subsidiary revenues from gold, diamonds, and bauxite. Historically, its major attraction for the West lay in the slave trade and gold. Although there is no resident white population, the coastal areas reflect their long association with the West and access to alternative ways of life. There are large towns with suburbs, slums, schools, and prisons.

The rich central area of the Gold Coast, the Ashanti Con federacy, represents a military theocracy which at one time dominated most of the Gold Coast. Finally defeated by the British in 1901, much of the confederacy is intact, with deep loyalties to the Golden Stool and the Asantehene, both symbols of authority, religion, and the cultural tradition.[3]

The Northern Territories contain more widely diverse tribal and linguistic groups than the central and southern regions. In the north trade routes to the Middle East go back many centuries, when caravans crossed the desert to trade in salt, kola nuts, and slaves. Traditional cultural patterns are increasingly intact as one moves northward from the coast. By and large, traditional patterns of life in the Northern Territories continue undisturbed; the major strains remain those of struggle for subsistence. The northerners fear the southerners, partly for historical reasons, while the southerners, in the main, have contempt for the northerners. The latters' fear of domination by the south is one factor in their hesitancy to offer wholehearted commitment to "Self-government Now."

The kinds of conflict situations which derive from cross-cultural pressures and orientational antagonisms are therefore aggravated by the regional splits inherent in the territory of the Gold Coast. In the discussion which follows little will be said about these regional difficulties in the Gold Coast, since they do not yet form a crucial obstacle to the formation and operation of secular governmental institutions. As potential problem areas for secular government and particularly as bases from which opposition can become effective, however, they are worthy of

3. See W. F. Ward, *A History of the Gold Coast* (London: Allen & Unwin, 1948).

particular notice. In Nigeria the problems raised by regional differences have made central government inoperative and have been crucial to the lack of consensus about the terms of membership in a national Nigerian society.

INTEGRATIVE FOCI

A. TRADITIONAL SYSTEMS OF AUTHORITY

Some picture of the ideally integrated authority system is significant for an understanding of political behavior and political affiliations in the various political structures which have been developed in the Gold Coast. Aside from the usual works by Rattray, the work done by Busia is an extremely able presentation of the traditional authority system in Ashanti.[4]

The two traditional systems of authority which we shall discuss are by no means the exclusive authority systems. One represents the system which by and large holds for the central and southern parts of the Gold Coast (i.e., the Ashanti Confederacy and the Colony proper). The other represents an example of one of the three similar dominating systems in the Northern Territories, having particular relevance because of the representation of the Northern Territories in the central government. Each of the traditional authority systems touched upon is highly organized, with specific and elaborate political organizations. For some of the less organized systems of authority the works of Cardinall, Rattray, and Fortes are readily available.[5]

The system characteristic of the coastal[6] and Ashanti areas provides for the election of chiefs (enstooling), chosen from a royal lineage by the queen mother and approved by elders and commoners. In swearing his "great oath," a chief was bound to represent the limitations of his office. In methods and procedures of choice a somewhat "democratic" system is used. Within the limitations of his office a chief could be "autocratic." By

4. K. A. Busia, *The Position of the Chief in the Modern Political System of Ashanti* (London: Oxford University Press, 1951).

5. A. W. Cardinall, *The Natives of the Northern Territories of the Gold Coast* (London: G. Routledge & Sons, 1920); R. S. Rattray, *Tribes of the Ashanti Hinterland* (London: Oxford University Press, 1932); M. Fortes, *Dynamics of Clanship among the Tallensi* (London: Oxford University Press, 1945).

6. Largely Akan and groups having organizational forms somewhat similar, such as the Ga, the Ewe, and the Krobo.

overstepping his authority, however, he could legally be "de-stooled" according to customary law.[7] In almost every impor-tant decision affecting the tribe, the chief was obliged to dis-cuss with his council. The council was made up of lineage heads or their representatives, and the major social organization was composed of lineage clusters. The lineage elders, occupying specific political and/or military positions, formed advisory and decision-making bodies. Indeed, the chief could not speak di-rectly for the tribe but rather through a linguist, with whom the elders could disagree without undermining the fiction of the chief's sovereignty. The chief, in the main, derived his authori-ty from (1) his military capacities; (2) his royal lineage, which traced (matrilineally for the Akans) back to common religious and mythological orientations of the tribe; (3) his custodianship over land; and (4) his adjudicating responsibilities. The residual trusteeship over land gave him powers of economic allocation. His military capacities gave him formal organizational powers in the relationship to lineage affiliations in military formations. The royal lineage gave him nonempirical sources of authority through deference and religion, reinforcing the authority of his adjudicatory powers in which decisions were considered binding upon the members.

The system in the Northern Territories is a threefold varia-tion on original Moshi practice. The Moshi came down from the southern Sudan, dominating the local populations, setting up a "symbiotic" economic relationship, and, in many cases, receiv-ing the allegiance of the indigenes. The three groups, the Dagomba, the Mamprussi, and the Moshi, have a patriarchal system of political authority involving the elections of chiefs from lineage heads arranged in hierarchical status groups. Ac-ceptable lineage heads are elected over a period of time to higher and higher office, with final selection of the paramount chiefs made from the three liege posts directly below the paramount chief in the hierarchy. By the time a chief is eligible for the top posts, he is an old man. Although a chief is obliged to discuss with his council, his authority is far more absolute than in the central and coastal areas of the Gold Coast.

7. See Busia, *op. cit.*, and R. S. Rattray, *Ashanti Law and Constitution* (London: Oxford University Press, 1929).

Important elements in the social system which support tribal and chieftainship forms of authority are a specific set of tribal role structures. The maintenance of tribal authority is intact to the degree to which these role structures are intact and operative. Some of these important role structures can be characterized in terms of certain cognitive relationships (from the point of view of the members). The affective content applied to these cognitive relationships determines to a considerable extent whether or not they are able to persist or will crumble under the impact of other cultural influences. The allocation of duties, prerogatives, and rights within the tribe depends to a large degree upon the cognitive and affective content of the elder-youth relationships, the royal-nonroyal lineage relationships, the slave-nonslave relationships, and the elder-commoner relationships.

Much of the content of these relationships has been changed by European culture and incipient Europeanization of Africans. That which survives presents difficulties for the development and maintenance of secular systems of authority.

By and large, however, the integration achieved through tribal authority was the consequence of particular formalized roles, given ritual precision, and clustered on the basis of lineage and rudimentary division of labor, in which the needs of the members could be met. Insofar as the tribe had successfully dealt with problems in order to survive, often against great odds, the functions of protection and preservation were enshrined by a mythical past. From this past came the ultimate sanctions of norms and acceptable behavior. The emphasis upon age, which in the north reached the proportions of a gerontocracy, gave credence to the identification of wisdom with age. The concept of "progress" as an orientational symbol did not exist. Any demand for formal role changes emphasized the essential conservatism of tribal authorities. Any changes in environment with which they could not cope by traditional means left them with a remarkable degree of helplessness.

### B. THE SECULAR SYSTEMS OF AUTHORITY

Under the recent constitutional changes, full internal self-government, except for the reserve powers of the governor, has been achieved by Gold Coast Africans. Coexistent with the traditional forms of authority are secular forms of authority. The central government follows in the British parliamentary tradition. The rules and procedures of the Legislative Assembly are derived from the practice of the House of Commons. Members of the assembly are chosen by an elective system. A cabinet and a prime minister, chosen on the basis of majority party membership in the assembly, are responsible for the operations of government. A Gold Coast civil service coexists with the Colonial Service officers, who are gradually being replaced by Africans. This system makes the ultimate decisions, passes the bills and ordinances, and takes the exceptions considered binding upon the entire population of the Gold Coast.

The only formal recognition of chieftainship in secular parliamentary government appears in territorial councils having advisory powers only. Each of the four areas of the Gold Coast has its council of chiefs, only one of which, the Asanteman Council, has any traditional precedent. They represent a remnant from the days of indirect rule. These councils—the Northern Territories Council, the Asanteman Council, and the Joint Provincial Council (for the Colony proper)—elected representatives to the Legislative Assembly until 1954, when direct election in 104 constituencies was inaugurated.[8]

Prior to the present "Nkrumah" constitution, some members of the assembly were elected by indirect election through electoral colleges or, in the case of municipalities, by direct election. All members of the Legislative Assembly, regardless of their methods of selection, however, sat as equal members of the assembly and were expected to participate in parliamentary processes. However, in the past the method of selection reflected the area which members represented, determining the roles which they were expected to play and the affiliations which they held. Now the method of election is identical for all members, the same kinds of affiliation still holding within a more formalized pattern of political parties.

The formal requirements of membership and participation set one pattern of role prescriptions in which procedural factors

8. A fourth territorial council was established for the Trans-Volta Togoland region.

are paramount. The place from which members come sets patterns of representation and responsibility. The affiliations which they hold determine (*a*) the dominant reference groups to which they belong, (*b*) the criteria by which they will make decisions, and (*c*) the parliamentary groups which the members will form in the assembly.

The procedural factors wield the members into a single organizational body united on ultimate objectives (i.e., the making of decisions on bills and ordinances). The place from which they come is particularly significant in the representation of local and regional interests. In the case of members from the Northern Territories and members of territorial councils, of major importance is the strata of the population which they represent. The affiliations which they hold are particularly significant for members of political parties and territorial council members, since the one involves party discipline and a party program, and the other means that representation of chiefs can indirectly enter into party politics. For example, one of the members of the Asanteman Council is Dr. K. A. Busia, the chairman of the Ghana Congress party, for a time the leading opposition party in the Gold Coast.[9]

The parliamentary system therefore imposes structural and procedural integrative bases by wielding diverse elements into a procedural chamber in which the decisions taken are considered binding upon the members at large. Open normative conflicts at the central government level are avoided principally by the participation of various significant subgroups such as chiefs, political parties, etc., in the processes of government and by the dominance of a particular group which holds the affiliation and sanction of the majority of the members of the system, that is, the Convention People's party. This factor, of central importance, will be discussed later on.

A second secular system is imposed under the Local Government Ordinance of 1951.[10] This ordinance establishes local councils with a two-thirds elective membership and a one-third traditional membership. The councils are replacing the native

9. In the general election of 1954 Busia was the only member of his party returned.
10. See Local Government Ordinance of 1951 (Accra, January, 1952).

authorities system which had been set up under the period of indirect rule. The secular authority which chiefs had been given from British (not traditional) sources has in effect been abolished, and the dominance of a two-thirds elective membership on the local councils involves the direct injection of party politics at the local level. In effect the authority of the chiefs becomes merely residual authority maintained by affective bonds attached to ceremonial or religious aspects of social and economic life and the same adjudicative functions.

The secular parliamentary system plays the following integrative role. The decisions to be made devolve around problems arising in a larger focus of social and economic change and of cultural clash than in the past. Decisions made affect all the members of the Gold Coast society, necessarily superseding the tribal focus. For participation in these decisions nontraditional members, or traditional members playing nontraditional roles, engage in a series of parliamentary processes. Serious sanctional and normative conflicts have not arisen from the establishment of central government primarily because central political organs had no counterpart in the traditional authority organization. However, while minor normative conflicts do appear, none of the traditional sources of sanction for the secular system emerges from the traditional system. In order for the development of positive support of central government, rather than wholesale apathy, nontraditional sources of orientation and affiliation must develop. Nontraditional orientation and affiliation necessitate the breakdown of traditional modes. Any breakdown of traditional modes is resisted by the chiefs. The institutionalization of central secular organs of government depends first upon mass alienation from the tribe, the chief, and traditional authority, to the larger prescriptions of central government. The construction of organs of central government does not, in and of itself, incur normative conflict. As a consequence, relative procedural harmony is possible. However, disaffiliation from tribal norms, which previously occupied the central position in the traditional value hierarchy, draws fire from the chiefs. Their protective functions are violated. Either they withdraw from participation by not helping to administer an act or ordinance, or they foment active opposition to a measure where they think this will be helpful to their own power; for example, in taxation. While the representatives of chiefs, or the chiefs themselves, are willing to participate in the Legislative Assembly, they are not willing to carry out decisions harmful to their traditional power.[11]

The Local Government Ordinance, in its range of authority, parallels the territory and population over which the chief rules. It strikes directly at chieftainship by stripping the chiefs of almost all nontraditional authority. At present local government and traditional authority are competitive. The one involves traditional norms and sanctions over lineage, clan, and family members. The other involves secular norms over the same people whose social structures remain largely traditional.

The simultaneous persistence of two integrational foci, traditional and secular, poses a crucial problem for the development of a national society. On the one hand, we have the structures, procedures, and behavioral limitations of traditional systems which remain intact in varying degrees in different parts of the country. On the other hand, we have the structures, procedures, and behavioral requirements of a secular parliamentary system upon which the emergence of a viable national society depends.

### FACTORS IN AUTHORITY SHIFTS

In identifying the predominating political systems in the Gold Coast, we have found that one applies to traditional types of authority and the other to secular types of authority. The one is superseding the other. How has this process occurred? In the development of secular government enough support by decision-making participants has been found in the Gold Coast so that basic questions over the terms of government have not hampered the derivation of consensus. In other words, a work load has been imposed upon the cabinet and the members of the

11. There is a strong feeling among chiefs that they are "above politics." Since the Nkrumah constitution, however, the territorial councils have seen revived "political" activity on the part of chiefs of particular importance in the National Liberation Movement, backed by the Asanteman Council in Ashanti, which is striving to abolish the current unitary constitution and replace it with a federal system allowing greater regional authority.

Legislative Assembly which has been dispatched in the debate and passage of bills necessary to carry out a program. There have been no wholesale walkouts from the assembly. The members have joined in debate under certain rules. The laws and ordinances which they have passed have been operationally binding upon all the members of the Gold Coast. The Legislative Assembly, in which the expression of law is the expression of change, has been able to come to decisions and to effectuate these decisions with popular support.

Yet this does not touch upon the larger issues of the development of a democratic national society. Any political system depends not only on the formal enactment of laws but on the degree to which a particular form of authority becomes part of the norm structure held by the members of the system. It depends upon the proportion of people who see in government not only a formal, and, for the Gold Coast, an alien structural mechanism by which decisions are made, but also a vehicle for the realization of their expectations, an expression of their membership and solidarity in a larger social unit, and expression of a political value complex concerning the use of power. The shift from local traditional allegiance to the allegiance of members to a larger political and social entity involves three orientational variables. These can be called (1) tribal and secular *goal* orientations; (2) tribal and secular *behavioral alternatives;* and (3) tribal and secular *political norms.*

The first deals with the range of perceived objectives. The second deals with the range of role prescriptions available to members. The third deals with the sources and limits of sanctioned authority. Each one of these represents societal cohesives crucial to the maintenance of the older systems of authority. When these orientations no longer appear satisfactory or appropriate to the people themselves, either apathy results or a reintegration of belief patterns must take place.

In terms of these variables, traditional authority refers to restricted membership units. The membership units refer to solidarity units having a highly parochial system of cultural integration. The range of perceived objectives is local and intimate, pertaining to threats to existence within a circumscribed pattern of life. The behavioral alternatives are limited to a narrow range of role prescriptions based less on choice than on particularistic criteria such as "blood" affiliations, lineage mythology, and a limited division of labor. The limits of sanctioned authority impose disabilities upon aggressive elements who seek either to change or to find outlets for energies. The sources of authority are in the past, and chieftaincy does not extend beyond the tribe or the confederacy.

The interjection of Western cultural patterns upon traditional systems supplied alternatives to the traditional content of the orientation variables. In particular the criteria by which the British judged the African became, for many Africans, the criteria by which they judged themselves. Modes of behavior and Western standards of subsistence and social organization became attractive alternatives to tribal life and society. The system of indirect rule changed the source of a chief's legitimate authority from internal tribal support to the external and foreign support of Great Britain. Many traditional inhibitions upon behavior were released as a consequence, particularly in areas where British authorities directly mixed into problems and issues of social life. Alternative religious, legal, and political codes were introduced, and some fundamental prerogatives of chieftainship such as human sacrifice were abolished. Education, commerce, and the introduction of a money economy provided alternative objectives, prestige levels, and specific items of desirability which could not be provided within the traditional pattern of life.[12]

It is quite obvious that the Europeans, particularly the British, established themselves as the fount from which benefits, development, and the material products of Western civilization would flow. Nationalism owes its success in part to the inabilities of a colonial government to devote its full time to fulfilling the desires which it has awakened. The resulting breakdown of chieftainship increasingly was expressed in demands for larger

12. For excellent summaries of the background of British administrative rule see F. M. Bourret, *The Gold Coast* (2d ed.; London: Oxford University Press, 1952); R. Buell, *The Native Problem in Africa* (New York: Macmillan Co., 1928); Lord Hailey, *Native Administration in the British African Territories* (London: H.M. Stationery Office, 1952), Part III.

participation by Africans in the decisions affecting their own lives. The fundamental prerequisite to the establishment of non-traditional forms of authority is the basic inability of traditional systems to satisfy a range of newly perceived needs deriving from a differing material and cultural tradition.

The problems of Gold Coast social life can no longer be satisfied within the means of traditional authorities. Only temporary satisfaction was provided by the co-operation of chiefs and British authorities during the period of indirect rule. Yet, when central government authority in a legislative council, an executive council, and an administrative service was opened to Africans, it only served to increase the range of expectations rather than fulfil them.

Until the appearance of Kwame Nkrumah, the young nationalist leader who broke away from the older nationalists to form a mass political party, the range of political expectations by younger elements, dissatisfied with old ways of life, did not seriously encompass political office. Rather these disaffected elements formed a group seeking the means to prestige and wealth. From the point of view of the old system, they represented culturally "displaced persons." Around Nkrumah and the Convention People's party rallied the younger elements of the population—the disadvantaged, the ambitious, the idealistic. The first general election in 1950 gave Nkrumah and the C.P.P. an overwhelming majority, and the public was dramatically introduced to parliamentary government. Their leader was prime minister.[13] Their party controlled the decisions over the chiefs and the older nationalists, both of whom were increasingly divorced from the aspirations of the "young men," either through limitations imposed by customary tradition or through educational and financial elitism. For large numbers of the young active nationalists, that which had been denied became accessible. That which had seemed far away was given as the fruit of political victory.[14]

The electoral procedures became weapons of mass revolt. The

13. At the time his formal title was "Leader of Government Business."

14. See J. H. Price, "The Gold Coast Election," *West African Affairs* (London), 1952, *passim*.

elected members of the assembly by and large are associated with the Convention People's party. Techniques of mass communication and indoctrination aroused manifest hostility against Great Britain and latent hostility against the chiefs. Those who had been the rascals became the heroes.

Behind all this was the fact that Gold Coast life, in rural and municipal areas, could no longer find satisfactory expression in tribal political structures. In particular those who had accepted Western valuations of subsistence standards, occupational goals, and social customs hardly looked to the traditional forms of life for emotional and economic sustenance. Access to politics suddenly became access to power formerly held by the British and the virtual elimination of the chiefs and older elites from public life.

The Convention People's party as the major expression of nationalism in the Gold Coast derives its major strength from the five following sources: (1) tensions and malintegrations deriving from value conflicts and changing goal orientations; (2) limited access by the African to publicly perceived roles and symbols of "prestige" and "success"; (3) psychological disabilities suffered by Africans when judged by nonindigenous standards; (4) hostility to tribal and rural life as obstacles to Western patterns of behavior and Western standards of subsistence; and (5) resentment against racial and cultural domination by Great Britain.

The amalgam of these and other pressures[15] has given the nationalist movement an impetus since the war which has carried the Gold Coast, via the Convention People's party, to the threshold of independence. A mass nationalist movement has evolved in which the hopes and desires of a large variety of people are bound up and organized into a political party which has set its program against domination of chiefs and of the West.

#### INSTRUMENTAL FOCI

In its operations nationalism is increasingly expressed through parliamentary channels. This has developed partly because the British have been willing to relinquish power only

15. Particularly economic pressures such as inflation.

through the devolution of parliamentary responsibility. It has developed partly because the standards and self-images held by secular political leaders are modeled, in crucial respects, after the hierarchy of roles and offices of the British system of government. Insofar as these parliamentary structures satisfy the needs and motives of the nationalist leaders and provide an area for successful problem-solving, they will probably continue to take on more and more meaning in Gold Coast political life. The disabilities suffered by Africans in the performance of European roles have been diminished as nationalist politicians see the support given them by the voting public. They take pride in their accomplishments and their leader.

The British themselves have provided a major basis for spiritual unity and solidarity for the Convention People's party. Each change toward more self-government is phrased as a great victory for Kwame Nkrumah. Each step is played on as a strike against the imperialists. At the same time, the Nkrumah government has not been averse to keeping the British around. With substantive internal authority increasingly in his hands, Nkrumah still needs trained British personnel to staff the administration. Furthermore, he can blame them for mistakes which his government might incur. By playing the parliamentary game, the Nkrumah government would run grave risks in immediately assuming the full burden of responsibilities for decisions which affect the lives of the voters. By phrasing his participation "limited" and by calling the 1950 constitution bogus and fraudulent, he can shift the burden of blame to the British while reaping the rewards of electoral victory and parliamentary successes.

That the British have seen the essential wisdom of allowing parliamentary institutions to be used in this fashion is a credit to their own history. The Convention People's party, instead of being denied access to the positions of formal authority, have been rewarded with responsibility. With the installation of Kwame Nkrumah as prime minister, a major conflict was averted. It was the only step which would have made possible the endowment of parliamentary institutions with affiliatory meaning in the Gold Coast.

# POLITICAL DEMOCRACY IN THE GOLD COAST

The use of parliament to further the aims of nationalism has been successful partly because it has become the only legal and effective means by which the nationalists could promote their own ends. The alternative would have been an outright clash between the nationalist elements of the Convention People's party, on the one hand, and the British and the chiefs, on the other.

However, a major factor in the acceptance of parliamentary channels and the observance of rules of parliamentary processes has been its endowment with "legitimacy" by the major non-traditional source of political norms. This source derives from one man, Nkrumah. His authority is almost unquestioned. He can do no wrong for large masses of the public. He occupies a unique position as a nationalist leader in the Gold Coast.

Clustering around the figure of the prime minister, the "life-chairman" of the C.P.P., but in no way equal in stature insofar as the public is concerned, are the hard-core party leaders—the "old fighters." Some of them would correspond to the "old Bolsheviks" of the Russian revolution. Many are less effective as parliamentarians than as agitators, and some are a source of embarrassment to the party in its present parliamentary role.[16] However, the hard core is an effective party management organ which, by constant agitation and travel to all parts of the Gold Coast, keeps alive the "revolution" and enhances the populari-ty of the prime minister. These old fighters, some of whom are quite young, the British obliged by incarceration shortly before the new constitution. This precedent most of the opposition leaders neglected. Nkrumah and many of the party leaders were rewarded with martyrdom. The wearing of "P.G." or "Prison Graduate" on their caps when rallies are held is a vital symbol of their roles as martyrs. The theme of Nkrumah's suffering for the people has become one of the most effective sources of his strength. How much of public resentment, frustration against poverty, against tribal restrictions, and against unfulfilled

---

16. Several such figures have been dropped from the new cabinet installed after the general election of 1954.

hopes, finds an outlet in Nkrumah's fight, incarceration, and subsequent assumption of the office of prime minister, it is difficult to say. But there is little doubt that it has played a major part in rallying latent nationalism. It lends support to Nkrumah's role as a "charismatic" leader, to use Weber's term. It serves as a focus for a genuine orientational shift away from traditional authority and local particularism to a sense of participation in a crusade for "Freedom," the C.P.P.'s slogan.

Party discipline, normally difficult to maintain as the opposition demonstrates, has in part developed out of the tremendous stature of Nkrumah and the practical impossibility of any other leader gaining a mass following. At the same time the parliamentary party of the C.P.P. is welded together by a feeling of participation in a cause, loyalty to Nkrumah, and a faith that any modification of the party objectives in the light of parliamentary limitations is a brilliant tactical maneuver on the part of the leader and therefore not a seduction of their cherished ends.

Nkrumah is able to inculcate devotion to himself both in the party organization and in large segments of the public. In interviews in both rural and urban areas it was found that people were in favor of a man or a measure if Nkrumah was. They were opposed if Nkrumah was opposed. "Seek ye first the political kingdom, and all things will follow," Nkrumah has promised. In effect, the political kingdom has become parliamentary government as run by the Convention People's party. There is little effective opposition. The chiefs, in order to maintain what authority they have left, have attempted to put themselves "above" politics, since they have no customary basis of parliamentary participation. Rather their opposition has now been manifested in "separatist" movements.

The secular opposition to the Nkrumah government finds itself almost impotent. It gathers most of its strength from intellectuals who are not dazzled by "charisma" and who see in Nkrumah an ultimate threat to democratic politics. They oppose some of the "ruffians" in the C.P.P. and are often stoned for their troubles. At the same time, most of these intellectuals are denied membership in the C.P.P. They are either deliberately kept out or, if they are C.P.P. members, rarely rise to positions of eminence. Nkrumah recognizes clearly that his "gift of grace" within the party is the surest prerequisite of his leadership.

In order to find some support, the secular opposition has formed a tacit alliance with the chiefs. Members affiliated with the territorial councils, the customary advisory organs composed of chiefs and their representatives, tend to oppose the C.P.P. and the person of Nkrumah. Most of the secular opposition is related to these territorial councils either by family ties or by considerations of practical politics.

The operation of various groups in the assembly tends to reflect the uneven development, detribalization, and levels of aspiration of different parts of the country. Where the traditional system is most intact, in the Northern Territories, the alliance between chiefs and the British administrators is still a potent element in the opposition. In the assembly northern politicians tend to be under the general domination of the chiefs. The northern representatives have uneasy tenure with the Nkrumah government. They are being assiduously wooed by Nkrumah, even though they constitute the opposition and form an effective bloc in the assembly.[17]

### B. THE MAINTENANCE OF PARLIAMENTARY LEGITIMACY

It is questionable whether or not effective use of parliament by the Convention People's party would continue if the parliamentary party found itself consistently outvoted by an opposition coalition. It is also questionable that Nkrumah would continue to participate in parliamentary government if it no longer suited his objectives. At the moment, however, there is little chance of an effective opposition. The lack of party support, funds, and effective leadership are continual handicaps to the Ghana Congress party and the Northern People's party, which comprise the main political opposition at present.

At the same time there are subgroups within the Convention People's party whose orientation is more to Nkrumah and to

17. If the Northern People's party and the followers of the National Liberation Movement (at present largely an Ashanti phenomenon) should ally, their challenge to Nkrumah and the C.P.P. would indeed be great.

political power than to norms of political democracy. Some of these groups are highly organized and well versed in Leninist and Stalinist tactics (rather than Marxist theory). They are sponsored by Nkrumah and give him a range of alternatives for nondemocratic action, once the British leave, if his personal authority is attacked strongly in the parliament or his charisma is undermined by his continuing operation within a parliamentary framework of government.

Partly in order to head off a possible effective coalition of chiefs and opposition, the Local Government Ordinance of 1951, passed by the C.P.P. majority, deprived the chiefs of their substantive control over finance and over decision-making within the tribal areas on noncustomary issues. Local tribal opposition both to the C.P.P. and to implementation of measures passed in the assembly has been phrased as undemocratic. The organization of local council elections has in effect been organizational drives by the C.P.P. Local party units have been formed around the nomination and election of candidates to the local councils. Through the formal means of electoral law the C.P.P. has reached out into almost every local area, making manifest any latent hostility to the chiefs and promising benefits and development to the local population. If a powerful chief is in opposition to the C.P.P., local party units may initiate "destoolment" proceedings, often based on spurious charges, but carefully phrased in traditional terms. Most of the "royal" troublemakers for the C.P.P. have been gotten rid of in this way. Those who remain are subject to constant attack. A particular example of this is in the Wenchi Constituency, where the "Wenchihene," or paramount chief, is the brother of the leader of the Ghana Congress party. As a source of income and voting strength for the Ghana Congress party, the Wenchi area is crucial to its survival. Two rival royal families exist in this state, and the C.P.P. has intervened on the side of the royal family at present not occupying the stool. Efforts to destool the Wenchihene and replace him with the rival pro-C.P.P. chief have inflamed bitter separatism in the Wenchi State, and the association of the Wenchihene with the Ghana Congress party has been used by the C.P.P. to identify both with reaction, chieftainship, and British hegemony.

The secular opposition assumes that, as the British withdraw, the mistakes and failures of the Nkrumah regime will be blamed upon him directly. It assumes that the political kingdom will carry fewer blessings and more tyranny than British rule. The opposition seeks to capitalize on a mass disenchantment.

It is by no means given, however, that Nkrumah would sit back and allow such developments to occur. There is good reason to believe that the organizational alternatives deriving from his charismatic leadership and his effective party organization could mean the sacrifice of parliamentary institutions. There is also good reason to believe that party organization and party strength are more important considerations to the C.P.P. than the particular forms of decision-making. At the same time Nkrumah himself is aware not only of the historic importance of his role but of the fact that its fulfilment in the British parliamentary tradition will reflect the greatest credit upon himself. The major factor in the "success" or "failure" of parliamentary government in the Gold Coast lies in Nkrumah's willingness to continue to endow it with effective legitimacy, a power which only he holds.

Nkrumah's willingness to continue within the parliamentary framework depends largely on his ability to make sure that a mass disenchantment does not occur. The institutionalization of parliamentary structures depends upon the extension of Nkrumah's gift of grace to these institutions. A genuine opposition can develop only as a consequence of the diminution of Nkrumah's charisma and the concomitant loss of power of C.P.P. members for whom election represents merely an affirmation of loyalty to the prime minister by the voters. When the British leave, however, and can no longer be blamed for failures of his government, and when the gap between C.P.P. promises and C.P.P. accomplishments grows, there is good question of how long charisma can be maintained. Further, the more Nkrumah continues to play the parliamentary game, the greater is his vulnerability as he serves as a target in the assembly. At present to assail Nkrumah is tantamount to political suicide. But the parliamentary framework demands certain processes of decision-making. It takes on a legitimacy of its own. Nkrumah must make internal decisions which will satisfy the needs of the

# AFRICA IN THE MODERN WORLD

members of the Gold Coast. Certainly he must make provisional decisions which will give him continued support. Yet the enactment of some of the most popular proposals in his program will change the organizational and substantive bases of the society. For example, if the proposed Volta Aluminum Scheme[18] or the Ten-Year Development Plan is successfully completed, problems for the Nkrumah government will multiply rather than diminish. Strains in the social structure caused by changes in occupation, a more extensive division of labor, urban migration, overcrowding, etc., will provide major headaches to the government. These headaches are difficult to cure. The unifying symbol of Gold Coast nationalism—self-government—will soon be a historical bond rather than a goal to which social action is oriented. When the road to self-government branches off into the highways of economic and social reconstruction, the programs designed to settle present problems will create new and more complex problems. In the decision-making process of parliament it is difficult to see how personal charisma can be maintained without making the parliament a rubber stamp.

THE INSTITUTIONALIZATION OF PARLIAMENTARY DEMOCRACY

We have discussed, so far, the types of authority systems which have currency in the Gold Coast. One we have called "traditional" insofar as it deals with the indigenous systems of power and responsibility suitable to tribal society. The indigenous systems are oriented to the past and are held together by factors such as age, lineage, and blood ties. The other we have called "secular" insofar as it derives from a legal rather than a theocratic source. It is universalistic insofar as popular election and criteria of choice are based in the main on broad criteria open to anyone in the Gold Coast. We have indicated that much of the substance behind the shift away from traditional authority derives from changes in goal orientations, the opening-up of new behavioral alternatives, particularly those offered by participation in politics, and the lifting of traditional limitations in regard to permissible behavior (i.e., a shift in

18. For a good discussion of the Volta Scheme see R. B. Davison, "The Volta River Aluminium Scheme," *Political Quarterly*, XXV, No. 1 (1954), 55–67.

[ 134 ]

political norms). The shift in goal orientations derives from the limits on the patterns of expectation and the values regarding specific desirability of ends which are inherent in tribal societies. The shift in behavioral alternatives derives from changes in the socioeconomic environment such as the extended division of labor, the possibilities of migration to urban and nontribal areas, and the multiplication of role structures outside the narrow prescriptions of tribal life. The shifts in political norms derive from the formation of central government, a wholly nonindigenous institution, having a range of normative demands which are associated with the two variables mentioned above.[19]

Under the title of "secular authority," however, we have dealt with one source of the normative shift away from traditional authority and toward secular authority. This shift has taken place via the charisma of Nkrumah. Through Nkrumah, parliamentary institutions have provided a means for the satisfaction of the multiplicity of desires and wants of those disaffected elements who no longer find traditional authority satisfactory. The authority of the man has been substituted for the authority of the chief, and the form through which the authority of the man has been expressed is parliamentary.

Ultimately, however, parliamentary institutions do not derive their strength solely from the substantive source of authority through which public sanctions are shifted away from the traditional patterns of politics toward the secular. It is hardly sufficient that the public supports whatever Nkrumah supports, including the form by which decisions are made. As important for the future of democratic institutions are the actual criteria by which decisions are made. These criteria must involve terms of decision-making in which the norms of rational choice prevail. Issues must be judged on the basis of argument and persuasion and the element of personal nonrational influence reduced to a minimum. Insofar as this type of norm does exist in the Gold Coast, it is found to some degree in the assembly. For most of the interested public, however, the results of decisions center around whether Nkrumah won or lost.

19. See W. Moore, "Social Consequences of Technological Change from the Sociological Standpoint," *International Social Science Bulletin*, Vol. VIII, No. 13 (1947).

Rational choice as a predominant criterion for decision-making displaces charismatic factors, as parliamentary democracy becomes institutionalized. The one is incompatible with the other. What has occurred in the Gold Coast is the use of charisma to transfer sanctional allegiance away from the chiefs to an individual. The individual has directed sanctional allegiance to the parliament. The question is whether or not sanctional allegiance to the parliament will create a public acceptance of norms of critical rationality in which charisma will be destroyed. If such a final shift occurs in terms of public orientations, the prospects for the institutionalization of parliamentary government are favorable indeed.

One major factor in favor of this shift is that the kinds of issues which are now coming up for discussion, a national Gold Coast bank, the Volta Aluminum Project, slum clearance, housing, and the like, are not issues of nationalism. Constitutional issues are issues of nationalism insofar as they are directly involved with authority and the form in which authority will be expressed. With constitutional issues out of the way, it will be increasingly difficult to make charismatic capital out of the technical issues which are by and large ahead of the Nkrumah government at present. If the attention of the public is directed more and more toward policy issues which demand careful thought and public debate, not only will the issues themselves tend to determine the kind of approval or disapproval which derives from national examination of a problem but the opposition will undoubtedly get a hearing.

Ultimately the burden of institutionalization of parliamentary democracy would appear to rest, on the one hand, on the adoption of political norms regarding substantive rationality. On the other hand, it would depend upon Nkrumah's willingness to watch the diminution of his charismatic authority. This last could occur only if Nkrumah's effective authority is not seriously threatened.

It is held here that a reintegration of Gold Coast political life around parliamentary institutions is occurring. The charismatic factor is the transitional instrumentality by which the shift has occurred. Without the charismatic factor either apathy or local separatism probably would have occurred. In order for charisma to "wither away," the criteria for decision-making must become rational, and the decisions made must be adequate to satisfy the perceived needs of the members of the system.[20]

Surprisingly enough, one of the resources of potential value for the reintegration of political life around parliamentary institutions lies with the chiefs. With their power broken or abdicated, neither the chiefs nor the British at present represent threats to the Convention People's party as they did in the past. But both are important in the establishment of genuine parliamentary institutions. Both must clearly play subordinate parts, however, to the authority center, the C.P.P.-dominated assembly.

Whereas in highly industrialized systems much of the economic and social reserves derive from nongovernment sources, in the Gold Coast government is the major internal source of investment funds or capital, and the major agency for social development (e.g., housing and medical and health facilities). Under Nkrumah, government has so far served to strengthen the nationalist movement and stabilize structures of political expression in Western patterns. It has not yet dealt with major issues of reconstruction out of which a new pattern of national society, in its social, economic, and political integration, can be realized. The British are particularly important with respect to the provision of technical skill, economic aid, and educational training to aid the government in handling its problems.

But the adaptive value of tribal structures can play an equally significant part in preventing a wholesale departure from democratic goals and methods by Nkrumah or in averting public dissatisfaction with the Convention People's party, which might put an end to parliamentary democracy. The traditional systems of "social security," the family system, and the functions of adjudication still held by the chiefs tend to remove some of the daily pressures of decision-making and other demands placed on the central government. If the chiefs and el-

20. For a full treatment of some of the assumptions involved in this discussion see M. Weber, *The Theory of Social and Economic Organization* (London: William Hodge & Co., 1947).

ders aid in general development by using the forms of tribal co-operation as agencies of local development, they can remove public pressure on the central government and redirect it to the traditional authorities and their local secular associates. Community participation, combined with ceremonial and religious aspects of traditional culture, not only can keep African culture alive but can serve as an agency for the integration of traditional authorities with local secular authorities in accordance with the modern needs of rural and tribal areas. In this view a wholesale repudiation of the chiefs puts an impossible burden on the central authorities at a time when their burdens are growing. By lending their support to communal projects and self-help, the chiefs can find modern uses for their roles. In effect, local problems may be solved best by local solutions.

Assuming that traditional authorities can help to reduce the burden which will be placed on the central authorities, the government must have the resources and equipment to make and carry out decisions which will satisfy the needs of the public. They must carry them out in a way which lies within the sanctional limitations of emerging political norms. The history of differences and mutual restraints upon behavior which characterize all tribal systems provides a favorable climate within which parliamentary structures can take root. This has already made its mark in affecting the types of acceptable actions which politicians can demonstrate. Remarkably little bloodshed and violence have occurred considering the far-reaching changes which have taken place in Gold Coast social and political life in the last few years. A voluntary boycott and a few demonstrations have been the only mass movements for political and economic reform. "Tribalism" as co-operation, and as self-imposed limits on permissible behavior, remains an adjustive mechanism where it has not been destroyed utterly or is not a major inhibition to the goals and desires of the members.

The problem of transition from traditional to secular systems of authority and manifestations of the broader issues of over-all cultural clash and change are deeply significant to the construction of democratic politics in West Africa. The major advantage of charisma is that it unifies the perceptions, motivations, and energies of the more aggressive nationalist elements within a framework of parliamentary institutions. In the British colonies this is the only alternative to outright conflict. If, subsequently, parliamentary democracy can be institutionalized in its normative prescriptions, parliamentary government can become a vehicle for progressive social change.

In sum the traditional systems represented substantive integration of members around a complementary system of norms, objectives, and role structures. The secular parliamentary system represents procedural integration within the requirements of a legal framework of secular politics. The elements of charisma carried by Nkrumah and the use of secular government to further the ends of nationalism have brought the Gold Coast a long way toward transforming procedural integration into substantive integration. It has been an important step in the process of creating parliamentary democracy in the Gold Coast.

It is clear that parliamentary democracy cannot develop simply through a devolution of authority to Africans organized with a parliamentary structure. If nothing else, the experience of the old Legislative Council proved this in the Gold Coast. It is being demonstrated again today in Nigeria. In the Gold Coast the personal leadership of a man and the effective organization of a political machine have carried the public into the democratic process. This has transcended regional differences, divided loyalties, and conflicting cultural norms to the extent that parliamentary democracy in the British tradition appears to have excellent prospects.

# POLITICAL DEVELOPMENT IN FRENCH WEST AFRICA

KENNETH ROBINSON

*Nuffield College, Oxford*

## INTRODUCTION

THIS paper is intended to outline some of the changes made in the political structure of French West Africa since the end of the second World War and to attempt some assessment of the development of political parties in that period. As it is difficult to assess the changes brought about by the war, the constitution of the Fourth Republic, and later legislation without some knowledge of the earlier history of the area, some account of this has been included. No definitive treatment is possible either of the earlier period or of the more recent developments without much more research, both in the field[1] and in the records of the local assemblies.

French West Africa is a group of eight overseas territories,[2] each with its own governor, budget, and, since 1946, elected assembly but subject to the general direction and authority of a governor-general, high commissioner of France, and dependent for many services on a general budget and a "grand council" for French West Africa as a whole, made up of representatives elected by each territory. The eight territories are Mauretania, Senegal, French Sudan, French Guinea, the Ivory Coast, Dahomey, Upper Volta, and Niger. (The two trust territories of Togoland and the Cameroons are entirely separate political and administrative units which are not part of French West Africa.) Each territory is divided for administrative pur-

---

1. The author last visited French West Africa in 1950. This visit was made possible by a grant from the Committee for Colonial Studies of Oxford University. The French authorities gave the author every help.

2. For the implications of the constitution of 1946 in respect of French colonial areas see K. E. Robinson, *The Public Law of Overseas France since the War* (rev. ed.; Oxford: Institute of Colonial Studies, 1954), originally published in the *Journal of Comparative Legislation*, Third Series, Vol. XXXII (1950).

POLITICAL DEVELOPMENT IN FRENCH WEST AFRICA

poses into *cercles*, under an administrator, usually referred to as a *commandant du cercle*. A *cercle* may be divided into subdivisions under a *chef de subdivision*. Table 1 shows the area, population, and administrative divisions of each territory.

This vast area (some fourteen times the size of France) has for the most part been under effective French control only since the last decade of the nineteenth century, though French interests were established in some coastal areas for centuries, and

TABLE 1*

AREA, POPULATION, AND ADMINISTRATIVE DIVISIONS

| TERRITORY | AREA (000 SQUARE KILOMETERS) | POPULATION | | No. OF "CERCLES" | No. OF SUB-DIVISIONS |
|---|---|---|---|---|---|
| | | African | Non-African | | |
| Niger.......... | 1,219.0 | 2,125,800 | 1,530 | 10 | 25 |
| Dahomey...... | 115.8 | 1,532,400 | 2,200 | 9 | 24 |
| Upper Volta.... | 315.8 | 3,106,300 | 2,300 | 11 | 24 |
| Ivory Coast.... | 319.5 | 2,159,500 | 10,500 | 16 | 46 |
| Sudan......... | 1,192.2 | 3,341,100 | 5,800 | 16 | 33 |
| French Guinea.. | 280.9 | 2,253,700 | 6,900 | 20 | 26 |
| Mauretania..... | 943.0 | 566,100 | 770 | 10 | 23 |
| Senegal........ | 210.0 | 2,059,600 | 33,100 | 11 | 27 |
| Total...... | 4,596.2 | 17,144,500 | 63,100 | 103 | 228 |

* Source: area and administrative divisions: *Annuaire statistique de l'Afrique Occidentale française* (Paris, 1949), Vol. I; estimated populations: United Nations, *Non-self-governing Territories* (New York, 1953), Vol. II.

those in Senegal have been in undisputed French control since the end of the Napoleonic Wars. The extent and depth of French penetration and of the Western social forms which tend to accompany it vary widely in French West Africa even today, and this variation was even more striking before 1939. In the half-century from 1895, which witnessed the first attempts at the establishment of a "Federation" of French West Africa, to 1945, when the end of the second World War released new forces of social and economic change, the political history of French West Africa is essentially administrative history—the history of the impact of metropolitan ideas and interests on the practical day-to-day problems of administration in a poor, thinly populated, and undeveloped country. The form which political movements in such colonial countries take seems to de-

pend largely on two factors: the character of the political organization established by the colonial power and the extent to
which, at any given time, indigenous social institutions are disintegrating as a result of economic and social change induced by
Western contact. The institutions which were established by
the French during this period did not, perhaps, encourage—indeed, they scarcely permitted—the development of indigenous
political activities; but, equally, the extent of economic and social change was hardly enough to stimulate as yet any serious
challenge to the social order.[3] Let us now briefly consider these
two factors: the political structure set up by the French rulers
and the extent of social and economic change before the beginning of the second World War.

POLITICAL STRUCTURE IN THE INTERWAR YEARS

Before the second World War the system of government in
French West Africa was essentially "colonial," that is to say,
rule by officials of the metropolitan government, administering
policies determined by metropolitan ideas and, to a large extent, metropolitan interests—policies in the elaboration of
which few, if any, of the inhabitants of the territory played any
part. Fundamental to the system was the sharp distinction between French citizens and French subjects. All Frenchmen from
France were, of course, French citizens, exercising as such special privileges, subject only to French law administered by
French courts. Native-born Africans, with the exception of a
specially favored group in Senegal,[4] were French subjects and
could acquire citizenship only by a process akin to individual
naturalization. As subjects they were subject to a special dis-
ciplinary regime known as the *indigénat*, the Native Status

3. In both respects comparison may be made with the situation in British West
Africa between the wars, though the contrast is usually overemphasized. Particularly
in the Gold Coast Colony proper (i.e., southern Gold Coast) political institutions and
economic development resulted in more self-conscious political activities (R. L. Buell,
*The Native Problem in Africa* [New York, 1928], Vol. I, chaps. xlv and li; M. Wight,
*The Gold Coast Legislative Council* [London, 1947], pp. 163–207; C. K. Meek, W. M.
MacMillan, and E. R. J. Hussey, *Britain and West Africa* [London, 1940], pp. 94–115;
G. Padmore, *Africa, Britain's Third Empire* [London, 1949], pp. 193–215 [partisan, but
stimulating]). For the relative lack of such political activity in Nigeria before 1939 see
J. Wheare, *The Nigerian Legislative Council* (London, 1949), esp. pp. 143 ff.

4. See below, pp. 143–45.

Legal Code,[5] in accordance with which they could be punished by short periods of imprisonment or by fines for offenses defined, not by ordinary law, but by administrative regulations. These sentences were awarded summarily by French administrative officers. Subjects were also liable to a longer period of military service than were citizens and in practice were liable to compulsory labor service under the system whereby conscripts were divided into two groups, one sent on military service and the other, called the *deuxième contingent*, employed on works of public concern under more or less military conditions. Compulsory labor, regarded as equivalent to the metropolitan system of *prestations* or contributions in kind for the maintenance of roads,[6] was also exacted by requisitioning labor through the chiefs. On the other hand, subjects, unlike citizens, were not required to accept French private law in regard to such matters as marriage, inheritance, and succession, which were dealt with by native courts over which an administrative officer presided, with two African assessors chosen for their knowledge of the particular customary law involved in the case.

In the old French coastal settlements in Senegal, the system of government presented certain special features which were the outcome of the fact that, unlike the rest of the area, they had been French territory in the earlier years of the nineteenth century, and to them had been applied, from time to time, the assimilationist policy of successive metropolitan governments.[7] In 1833 Parliament had provided that "any person born free or having legally acquired his liberty enjoys in the French colonies (1) civil rights (2) political rights under conditions prescribed by law." No subsequent legislation defined the political rights of the natives of the four communes of Rufisque, Dakar, Gorée,

5. For an interesting discussion of the prewar system see R. Delavignette, *Service africain* (Paris, 1946), English trans. *Freedom and Authority in French West Africa* (London, 1950).

6. For *prestations* in present-day France see B. Chapman, *Introduction to French Local Government* (London, 1953), pp. 182–83.

7. See Lord Hailey, *An African Survey* (London, 1937), pp. 193–200; Buell, *op. cit.*, pp. 946 ff.; and K. E. Robinson, "French West Africa," *African Affairs*, L (1951), 123–31.

and Saint-Louis, the only parts of Senegal which had been annexed in 1848, when the Second Republic, resuming the assimilationist tradition of the Great Revolution, provided for the election of deputies to the French Parliament by the colonies, including Senegal, and for the exercise by inhabitants of Senegal of the franchise on the same conditions as in France. In Senegal it was from the outset recognized that these franchise rights would not involve the complete assimilation of the native inhabitants to French civil law, and they continued to remain subject to Moslem private law, though the privilege was restricted to persons born and resident in one of the four communes. When the Third Republic re-established the system of colonial representation in Parliament, which had been suppressed under the Second Empire, the *originaires* of the four communes of Senegal were once more allowed to vote for the election of the Senegal deputy. From then until 1916 there was a series of attempts by the administration to restrict these rights[8] and much legal controversy as to whether the *originaires* were in law French citizens though retaining their *statut personnel* as Moslems (in which case they could, for example, vote elsewhere) or merely exercised, within the communes, a peculiar franchise privilege which did not in itself amount to citizenship. In 1916, however, the French Parliament declared by law that the *originaires* and their descendants were French citizens. In spite of some attempt to argue that, if they were indeed French citizens, they must be subject to French private law, they continued in practice to retain their privileged positions as citizens, on the one hand, exercising the franchise and free from the special native legal code (*indigénat*), while, on the other hand, remaining subject to their own Moslem law in such matters of private law as marriage and inheritance. They took part, and indeed constituted the overwhelming majority of the voters, in the elections of the deputy for Senegal. Until 1914 they had been content to return a European, but in that year M. Blaise Diagne, an African, was elected.

Not only was the right of Senegal (and the other older colonies) to parliamentary representation restored by the Third Republic, but in 1872 Saint-Louis and Gorée were created com-

8. Buell, *op. cit.*, pp. 949–51.

munes, with elected councils and mayors and powers similar to those of communes in France. A commune of Rufisque was created in 1880, and Dakar, separated from Gorée in 1887, at length swallowed its parent in 1929. Some of the powers of an ordinary French commune were transferred to French administrative officials during the interwar years, and the establishment in 1924 of a special administrative district for the city of Dakar also resulted in a diminution of the powers of the commune. Nevertheless, within their limited sphere, these were wholly elected councils exercising some local government functions, and they formed an important basis for political action. M. Diagne was mayor of Dakar for many years, while his postwar successor, M. Lamine Gueye, was mayor of Saint-Louis in the twenties and has been mayor of Dakar for many years.

The assimilationist philosophy of the earlier years of the Third Republic also resulted in the establishment in Senegal of a *conseil général*, modeled on that of a department in metropolitan France. Its scope was limited to the communes, the territory then under direct administration, as opposed to the remainder of Senegal then regarded as a protectorate. In 1920 the former area had a population of about 175,000, the latter about 1.5 million.[9] All the twenty members of the General Council were elected by the French citizens, who included, as we have seen, all those born in the communes, and most of them soon came to be Africans. Subject to the usual metropolitan rules about providing for obligatory expenditure,[10] the council's assent was required for the budget. In 1892, however, a separate budget was established for the protectorate, and its finances thus removed from the control of the General Council. The establishment of the so-called "Federation of French West Africa" in 1904 and the creation of a federal budget in 1905 further limited the revenue available for the budget of that part of Senegal under the authority of the General Council. Serious disputes with the administration occurred over the budgets of 1917 and 1918[11] and led to demands for the extension of the jurisdiction of the council to the whole of Senegal. This was

9. *Ibid.*, p. 967.
10. For these in present-day France see Chapman, *op. cit.*, pp. 74–75.
11. Buell, *op. cit.*, p. 969.

opposed by the administration on the ground that the council was, in fact, representative only of the communes; and, accordingly, in 1920, the council was replaced by an enlarged body, called the Colonial Council, whose jurisdiction was extended to the whole of Senegal and whose membership included, besides the twenty members elected by the citizens, twenty chiefs elected by the provincial and cantonal chiefs in a meeting called by an administrative officer. In effect this was an attempt on the part of the administration to provide for itself something closely approximating to the official majority in the legislative councils of British West Africa at that time, especially if it is true that, as Buell asserts, "the chiefs were more regular in their attendance and voted more solidly than the citizens."[12] The arrangement was not a success and frequently resulted in what Hailey describes as "unfortunate bickerings."[13] In 1925 the number of citizen members was increased to twenty-four, while that of the chiefs was reduced to sixteen; later these were increased to twenty-six and eighteen, respectively. In 1939 the number of members was further increased by the addition of eighteen members who were French subjects, born in Senegal, or descended from persons born in Senegal, and had completed their military service. These were elected by all French subjects who fulfilled the same conditions.

The powers of the council were similar to those of the *conseil général*, which it had replaced. It could, of course, be consulted by the administration on any matter and could express its opinions on administrative questions. It could take decisions on a number of matters such as the "disposition and management of public property, the acceptance or refusal of gifts to the colony, the classification of roads, and the contribution of the colony to work being executed by the State."[14] Such decisions entered into effect after two months unless the lieutenant-governor had asked for their "annulation pour excès de pourvoir, pour violation des lois et des règlements ayant force de loi."[15] In certain

12. *Ibid.*, p. 976.
13. *Op. cit.*, p. 198.
14. Buell, *op. cit.*, p. 971.
15. Decree of December 4, 1920, Art. 42.

other matters the council was empowered to take decisions, but such decisions required the approval of the governor in council of government before they took effect. The most important of these were those relating to taxation. Finally, the council had power to decide the budget for the whole of Senegal (now again combined into a single budget).

English writers have tended to underemphasize the powers of *conseils généraux* and of this council, which was closely modeled on them. Buell, however, writing in the late twenties after a careful examination of the actual working of these institutions, concluded, quite correctly in my judgment, that

the members of the Colonial Council have more power than the unofficial members of any other consultative assembly in Africa, including the Legislative Councils found in British territory. They can block the imposition of new taxes and withhold about half the expenditures of the government. The Colonial Council may thus deadlock the efforts of the administration to carry out a development programme. On the other hand, the Council has no direct means of getting rid of the administration, since it cannot hold up obligatory expenditures . . . in other words, the Colonial Council presents all the disadvantages, from the standpoint of political science, of a legislative controlled from outside.[16]

But interesting as were these legacies of an earlier age in which assimilationist policies had carried the day, and important as the future was to show them to be as foreshadowing the shape of things to come, they were the concern of a tiny minority of the inhabitants of French West Africa. Of its total population, then estimated at some 14.5 million, some 78,000 were citizens in 1936 by virtue of their connection with the communes, while a further 2,000 in all parts of the federation had acquired citizenship by naturalization. We must now briefly examine the regime under which the vast majority of the inhabitants were administered. In each of the territories except Senegal,[17] the lieutenant-governor, as he was then called, was assisted by a *conseil d'administration*,[18] which he was required to consult regarding the territorial budget, direct taxation, loans, the disposal of government property and land, and similar admin-

16. *Op. cit.*, p. 971.

17. After 1933 Upper Volta ceased to exist as a separate administrative unit. It was re-established as an overseas territory in 1947.

18. Hailey, *op. cit.*, pp. 201–2; Buell, *op. cit.*, pp. 981–82.

istrative matters. In Dahomey, the Ivory Coast, the French Sudan, and French Guinea these bodies contained three official members, the member of the Conseil Supérieur de la France d'Outre Mer[19] (elected by the French citizens in each of these colonies); two members, being French citizens, elected by the chambers of agriculture and commerce, respectively; and three members, being French subjects (i.e., native noncitizens), elected by a special electorate consisting of noncitizens holding certain civil service posts, chiefs of provinces and cantons, licensed traders, owners of registered urban property worth 5,000 francs, and farmers cultivating areas of a size fixed by the lieutenant-governor, as well as holders of the Legion of Honor and other titles, and Africans who had rendered exceptional services to France. The *conseils d'administration* in Niger and Mauretania had only nominated unofficial members besides the officials. It has been usual for British writers to contrast these advisory councils unfavorably with the legislative councils of British territories, but, as Buell pointed out, the basis of representation was much wider than in Nigeria, Sierra Leone, and the Gold Coast, where, except for the members elected by the chiefs in the Gold Coast, the principle of election was confined to urban areas. It will be seen later that this experiment in the creation of an African electorate formed the basis of the electoral law of 1946.

At the federal level the governor-general was assisted by a *conseil du gouvernement*. It consisted of sixteen official members: the deputy for Senegal; the four members of the Conseil Supérieur de la France d'Outre Mer elected by the French citizens in Dahomey, the Ivory Coast, the French Sudan, and French Guinea; the president and one noncitizen member elected by the noncitizen members of the Colonial Council of Senegal; two un-

19. An advisory body sitting in Paris. An African author says of these elections: "Etaient électeurs et éligibles tous les citoyens français agés de 21 ans. Les femmes n'étaient ni électrices ni éligibles. Les autochtones de la Colonie, à l'exception d'un très petit nombre d'entre eux naturalisés français n'avaient pas voix au chapitre. De ce fait le collège electoral était très restreint et les élections ne traduisaient nullement la volonté du pays. En Côte d'Ivoire, les électeurs étaient surtout des Européens ou des Africains natifs des quatres communes du Sénégal. Et cette majorité d'étrangers ne voyait pas toujours les choses sous le même angle que les autochtones" (F. J. Amon d'Aby, *La Côte d'Ivoire dans la cité africaine* [Paris, 1951], p. 53).

official members (one citizen, one noncitizen) elected by each of the *conseils d'administration* in the other territories; together with members elected by the chambers of commerce in Senegal and the municipal council of Dakar. This body met annually and heard a general report and exposition of policy from the governor-general, considered the budgets of the federation and the individual territories, and had to be consulted on public works, loans, and taxation.

Finally, mention should be made of the existence, at the local government level, besides the old *communes de plein exercise* of Senegal, which have already been discussed, of municipal bodies in most of the remaining towns called *communes mixtes*. These consisted of an appointed official as mayor, together with a council which might be either nominated or elected by citizens together with certain categories of noncitizens,[20] or elected by both citizens and noncitizens on the basis of universal suffrage. None of this last category was in fact established before the second World War. In the rural areas advisory councils of *notables* were established, but their functions were shadowy, and they had no separate budgets or funds of their own.

Outside the special regime of the Senegal *communes de plein exercise*, this system did nothing to stimulate political activity on Western lines, though the existence of the Senegalese citizens who had not been required to accept French private law as the price of citizenship, as well as the institutions associated with their citizenship, doubtless did something to suggest that a similar result might one day come about elsewhere, just as the existence in the legislative councils of Nigeria and the Gold Coast of one or two members elected for urban constituencies by ballot operated in a similar fashion there. Both British and French administrations in the interwar years sought, within the different presuppositions of their respective systems, to limit the scope (and the power of attraction) of such examples of the policy of *identity*—the policy seeking in principle to establish in the colonial territories institutions identical with those at home. In Senegal this attitude resulted in an attempt to alter the bal-

20. The categories were traders paying a license fee of at least 200 francs a year and property owners.

ance of power as between "citizens" and the administration by
the reconstruction of the *conseil général* so as to include what in
practice was likely to be a majority of chiefs.[21] But scope for
some political activity remained in the elections of the deputy,
in the new Colonial Council, and in the basis for political organization afforded by control of the *communes de plein exercise* and
the opportunities for patronage afforded by municipal employment.[22] Between 1914 and 1940 only two people were elected
deputy for Senegal, M. Blaise Diagne, who was the first African
to be elected and who retained the seat until his death, when he
was succeeded by Galandou Diouf. The historian of Senegal,
André Villard, says of them:

> Les élections de 1914 amenèrent au Parlement le Goréen Blaise Diagne.
> Pendant vingt ans, ce personnage, d'une activité et d'une intelligence rare
> sera une de figures les plus curieuses de la vie sénégalaise. ... Des 1916, ce
> parlementaire jouissait en France d'un crédit extraordinaire. On le nomma
> haut-commissaire au recrutement des troupes. ... Diagne fit passer au Parle-
> ment la loi de 1916 sur la citoyenneté. Il intervint vigoureusement dans ce
> qu'on appela la bataille de l'arachide. Il devint même sous-secrétaire d'État
> aux colonies. Son action ne fut pas toujours très proportionnée aux possibilités
> réelles du Sénégal et on ne peut dire qu'il facilita en toutes circonstances l'ac-
> complissement de certaines lourdes tâches administratives ... après lui
> Galandou Diouf représenta le Sénégal au Parlement avec moins d'éclat.[23]

In the elections of the deputy, candidates adopted a French
party. Diagne was a member of the Republican Socialist group,
but, as Buell commented, "in Senegal these party labels mean
little. At present the only division between the native voters is
a personal one between the followers of M. Diagne and M. Lamine Gueye."[24] The general impression is of a political machine,
deriving its strength mainly from the influence it could bring to
bear in the metropole on the colonial minister and its ability to
exercise, in one way or another, substantial patronage, and organized round a leading personality, almost a political boss,
rather than any set of political principles or a specific party pro-

21. The similarity of the policy of Governor-General Merlin in Senegal and Governor Guggisberg in the Gold Coast in this respect is striking. For Guggisberg's reform
of the Gold Coast Legislative Council see Wight, *op. cit.*, pp. 66–75.

22. Cf. Buell, *op. cit.*, p. 961.

23. *Histoire du Sénégal* (Dakar, 1943), p. 179.

24. Buell, *op. cit.*, p. 957. M. Lamine Gueye became deputy for Senegal in 1946 and
was defeated at the election of 1951.

gram. But this is an aspect of the prewar situation which has, so far as the author is aware, been little investigated since Buell's pioneer work. The political biography of M. Diagne would be an interesting theme for research, and it should be possible to throw a good deal of light on the working of the Senegalese system not only from the records of the Colonial Council and West African newspapers but also from a study of his activities in Paris, in the proceedings of the chamber of deputies.

### ECONOMIC AND SOCIAL CHANGE

An attempt must next be made to assess the extent of economic and social change in the period between the wars and subsequently. This is, of course, a much more hazardous enterprise than the mere description of administrative and political institutions. But, in general terms, just as for the greater part of the area the prewar political system was essentially colonial, so the economy may be described as a typically colonial economy at a fairly early stage in its development.

A broad distinction may be made between the coastal areas, with a relatively highly developed agricultural production for export, and the interior zones, becoming increasingly arid as one moves northward from the Atlantic coast until the country shades gradually into the Sahara. Natural communications are poor, neither of the two major waterways, the Senegal and the Niger, being navigable for any considerable distance by sizeable vessels in the dry season, and the latter being broken up into relatively short stretches by falls. Before the war more than half the exports of French West Africa took the form of oilseeds, and about five-sixths of those were groundnuts. Other important exports were cocoa, coffee, bananas, timber, and the traditional "gum arabic"; apart from small quantities of gold, and a relatively new export of industrial diamonds from Guinea, there were no mineral exports, and little had been done either in geological survey or commercial search for exploitable minerals . . . the picture in 1938 was thus one of a typical colonial economy, including a number of areas, mainly in the coastal territories, in which monoculture had been pushed to the point at which subsistence food production had given place to imported foodstuffs. There was also a large internal area where poor communications and resulting concentration on the more accessible coastal areas had left indigenous society, with its mainly subsistence production largely, if not entirely, untouched by the pressure of the Western economy.[25]

25. K. E. Robinson, "Economic Development in French West Africa," *World Today*, VI (December, 1950), 536–37. See also J. Guillard, "Où en est l'économie de l'AOF," *L'Afrique et l'Asie*, No. 2 (2d Quarter, 1949), pp. 27–50.

Some features of this colonial economy are suggested in Tables 2 and 3: concentration on a small range of primary products for export, the import of consumption goods like cotton

TABLE 2*

SELECTED EXPORTS, 1938–51
(In Metric Tons)

| Product | 1938 | 1945 | 1947 | 1949 | 1951 |
|---|---|---|---|---|---|
| Groundnuts | 368,793 | ........ | 454 | 3,152 | ........ |
| Groundnuts (decorticated) | 169,400 | 94,809 | 191,723 | 208,134 | 166,725 |
| Groundnut oil | 5,681 | 33,503 | 35,908 | 55,405 | 53,448 |
| Other oilseeds† | 89,157 | 61,871 | 48,647 | 93,636 | 89,267 |
| Palm oil | 13,688 | 4,821 | 712 | 9,820 | 14,519 |
| Cacao | 52,729 | 26,943 | 28,048 | 56,132 | 55,477 |
| Coffee | 14,479 | 39,207 | 44,052 | 63,742 | 62,925 |
| Timber | 40,533 | 10,044 | 48,755 | 81,831 | 66,805 |
| Bananas | 65,128 | 270 | 33,023 | 61,012 | 69,868 |
| Total exports | 987,770 | 347,460 | 577,305 | 816,391 | 848,149 |

* Source: Service des Statistiques de la France d'Outre Mer.
† Excludes copra but includes shea-nut butter.

TABLE 3*

SELECTED IMPORTS, 1938–51
(In Metric Tons)

| Product | 1938 | 1945 | 1947 | 1949 | 1951 |
|---|---|---|---|---|---|
| Rice | 41,101 | 53 | 29,879 | 37,398 | 69,492 |
| Sugar | 21,002 | 5,699 | 28,364 | 26,911 | 43,317 |
| Cement | 113,313 | 35,946 | 74,587 | 139,262 | 312,213 |
| Coal | 97,540 | 103,959 | 100,758 | 110,307 | 162,495 |
| Gasoline, etc. | 51,416 | 71,917 | 73,114 | 150,182 | 273,752 |
| Cotton textiles | 9,781 | 5,899 | 14,200 | 9,038 | 16,024 |
| Iron and steel | 16,549 | 4,171 | 16,412 | 50,712 | 83,113 |
| Trucks, cars, parts | 2,463 | 1,171 | 8,726 | 17,977 | 21,774 |
| Total imports | 557,600 | 345,300 | 594,833 | 919,350 | 1,471,003 |

* Source: Service des Statistiques de la France d'Outre Mer.

piece goods, holloware, and certain foodstuffs and of capital goods such as cement, machinery, and trucks; and, finally, the imports of coal and petroleum products, reflecting French West Africa's lack of sources of power. They also suggest the character of some postwar development: little increase in exports, except coffee and timber; development of some processing industries (groundnut oil replacing groundnut exports); and large increases in capital goods imports, destined to be employed in the various constructional works undertaken as part of the postwar government-financed development plan.[26]

Before the war the territory which made the largest contribution to the wealth of French West Africa was Senegal. Next came the Ivory Coast. Table 4 shows one measure of the re-

TABLE 4*

PROPORTION OF TOTAL CUSTOMS REVENUE
ATTRIBUTABLE TO TERRITORIES

| Territory | 1938† | 1950 | 1951 | 1952 |
|---|---|---|---|---|
| Senegal................ | 163.4 | 4,766.2 | 5,744.3 | 6,261.4 |
| Ivory Coast and Upper Volta................ | 80.5 | 3,652.5 | 5,715.4 | 5,813.4 |
| French Guinea......... | 31.5 | 949.7 | 1,232.5 | 1,300.1 |
| Dahomey.............. | 32.2 | 690.5 | 987.3 | 852.2 |
| Niger................. | 4.4 | 201.8 | 290.7 | 418.3 |
| Sudan and Mauretania... | 19.5 | 319.0 | 266.3 | 276.3 |
| Total.............. | 331.5 | 10,679.7 | 14,236.5 | 14,921.7 |

* Source: Service des Statistiques de la France d'Outre Mer.
† Figures for 1938 in millions of francs; remainder in millions of francs C.F.A.

spective shares of the various territories in modern economic activity of French West Africa, namely, the proportion of total customs revenue attributable to the various territories. This shows how the Ivory Coast has developed, relatively to Senegal, and also the development of French Guinea in recent years. The table brings out clearly the predominance of Senegal and the Ivory Coast in the economy of the areas as a whole. It is not surprising that political activities have, since the war, also been most striking in these two territories.

Another index of Westernization is afforded by the numbers of children attending schools. Prewar and postwar figures for the various types of schools cannot, however, be satisfactorily compared, because the educational system has been considerably changed since the war and the types of schools and the courses given in them brought more completely into line with

26. See, besides my article on economic development already cited, the official volume, *L'Équipement de l'Afrique Occidentale française* (Paris, 1951).

those of metropolitan France. Tables 5 and 6 suggest, however, what a small proportion of the population had, before 1939, been brought within the Western educational system,[27] in either

TABLE 5*

TOTAL SCHOOL POPULATION

| Year | School Population |
|---|---|
| 1937–38 | 68,416 |
| 1947 | 105,607 |
| 1950 | 163,323 |
| 1951 | 177,315 |

* Source: 1937 and 1947: *Annuaire statistique de l'Afrique Occidentale française* (Paris, 1951), Vol. II; 1950 and 1951: United Nations, *Non-self-governing Territories* (New York, 1953), Vol. II.

TABLE 6*

PUPILS IN PRIMARY SCHOOLS, BY TERRITORIES
1937–38 AND 1948–49

| TERRITORY | 1937–38 | | 1948–49 | |
|---|---|---|---|---|
| | Private | Government | Private | Government |
| Niger†‡ | | 1,595 | 20 | 4,647 |
| Dahomey | 6,853 | 8,252 | 14,265 | 11,740 |
| Upper Volta‡ | | | 4,954 | 7,962 |
| Ivory Coast‡ | 2,739 | 9,619 | 6,924 | 16,222 |
| Sudan‡ | 280 | 13,067 | 1,339 | 20,430 |
| French Guinea | 952 | 7,773 | 1,526 | 12,549 |
| Mauretania | | 476 | | 1,860 |
| Senegal | 1,457 | 15,353 | 3,631 | 23,287 |
| Total | 12,281 | 56,135 | 32,709 | 98,697 |

* Source: *Annuaire statistique de l'Afrique Occidentale française* (Paris, 1951), Vol. II.

† The figure given in the *Annuaire statistique de l'Afrique Occidentale française* for government primary-school pupils in Niger is 10,647. According to United Nations, *Non-self-governing Territories* (New York, 1950), Vol. II, the corresponding figure for the preceding year was 3,234; and, according to the handbook issued by the Ministry of Education in 1951, the figure for 1948–49 should be 4,647, which has been substituted above.

‡ Owing to the inclusion in 1937 of parts of Upper Volta in the Ivory Coast, Niger, and Sudan, the figures are not in these territories strictly comparable.

government or mission schools, and how relatively small it still remains despite an increase of about 150 per cent in the school-going population between 1938 and 1951.

Another and most important indicator of economic and, still

27. For purposes of comparison, the number of children attending primary schools alone in the Gold Coast was, in 1950, 272,600 (population about one-quarter of that of French West Africa).

more, social change is the growth of urbanization. Unfortunately, satisfactory figures to illustrate the extent of this phenomenon in French West Africa do not seem to be available. The rate of growth of Abidjan, Bamako, and Dakar has, however, been accelerating in recent years and has reached formidable proportions. The interrelation of the social and economic causes of urbanization and internal migrations and their political consequences is a fascinating and important field for research. For the present we can only note that direct observation suggests

TABLE 7*

APPROXIMATE POPULATION OF CERTAIN TOWNS

| Town | 1921 | 1945 | 1951 |
|---|---|---|---|
| Dakar........ | 32,000 | 132,000 | 250,600 |
| Saint-Louis.... | 18,000 | 51,000 | 62,200 |
| Abidjan....... | 5,000 | 46,000 | 86,000 |
| Conakry...... | 9,000 | 26,000 | 52,900 |
| Bamako....... | 14,000 | 37,000 | 101,000 |

* Source: 1921 and 1945: *Annuaire statistique de l'Afrique Occidentale française* (Paris, 1951), Vol. II; 1951: Service des Statistiques de la France d'Outre Mer.

that the growth of towns has been on a very considerable scale and that the various social, economic, and cultural maladjustments which have commonly been associated with this form of social change, in Africa as elsewhere, are such that a large proportion of the migrants provides suitable material for political organizations of a Western type and for appeals to "radical" policies.[28] The movement into the towns had begun between the wars, as is shown in Table 7 but it has greatly increased since the end of the second World War and, like the other factors selected to indicate social change, seems likely to continue to increase in the future.

Table 8 shows the number of African wage-earners in 1947.

28. For some discussion of urbanization in French West Africa see J. Richard-Molard, *L'Afrique Occidentale française* (Paris, 1952), pp. 213–16; G. Balandier, "Le Développement industriel de la prolétarisation en Afrique noire," *L'Afrique et l'Asie*, No. 20 (4th Quarter, 1952), pp. 45–53; M. Gosselin, "Bamako: Ville soudanaise moderne," *L'Afrique et l'Asie*, No. 21 (1st Quarter, 1953), pp. 31–37; and for the relationship of such social mobilization to nationalism see Karl Deutsch, *Nationalism and Social Communication* (New York, 1953), esp. pp. 100–104.

It will be noticed that almost two-thirds of the total were to be found in the Ivory Coast and Senegal.

To sum up, before 1939 the impact of the Western economy in French West Africa was relatively slight and its distribution very uneven. Since then the pace of social change has undoubtedly increased considerably, and this acceleration is at the moment probably cumulative. If, for example, a comparatively small proportion of the population had, by 1950, received any schooling of a Western kind, it should be realized that in 1951

TABLE 8*

AFRICAN WAGE-EARNERS
BY TERRITORY IN 1947

| Territory | No. of Wage-earners |
|---|---|
| Niger | 4,945 |
| Dahomey | 12,046 |
| Upper Volta | ...... |
| Ivory Coast | 76,629 |
| Sudan | 29,028 |
| French Guinea | 35,206 |
| Mauretania | 2,511 |
| Senegal | 71,301 |
| Total | 231,666 |

* Source: *Annuaire statistique de l'Afrique Occidentale française* (Paris, 1951), Vol. II.

there were 1,645 schoolteachers in training, as compared with a total of 4,829 actually employed. This implies large increases in the provision of schooling during the next few years. Similarly, it may be confidently predicted that the numbers of Africans living in towns and earning wages will continue to increase rapidly. Much of the relative lack of radical, popular, or "nationalistic" political activity in French West Africa, as contrasted with parts of the Gold Coast and Nigeria, is to be ascribed, not so much to differences in the policies of the colonial powers as to the much smaller degree to which "social mobilization" had occurred in French West Africa before 1945. As economic and technological change continues, the proportion of the adult population likely to be within the range of such activities is constantly increasing.

# POLITICAL DEVELOPMENT IN FRENCH WEST AFRICA

It is not possible in this paper to discuss the nature of the changes made in 1946 in regard to the political organization of the French Empire or the complex reasons why they took the form they did or to attempt to elucidate the confused drafting and often contradictory provisions of the articles of the constitution of 1946 which deal with the French Union.[29] The constitution contemplates four categories of overseas dependencies, namely, associated states and associated territories, which are not parts of the French Republic and form with it the French Union; and overseas departments and overseas territories, which are parts of the Republic, "one and indivisible."[30] All the former colonies comprised in the Federation of French West Africa are, constitutionally, overseas territories, in which, in general, the system of government established by the new constitution resembles that of the old communes in Senegal. All the overseas territories in French West Africa are represented by deputies in the French National Assembly and by senators in the Council of the Republic, as well as in the newly created Assembly of the French Union, an advisory body half of whose members represent metropolitan France and the remainder the associated states, overseas departments (including Algeria), overseas territories, and associated territories.

All the inhabitants of the overseas territories were declared to be French citizens, but it was made clear that this did not make them subject to French private law and that they remained under their own customary law in all such matters.[31] Such *citoyens de statut local* were to exercise their rights as determined by separate laws; that is, in practice they were not entitled automatically to the franchise on the same basis as *citoyens de statut français*. At the same time, forced labor was abolished,[32]

29. For this see my article, "The Public Law of Overseas France since the War," cited in n. 2. To the references to the extensive literature there cited H. Deschamps, *L'Union française* (Paris, 1952), may be added.

30. Constitution, Art. 60.

31. *Ibid.*, Arts. 80 and 82.

32. Law of April 11, 1946.

metropolitan legislation regarding freedom of meeting and association extended to all overseas territories,[33] the *indigénat* abolished so far as criminal law was concerned, and the criminal courts alone empowered to deal with penal cases.[34]

In all the overseas territories the French Parliament of course remains competent to legislate, but metropolitan laws do not apply to them unless this is expressly stated or is evident from the subject matter of the law. In other matters the executive remains entitled to legislate by decree but must consult the Assembly of the French Union before enacting any such decree, even if its purpose is merely to apply a particular metropolitan law to the territories.[35]

Finally, there was established in each of the French West African territories a "local representative assembly" whose procedures and powers are substantially similar to those of a *conseil général* of a department, the most important of them being the power to vote the budget of the territory, subject, of course, to the inclusion of provision for meeting the obligatory expenditure.[36] For French West Africa as a whole a *grand conseil* was established, representative of the territorial assemblies and exercising, roughly speaking, similar powers to those of the territorial assemblies in matters of interest to French West Africa as a whole, including the "federal" budget.[37]

The most noticeable gap in the structure thus established is the absence of any new arrangements in respect of local government in the territories themselves, particularly striking in contrast to the intense activity in British African territories since the war, aimed at the development in rural areas, as well as urban, of representative institutions of local government. It was explained above that the prewar law relating to the *communes mixtes* made provision for a category of municipality in which the mayor was an administrative officer appointed by the exec-

33. Decrees of March 13 and April 11, 1946.

34. Decree of April 30, 1946.

35. Constitution, Art. 72.

36. Law of October 7, 1946, and decree of October 25, 1946, since amended by law of February, 1952.

37. Law of August, 1947.

utive, but the council was wholly elected by universal suffrage, and it was remarked that no *commune mixte* in this category was set up before the war. Since 1946, however, new *communes mixtes* have been established in a number of urban areas, and many of the older ones have been promoted to the category in which the members of the municipal council are elected by universal suffrage. Quite recently similar bodies have been established in rural areas in Togoland and the Cameroons but not, as yet, in any part of French West Africa.[38]

Clearly the key to a consideration of the significance of this new political structure lies in the franchise, in the arrangements for representation in the various assemblies, and in a more detailed examination of the powers of the territorial assemblies and the Grand Council. In all the French West African territories, the deputies in the National Assembly are elected, by all citizens entitled to vote, on a common roll (*collège unique*); that is, *citoyens de statut français* and *citoyens de statut local* vote together. For the elections to the territorial assemblies, however, they vote on a separate roll for separate constituencies, except in Senegal, where elections to the territorial assembly are also on the common roll. The senators in the Council of the Republic are elected by the deputies and the members of the territorial assemblies; in Senegal these electors form a single electoral college for this purpose, but in the remaining French West African territories the members of the territorial assembly elected by the *citoyens de statut français* form one electoral college, electing their own senators, and the *citoyens de statut local* a second electoral college, electing theirs. The members of the Assembly of the French Union and of the Grand Council of French West Africa are elected by the members of each territorial assembly voting together in a single electoral college.

Although in theory the *citoyens de statut français* might include Africans, they are in fact overwhelmingly European Frenchmen, and these arrangements thus insure in practice the representation of the French population of the territories in the territorial assemblies and in the Council of the Republic and ap-

38. Cf. *Civilisations*, III (1953), 106-7.

proximate to what in British East and Central African territories would be called "communal representation." Although
both the members representing *citoyens de statut local* (i.e.,
Africans) are in a majority in the territorial assemblies, the representation of *citoyens de statut français* (i.e., Frenchmen) is, of
course, entirely disproportionate to their relative number in
comparison with the numbers of *citoyens de statut local*. Moreover, as we shall see,[39] not all *citoyens de statut local* are entitled
to the vote, though the franchise was greatly widened in 1951,
as is shown in Table 10. These arrangements have accordingly
been strongly attacked, not only on general political grounds
by partisans of mathematical democracy, but also as a deroga-
tion from the provisions of Article 82 of the constitution, according to which the retention of *statut local* may not in any circumstances constitute a ground on which the rights and liberties of such citizens may be denied or reduced.[40] Nor do the
number of members assigned to the *citoyens de statut français*
in one territorial assembly as compared with another appear to
reflect their relative numerical importance in the different territories. Indeed, it is precisely in Senegal, where about one-third
or more of the French population of French West Africa is to
be found, that they have no separate representation at all.
Equally the total number of members in each territorial assembly does not appear to be at all closely related to the size of the
territory, its population, or its relative economic importance in
relation to the other territories of the group, as can be seen by
comparing Table 9 with Tables 4 and 10. A French critic
comments:

En définitive les chiffres adoptés sont purement empiriques et résultent de
tractations de séances ou de couloirs, les représentants de chaque territoire
mettant un point d'honneur à être aussi bien servis que ceux du territoire
voisin et le gouvernement écartant à la fois l'inégalité des territoires et la
multiplication des membres des assemblées. La préoccupation d'assurer au
premier collège un nombre suffisant de représentants ne fut pas non plus
absente de ces tractations. Dans tout ceci la préoccupation de donner aux
territoires des assemblées modélées sur les conditions propres à chaque territoire était manifestement absente.

39. Below, pp. 161–63.
40. For a valuable discussion of the issues involved and the arguments employed in
connection with the law of February 6, 1952, see P. F. Gonidec, "Les Assemblées
locales des territoires d'Outre Mer," *Revue juridique et politique de l'Union française*, VI
(1952), 327–38.

# POLITICAL DEVELOPMENT IN FRENCH WEST AFRICA

Similar criticisms may be made of the relative representation of the various territories in the metropolitan assemblies and a fortiori of the representation accorded to overseas territories in general in relation to that of the metropole itself. But politics is the art of the possible, and, so far as French West Africa is concerned, it is fair, taking the whole picture into account, to

TABLE 9

REPRESENTATION OF TERRITORIES IN ASSEMBLIES

| TERRITORY | TERRITORIAL ASSEMBLY, 1948* | | TERRITORIAL ASSEMBLY, 1952† | | GRAND COUNCIL‡ | NATIONAL ASSEMBLY§ | | COUNCIL OF THE REPUBLIC, 1946‖ | | COUNCIL OF THE REPUBLIC, 1948# | | ASSEMBLY OF THE FRENCH UNION** |
|---|---|---|---|---|---|---|---|---|---|---|---|---|
| | First College | Second College | First College | Second College | | 1948 | 1951 | First College | Second College | First College | Second College | |
| Niger............ | 10 | 20 | 15 | 35 | 5 | 2 | 2 | 1 | 1 | 1 | 1 | 3 |
| Dahomey.......... | 12 | 18 | 18 | 32 | 5 | 2 | 2 | 1 | 1 | 1 | 1 | 2 |
| Upper Volta††..... | 10 | 40 | 10 | 40 | 5 | 3 | 4 | ...... | ...... | 1 | 2 | 5 |
| Ivory Coast....... | 18 | 27 | 18 | 32 | 5 | 2 | 2 | 2 | 3 | 1 | 2 | 4 |
| Sudan............ | 20 | 30 | 20 | 40 | 5 | 3 | 4 | 1 | 3 | 1 | 3 | 5 |
| French Guinea...... | 16 | 24 | 18 | 32 | 5 | 2 | 3 | 1 | 1 | 1 | 1 | 4 |
| | | | | | | | | _Collège unique_ | | | | |
| Mauretania........ | 6 | 14 | 8 | 16 | 5 | 1 | 1 | 1 | | 1 | | 1 |
| | _Collège unique_ | | | | | | | | | | | |
| Senegal........... | 50 | | 50 | | 5 | 2 | 2 | 3 | | 3 | | 3 |
| Total.......... | .......... | | .......... | | 40 | 17 | 20 | 19 | | 20 | | 27 |

* Decrees of February 25 and October 25, 1946, as amended by law of August 21, 1948.
† Law of February 6, 1952.
‡ Law of August 29, 1947.
§ Law of October 5, 1946, as amended by law of April, 1948.
‖ Law of October 27, 1946, and decree of November 20, 1946.
# Law of September 23, 1948.
** Law of October 27, 1946, as amended by law of September 4, 1947.
†† The Upper Volta was re-established as a separate territory in 1947, and the representation of the Sudan, Niger, and Ivory Coast territories, of which it had been part, was amended in 1948.

recognize that these changes represented a courageous step toward a fuller participation in the political life of France as well as a considerable measure of local self-government.

Let us turn now to the electoral laws and the franchise qualifications for _citoyens de statut local_. It has already been pointed out that these fall short of the universal suffrage of metropolitan France or of _citoyens de statut français_ in overseas territories. The law of October 5, 1946, as amended by that of July 13, 1948, conferred electoral rights on those _citoyens de statut local_ who belonged to certain specified categories and were twenty-one years old. These were: (1) _notables évolués_, as defined in local regulations; (2) members and former members of local as-

## TABLE 10*

### ELECTIONS TO THE NATIONAL ASSEMBLY, 1946 AND 1952

| TERRITORY | POPULATION African | POPULATION Non-African | DEPUTIES 1946 | DEPUTIES 1951 | REGISTERED ELECTORS 1946 | REGISTERED ELECTORS 1951 | VOTES CAST 1946 | VOTES CAST 1951 | VALID VOTES 1946 | VALID VOTES 1951 |
|---|---|---|---|---|---|---|---|---|---|---|
| Niger | 2,125,800 | 1,530 | 1 | 2 | 57,266 | 94,986 | 26,149 | 56,594 | 25,819 | 55,839 |
| Dahomey | 1,532,400 | 2,200 | 1 | 2 | 57,153 | 332,867 | 33,573 | 147,350 | 32,977 | 145,333 |
| Upper Volta | 3,106,300 | 2,300 | | 4 | | 334,149 | | 251,138 | | 249,940 |
| Ivory Coast | 2,159,500 | 10,500 | 3 | 2 | 187,904 | 189,154 | 127,670 | 111,287 | 125,752 | 109,759 |
| Sudan | 3,341,100 | 5,800 | 3 | 4 | 160,464 | 916,944 | 95,243 | 340,207 | 94,803 | 337,989 |
| French Guinea | 2,253,700 | 6,900 | 2 | 3 | 131,309 | 393,628 | 96,099 | 224,182 | 95,564 | 221,256 |
| Mauretania | 566,100 | 770 | 1 | 1 | 16,271 | 135,586 | 9,539 | 52,181 | 9,451 | 51,425 |
| Senegal | 2,059,600 | 33,100 | 2 | 2 | 192,861 | 665,280 | 130,691 | 316,166 | 130,118 | 314,681 |
| Total | 17,144,500 | 63,100 | 13 | 20 | 803,228 | 3,062,594 | 518,964 | 1,499,105 | 514,484 | 1,486,222 |

* Source: 1946: *Journal officiel: Débats parlementaires, 1946 and 1947*; 1951: *Les Élections législatives de juin 1951* (Paris, 1953).

semblies (*conseils de gouvernement, conseils d'administration,* municipalities, chambers of commerce, chambers of agriculture and industry, agricultural unions); (3) members and former members for at least two years of co-operatives or trade-unions and of the committees of provident societies; (4) holders of decorations; (5) government officials and permanent employees of commercial, industrial, craft, or agricultural establishments legally constituted or having a regular "*carnet de travail*"; (6) members and former members of native tribunals; (7) ministers of religion; (8) servicemen and ex-servicemen; (9) licensed traders and planters, etc.; (10) chiefs; (11) owners of registered real property; (12) holders of driving or shooting licenses; and (13) literates in French or Arabic.

In 1951 the law of May 23 added three further categories: (1) heads of families or households who had paid the general capitation tax (*minimum fiscal*) either on their own account or on that of their families; (2) mothers of two children (*vivants* or *morts pour la France*); and (3) pensioners.

The law of February 6, 1952, relating to territorial assemblies amended this by removing the requirement that heads of households should be taxpayers. It also restored the rights of those who had been previously registered as electors but had been struck off without having been unqualified. This latter provision was no doubt inserted partly because of the allegations made after the 1951 elections that the administration had practiced what has been expressively described as "*malthusianisme électoral.*"[41]

It should be observed that these electoral arrangements which might seem strange to someone coming across them for the first time in the law of October 5, 1946, do not represent an entirely new device but are an extension of the arrangements for the Collège Électoral Indigène of prewar French West African territories which were discussed above. Although representing a large increase in the numbers enfranchised, they fall short of universal suffrage. The additions made in 1951, however, resulted in very large increases in the electorates in some territories. It will be remarked, from Table 8, that there were

41. Gonidec, *op. cit.*, p. 350.

very great divergences in the proportionate increase in the electorate as a result of the law of 1951, though, prima facie, there would seem no reason to suppose any great divergence in the proportion of the population belonging to these categories as between one territory and another. Some part of the explanation of these differences is no doubt to be found in the administrative problems involved in giving effect to a law which was finally passed only about three weeks before the general election in respect of which it was to be operative, but it would appear that in the Ivory Coast it was interpreted in a very restrictive manner or else that there were excessively large numbers of electors previously on the roll who were struck off for one reason or another.[42]

After the elections of 1951, when the National Assembly proceeded to the customary *vérification des pouvoirs* of the successful candidates, complaints were made of electoral abuses on the part of the administration in twenty-three out of the thirty constituencies in the overseas territories, including those in the Ivory Coast, Guinea, Niger, the Sudan, and Mauretania. These have been examined by a British scholar, who comments as follows:

> The complaints are of the same general pattern, although not all of them were made in each constituency. It was frequently alleged that the electoral rolls had not been published; that they had been fraudulently compiled—in Côte d'Ivoire by deleting the names of many supporters of the defeated candidates, and in other colonies by including the names of people who did not satisfy the legal conditions for the franchise; that poll cards were distributed to the wrong people and not supplied to registered electors—in Côte d'Ivoire they were sold for 200 francs each; that at the polling-stations registered electors known to be supporters of the "wrong" candidates were not allowed to vote, while supporters of the "right" candidates could vote even if not registered—"right" and "wrong" being decided by the governor of the colony or by his subordinates, who sometimes favoured different candidates. During the debate on the results in Mauritania, a U.D.S.R. deputy, protesting against abuses, said that the presiding officer at one polling-station was heard declaring that if a dog presented itself to him with a poll card he would allow

42. "Deux autres territoires démontrent qu'avec cette loi on peut faire les plus grandes fantaisies ou maintenir les plus vieilles et les plus dangereuses inerties. Le Soudan est passé à l'avant garde; la Côte d'Ivoire reste la plus retrograde, sur le plan électoral africain" (G. Gayet, "Évolution récente des collèges électoraux en Afrique occidentale," *Comptes rendus mensuels des séances de l'Académie des Sciences Coloniales*, XII [February, 1952], 57–73).

it to vote. M. Guy Petit intervened: "That is better than making the dead vote!" M. Kir: "It would be better to choose the deputy by drawing lots!"

Sometimes further abuses were alleged to have occurred on polling-day, such as that the sites of the polling-stations were suddenly changed and nobody informed except the supporters of the "right" candidates; that provisions for ensuring a secret ballot were inadequate or totally lacking; that supporters of the "wrong" candidates were intimidated by rowdies, the police, or the military; that the ballot-boxes were stuffed; that the local panels of polling officers were carefully packed; that the agents of the "wrong" candidates were excluded from the count by force, guile, or an improper interpretation of the regulations. Allegations of administrative pressure culminated in the complaints about an Algerian constituency where it was charged that there had been an administrative reign of terror.

Many of these complaints were dismissed by the bureaux concerned, which considered them either unimportant or unproved. Sometimes, however, the bureaux would admit that the complaints were both proved and important, but would contend that the irregularities were inevitable or had benefited more than one of the parties in the constituency. The electoral law which revised the franchise qualifications in the colonies had not passed through the Parliament until 23 May, less than four weeks before polling-day. In some places the administration had started work before the final passage of the law and had applied the initial text, which had later been amended; elsewhere, the administration had tried to apply the final text but had not had time to compile accurate new rolls, especially having regard to some of the new qualifications—such as the enfranchisement of "the mothers of two children who are living or have died for France." It had frequently been complained that at some polling-stations over 90 per cent, even a full 100 per cent, of the electors had voted for one candidate or list. The official explanation of this was that in some colonies a local chief would marshal his tribe to vote as he wished or else the chief alone would go to the station to vote on behalf of the whole tribe. Explanations of this kind were offered for most of those complaints which were not rejected as unimportant or unproved, and to some extent they are plausible.[43]

In many cases the complaints were dismissed by the bureaus of the assembly and not sustained in full debate. In those which were taken to a vote in the assembly, the decisions were dictated, as indeed were many of the complaints, by party allegiances.

Neither space nor the available data permit any detailed analysis of the elections in March, 1952, to the territorial assemblies. Tables 11 and 12, which set out the arrangement of constituencies and the results for each college in the Ivory Coast, have, however, been included as they bring out clearly

43. P. Campbell, "'Vérification des pouvoirs' in the French National Assembly," *Political Studies*, I (1953), 68–70.

## TABLE 11*

### TERRITORIAL ELECTIONS, 1952, IVORY COAST
### FIRST COLLEGE

| Constituency | Registered Electorate | Votes Cast | Valid Votes | Seats | Winning Vote |
|---|---|---|---|---|---|
| Abidjan and Grand Lahou | 5,045 | 1,322 | 1,200 | 11 | 1,200 |
| Grand Bassam.......... | 477 | 330 | 327 | 1 | 102 |
| Agboville.............. | 500 | 364 | 356 | 1 | 235 |
| Gagnoa, Daloa, and Sassandra.............. | 616 | 323 | 318 | 1 | 150 |
| Dimbokro, Abengourou, and Boudoukou...... | 310 | 127 | 108 | 1 | 108 |
| Man and Tabou........ | 191 | 150 | 144 | 1 | 103 |
| Bouaké and Katiola..... | 575 | 330 | 316 | 1 | 276 |
| Séguela, Odienné, Korhogo | 171 | 138 | 130 | 1 | 63 |
| Total............. | 7,885 | 3,094 | 2,899 | 18 | .......... |

* Source: *Journal officiel de la Côte d'Ivoire*, May 1, 1952.

## TABLE 12*

### TERRITORIAL ASSEMBLY ELECTIONS, 1952, IVORY COAST
### SECOND COLLEGE

| Constituency | Seats | Registered Electors | Votes Cast | Valid Votes | Party Chosen and Winning Vote |
|---|---|---|---|---|---|
| Abengourou......... | 1 | 10,507 | 3,597 | 3,575 | Union française, 2,539 |
| Abidjan............. | 2 | 22,902 | 12,900 | 12,776 | Union pour le Développement écon. Côte d'Ivoire (U.D.E.C.I.), 11,067 |
| Agboville........... | 1 | 8,794 | 4,752 | 4,697 | U.D.E.C.I., 4,126 |
| Boudoukou.......... | 2 | 9,734 | 2,499 | 2,486 | Union française, 1,595 |
| Bouaké............. | 5 | 14,911 | 5,049 | 4,987 | U.D.E.C.I., 4,357 |
| Daloa.............. | 2 | 15,156 | 7,983 | 7,874 | U.D.E.C.I., 5,395 |
| Dimbokro........... | 2 | 19,585 | 9,645 | 9,557 | U.D.E.C.I., 7,707 |
| Gagnoa............. | 1 | 15,758 | 8,221 | 8,071 | U.D.E.C.I., 7,200 |
| Grand Bassam....... | 1 | 7,780 | 4,890 | 4,845 | U.D.E.C.I., 3,488 |
| Grand Lahou........ | 1 | 10,319 | 6,312 | 6,269 | U.D.E.C.I., 4,734 |
| Katiola............. | 1 | 5,147 | 1,695 | 1,648 | U.D.E.C.I., 1,515 |
| Korhogo............ | 4 | 15,589 | 6,724 | 6,674 | U.D.E.C.I., 3,744 |
| Man................ | 3 | 14,816 | 7,853 | 7,761 | U.D.E.C.I., 5,213 |
| Odienné............ | 1 | 9,397 | 2,412 | 2,403 | Union française 1,441 |
| Sassandra........... | 1 | 8,954 | 4,465 | 4,408 | U.D.E.C.I., 3,894 |
| Séguela............. | 3 | 7,129 | 6,787 | 3,396 | U.D.E.C.I., 2,230 |
| Tabou.............. | 1 | 3,365 | 1,556 | 1,550 | U.D.E.C.I., 1,537 |
| Total.......... | 32 | 199,823 | 97,450 | 92,977 | .................... |

* Source: *Journal officiel de la Côte d'Ivoire*, May 1, 1952.

the extent of the weightage given to the representation in the territorial assembly of *citoyens de statut français* by the double college system and also show the extent of interest in these local elections in that territory, where just under 50 per cent of the voters went to the polls. (According to Professor Gonidec, this was the average for French West Africa, but in some constituencies there were 70 per cent abstentions.)[44]

It is not easy to convey any accurate impression of the powers and character of the territorial assemblies and the *grand conseil*. By contrast with those of a legislative council in a British territory, a model which Anglo-Saxon commentators often have in mind in considering them, it is important to recognize that they are not, and are not intended to be, legislative or parliamentary bodies but are patterned on the *conseil général* of the departments of metropolitan France. By contrast with these latter bodies, however, they deal with the affairs of much larger areas—areas in which, moreover, social and economic conditions are vastly different from those of metropolitan departments, and the budgets of which represent a much larger share of total public expenditure in the territory than do any departmental budgets in France—while their rights in regard to the rates and the basis of local taxation are inevitably much more important than those of any French local government body. Another important difference between these bodies and the legislative councils of British territories is that so much more of their time is occupied with what in British territories would be regarded as purely executive work (i.e., making decisions or giving advice, not on general policy, but on its application in specific instances). Finally, a much larger proportion of their work is settled in committee, and the discussion in the territorial assembly or the *grand conseil* merely gives formal approval of the proposals of the relevant committee. As a French author observes of the *grand conseil* of French West Africa:

Au premier étage travaillent les commissions; là s'établissent les premiers et nécessaires contacts entre les membres et les représentants de l'administration; là sont présentés, puis étudiés les differents dossiers. Là ont lieu les débats les plus vivants, et les plus instructifs qui se prolongent souvent la

44. Gonidec, *op. cit.*, p. 353.

nuit, et surtout au cours de la session budgétaire. ... Il s'agit de faire vite, car, en séance publique, le temps manque; en général, les autres conseillers font confiance à leurs collègues rapporteurs.[45]

As the powers of the *grand conseil* are fundamentally the same as those of the territorial assemblies, where the questions at issue concern French West Africa as a whole or interest more than one territory, it will be convenient to begin by describing the powers of the territorial assemblies. Subject to the control of the *conseil d'état* as regards their legality, the territorial assemblies have powers of decision in respect of the following subjects: (1) the purchase, sale, exchange, form of management, and insurance of territorial property, both real and movable; (2) leases of the goods of the territory; (3) cases to be prosecuted or defended in the name of the territory, unless urgent; (4) transactions concerning territorial rights; (5) accepting gifts or legacies to the territory; (6) the classification, direction, construction, and maintenance of roads for which provision is made on the territorial budget; (7) grants-in-aid of expenditure of territorial interest; (8) concessions in respect of works of territorial interest (except to foreigners), public works to be paid for from territorial funds, and territorial contributions to public works undertaken by the state or the government-general of French West Africa; (9) conditions of exploitation by the territory of public utilities and charges to be levied; (10) encouragement of production; (11) scholarships provided from territorial funds; (12) loans and guaranties secured on the assets of the territory; (13) assistance for children and the insane and social assistance insofar as it is a territorial matter; (14) division among the communes of their share of expenditure on children, on the insane, and on health services; (15) approval of municipal decisions about markets; (16) the basis, rules of collection, and rates of territorial taxes and the fixing of the maximum of *centimes additionnels* which may be levied by municipalities; and (17) the classification and direction of irrigation canals.[46]

The decisions of the assembly in all these subjects have effect if not quashed by the *conseil d'état* within two months after

45. C. Corby, "Le Grand Conseil de l'AOF," *L'Afrique et l'Asie*, No. 22 (2d Quarter, 1953), p. 46.

46. Decree of October 25, 1946.

notification of a demand for them to be set aside *pour excès de pouvoir ou violation de la loi* (i.e., as *ultra vires* or illegal). Such demands must be made within one month of the end of the session of the assembly in the course of which the decision was taken. In the case of decisions about the basis and rules of collection of taxation, such decisions are not effective until approved by the *conseil d'état*. Such approval must be given within ninety days of the receipt of information of the decisions by the Overseas Ministry, failing which they are considered approved. In the case of decisions about the rates of tax, *centimes additionnels*, loans and guaranties, such decisions are effective unless quashed by the *conseil d'état* within ninety days of their receipt at the Overseas Ministry and may be approved forthwith by the minister.[47]

The territorial assemblies must, in addition, be consulted about the following matters: (1) rural concessions of more than 200 hectares or forestry concessions of more than 500 hectares (there are special provisions for ministerial decision in cases of disagreement between the assembly and the local executive where very large concessions are involved); (2) mineral-prospecting licenses; (3) the administrative organization of the territory; (4) primary, secondary, technical, and vocational education; (5) land, mining, and forestry regulations; (6) the arrangements regarding state lands; (7) hunting and fishing regulations; (8) public works; (9) labor and social security; (10) development plans, so far as measures for their preparation and execution are concerned; (11) civil procedure (except judicial organization; (12) rent regulations; (13) regulations about *état civil* (i.e., registration of births, marriages, deaths, etc.); and (14) organization of chambers of commerce, etc.

The territorial budget is drawn up by the governor, and both the assembly and governor have the right of initiative in proposing expenditure, except insofar as they involve the creation of posts or expenditure in respect of the personnel of the public services, in regard to which the governor alone has the

47. A most interesting account of the relations between the *conseil d'état* and assemblies in the overseas territories is given by J. Ravenal, *Le Conseil d'état et les Assemblées des Territoires d'Outre Mer* ("Études et documents du conseil d'état," No. 4 [Paris, 1950]), pp. 49–63.

right to propose new expenditure. Provision must be made for obligatory expenditures, which are: (1) debts and pensions fund contributions of the territory; (2) local allowances, maintenance of premises of the governor and his secretariat, and allowances of civil servants belonging to services organized by laws and decrees; (3) grants or contributions to the general budget of French West Africa, for which provision has been made by legislation; (4) expenditure on justice, education, health, and the public forces; and (5) any expenditure imposed by express legislative enactment. If any such expenditure is struck out by the assembly, or insufficient revenue is provided to meet it, the governor may provisionally make the necessary increases by the omission of optional expenditure or the use of any free funds, and the amended votes are the included in the budget by decree of the *conseil d'état*.

The powers of the *grand conseil* are precisely the same in respect to the general budget and taxation, the revenue from which accrues to that budget. It can decide, subject to the same control by the *conseil d'état*, in matters concerning the same subjects where these affect more than one territory or French West Africa as a whole or require expenditure to be met by the general budget. In addition, it may decide on matters concerning the organization of savings banks, cheap housing and co-operatives (where more than one territory is concerned), the organization of tourism, and the rates of fees of justice. It must be consulted on all the subjects on which the territorial assemblies must be consulted, if more than one territory is involved, and on a few other subjects as well, including the prison regime and the organization of the legal professions and of agricultural and commercial credit.

It will be seen that the financial powers of the territorial assemblies and the *grand conseil* are considerable. The division of revenue between the territorial budgets and the general budget is, broadly, that direct taxes go to the former and indirect taxes to the latter. One of the most important and certainly one of the most delicate tasks of the *grand conseil* is to determine the amount of the rebates of revenue and the grants-in-aid to be made to territorial budgets from the general budget. In 1948, for example, these amounted to some $2\frac{1}{4}$ milliards of the total of the territorial budgets' revenue of some 6 milliards, while the total of the general budget was some $6\frac{3}{4}$ milliards, including the rebates and grants to the territorial budgets. Since then the relative importance of the general budget to the territorial budget, with all that this implies for the relative political importance of the territorial assemblies and the *grand conseil*, has probably increased.

To assess the real political importance of the territorial assemblies and the *grand conseil* is difficult, but, on the whole, Anglo-Saxon observers are probably more likely to underestimate than to overestimate this. If their formal powers are relatively limited, their influence is considerable; and, owing to the extent to which local politics and local political organizations are bound up with metropolitan parties, they are able, through the party organizations and their members in the French Parliament, to bring considerable influence to bear on the local executive, indirectly as well as directly through their legally defined powers.

THE DEVELOPMENT OF POLITICAL PARTIES SINCE 1946

It remains to attempt a brief survey of the development of political parties through and around this institutional framework. This is a subject on which detailed field research is essential and in which little work of any kind has been done.[48] The development and organization of local political parties, their relationship with metropolitan parties and with those of other parts of overseas France, and their activities in the various assemblies need careful study; so also does the growth of social institutions derived from Western examples and stimulated by the development of the Westernized sector of the economy, such as co-operatives, youth movements, trade-unions, and cultural and educational associations. Hodgkin points out that

48. A brief preliminary survey is in T. L. Hodgkin, *Political Parties in British and French West Africa* ("Information Digest, Africa Bureau," No. 10 [London, 1953]), pp. 13–16. The author is greatly indebted to Mr. Hodgkin for the loan of documentary material, newspapers, etc., relating to political parties in French West Africa. See also J. Delval, "Le R.D.A. au Soudan français," *L'Afrique et l'Asie*, No. 16 (4th Quarter, 1951), pp. 54–67.

a third factor which . . . assisted the growth of parties was the existence of a variety of organisations of other types,—the product mainly of the period 1935 to 1945—around which parties could be built. Trade Unions, Tribal Unions, Cultural Societies, Old Boys Associations, Ex-Servicemen's Associations, Youth Organisations, were among the most important of these. The leaders of such bodies provided a useful source upon which the newly formed parties could draw for their *militants*. Experience in organising a Trade Union or an Ex-Servicemen's Association could be carried over and applied to the problems of constructing a political party. This fact helps to explain the way in which the new parties have been able to find a local leadership capable of organising and running the Branch or the *sous-section*.

Studies of the growth, organization, internal dynamics, and interrelations of such bodies, as well as their connection with more specifically political movements, are essential to any satisfactory account of the recent political history of French West Africa and other similar countries.

The decision that all parts of overseas France—except, of course, Indochina—should be represented in the First Constituent Assembly can be seen, in retrospect, to have had a decisive influence on the shaping of political issues in these territories in the immediately postwar years. Given the political situation in France itself, the decision really made it inevitable that, whatever might be decided about the creation of new "federal" institutions for what was just beginning to be called the French Union, representatives of these areas should continue to find a place in the metropolitan Parliament itself. And this decision, in turn, has had a decisive influence on the character of political parties in French West Africa, insofar as they have become "deeply involved in the party-politics of Metropolitan France."[49]

It is not possible in this paper to trace the course of events in the two constituent assemblies, so far as overseas France was concerned.[50] As soon, however, as it became clear that the First Draft Constitution (which received a substantial majority of affirmative votes in all the overseas territories but was rejected in France itself) would be replaced by a constitution in which

49. Hodgkin, *op. cit.*, p. 14.

50. Some account of this will be found in M. Devèze, *La France d'Outre Mer* (Paris, 1948), pp. 221–82; D. Boisdon, *Les Institutions de l'Union française* (Paris, 1949), pp. 19–55; and W. Gordon Wright, *The Reshaping of French Democracy* (London, 1950).

fewer concessions were made to the egalitarian demands of the overseas representatives, an attempt was made to form a "common front" of West African political leaders and organizations, directed not to the satisfaction of "nationalist" or separatist demands but to securing equality of political rights and the abolition of any differentiations, whether of a legal or an administrative kind, between Frenchmen and the new French African citizens. To this end, a manifesto was issued signed by a number of political leaders, members or former members of the constituent assemblies, calling for a "rassemblement de toutes les organisations dont le développement rapide est le signe certain qu'elle poursuivent la réalisation de la démocratie politique et sociale en Afrique Noire."[51] The signatories included M. Lamine Gueye, mayor of Dakar and member of the constituent assembly; M. Fily Dabo Sissoko, member of both the constituent assemblies and, like M. Lamine Gueye, a Socialist; M. Houphouet-Boigny, member of the constituent assembly; and M. Gabriel d'Arboussier, a former member of the French Colonial Administrative Service who was also a former member of the constituent assembly. This document brings out clearly the main ideas on which apparently its authors considered it appropriate to base an appeal for African solidarity. After scarifying the reactionary tendencies alleged to have been displayed by the M.R.P. in the debates preceding the second constitution, it claimed that a common front had been brought into existence which united "toutes les organisations ouvrières, tous les mouvements culturels et religieux de l'Afrique Noire." It denounced federalism as no more than

le masque d'un régime d'autorité comme l'assimilation, que nous rejetons formellement n'est qu'une chape de plomb jetée sur l'originalité africain. Comme l'assimilation, il n'aboutirait qu'à figer l'Afrique dans son état d'organisation actuelle. ... En revanche, nous ne laisserons pas davantage tromper par le sentiment "autonomiste" qui se fonde sur une vue utopique des réalités africaines. ... Notre adhésion à l'Union Française que nous proclamons solennellement se justifie par une vue réaliste des problèmes politiques du monde, par une confiance dans le destin de l'Afrique et par la certi-

51. "Manifeste du Rassemblement Démocratique Africain, Septembre, 1946," in *Le Rassemblement Démocratique Africain dans la lutte anti-impérialiste* (Paris, 1948), p. 24.

tude que, malgré la réaction, nous obtiendrons les conditions libérales, démo-
cratiques et humaines qui permettront le libre développement des possibilités
originales du génie africain.[52]

The manifesto ended by calling for a congress to be held at
Bamako in the French Sudan in October, 1946. Some eight hundred people are said to have attended, but the movement had
already met with a check insofar as the Socialist leaders, M.
Lamine Gueye, M. Senghor, and M. Yacine Dallo, did not attend, and it was clear that they would not bring their parties
into the United Front. At the congress, the electoral law and
the principle of the double college were condemned as "œuvre
de division raciale et d'opposition colonialiste," and in language
which more clearly indicated the Communist direction the
movement would soon take "un instrument typique des trusts."
However, in the face of reaction, the new movement declared
its intention of doing everying possible to secure the election of
the largest number of members, of African origin, "démocrates
et progressistes."

The organization of the R.D.A. (which was not limited to
French West Africa but included French Equatorial Africa and
the two trust territories of Togoland and the Cameroons) consisted of territorial parties, each of which constituted a section
of the R.D.A. and was represented in a congress to be held annually which was the "plus haute instance du Rassemblement."
In the intervals between the meetings, the R.D.A. was controlled by a co-ordinating committee of the president, four vice-
presidents, the secretary-general, and one representative from
each territorial section.

The other major political party in French West Africa at the
time of the elections of 1946 was, as we have seen, the French
Socialist party, based essentially on its organization in Senegal.
It had, however, strong local organizations in French Guinea
and was soon to be formally joined by Fily Dabo Sissoko, the
leader of the Parti Progressiste Soudanaise. The Socialist plat-
form also included the extension of the single electoral roll, the
progressive abolition of the double college system, the effective
organization of universal suffrage, and the establishment of

52. *Ibid.*, p. 24.

identical judicial systems. The Socialist member for Senegal, M. Lamine Gueye, had indeed been responsible for the introduction of the Loi Lamine Gueye of May 7, 1946, which was later written into the constitution as Article 80, conferring equal citizenship on all the inhabitants of French overseas territories.

The elections of 1946 showed clearly the support which these two groups could muster. They resulted in six of the thirteen seats being won by the R.D.A., six by the French Socialist party or parties associated with it, and one by the small group led by M. Pleven (the U.D.S.R.).

For the next few years, the R.D.A. under the influence of the former colonial administrator, D'Arboussier, who had become its secretary-general, became steadily more violent and more strictly Communist in tone, especially after the French Communist party left the government. Its strongholds were the Ivory Coast, in parts of which M. Houphouet-Boigny enjoyed a large personal following, and certain parts of the Sudan, especially Bamako, Kayes, Sikasso, and Segou. Forbidden in 1949 to hold its second congress at Bobo Dioulasso in the Upper Volta, it was allowed to meet at Abidjan in January, 1949. In February, 1949, there were disorders at Treichville, the rapidly growing suburb of Abidjan, and in January, 1950, serious disorders at Bouaflé, in the Ivory Coast, which resulted in the dispatch of a parliamentary commission of inquiry. The program of the R.D.A. also changed a little: though its main themes continued to be the immediate abolition of all forms of discrimination, the immediate implementation of equal citizenship rights, and the employment of more Africans in government posts, it began to demand the development of political organs proper to Africa, whose relations with France were to be determined by bilateral agreements.

For some time, however, there had been signs that the R.D.A. was not entirely free from dissension. A considerable number of the members of the territorial assembly of the Ivory Coast elected on the R.D.A. ticket had by the beginning of 1950 detached themselves from it. The incidents in the Ivory Coast had a moderating effect on some members, especially when it became clear that the firm handling of the situation by the local administration would receive the full support of the metropolitan government; the administration undoubtedly exercised all the pressure it could against the R.D.A., and, on the other hand, the pronounced swing toward the right in France made the chances of a Communist government more remote at the same time as it increased the practical disadvantages of being associated with the Communist party. The parliamentary members of the party during 1950 progressively detached themselves from their Communist associates and finally supported the Pleven government, in December, 1950, on a vote of confidence. After various discussions with the parliamentary group known as the Indépendants d'Outre Mer, they attached themselves to the U.D.S.R., M. Pleven's party, and fought the elections of 1951 on that basis. M. Houphouet has thus explained his action in disaffiliating from the Communists:

> Le communisme n'étant pas le but, la masse africaine n'étant pas differencié en classes opposées, l'immense majorité du peuple français en dehors de la minorité de réactionnaires, égoistes et bornés n'étant nullement irréductiblement opposés à l'émancipation de l'Afrique, avions-nous le droit de faciliter la tâche des réactionnaires dans leurs menées contre le R.D.A., qu'il faisait passer pour communiste et anti-français enfin d'entrainer avec eux, dans la lutte contre nous, une large fraction du peuple français. ...
>
> C'est par un effort constant dans tous les domaines que nous bâtirons l'Afrique de demain. La route est longue qui mène à l'émancipation sociale. Ce n'est pas par des discours incendiaires, des oppositions systématiques, l'opposition entre Africains, travailleurs, semi-féodaux et néo-bourgeois que nous atteindrons ce but.[53]

The evolution of the R.D.A. finds a parallel in the other major political development since 1946 in West African parties. The two Socialist members elected by Senegal then were Lamine Gueye and Leopold Senghor. The latter is one of the most remarkable personalities in French West African politics. A poet, a *professeur agrégé de l'université* (the first West African to achieve this blue ribbon of French scholarship), and a leading figure in the National Assembly, he broke away from the Socialist party and founded his own party in Senegal, the Bloc Démocratique Sénégalais, and also founded a separate parliamentary group, the Overseas Independents (I.O.M.). No doubt differ-

53. "Réponse à D'Arboussier," *L'Afrique noire* (the R.D.A. newspaper), July 24, 1952.

ences of temperament and personality as between M. Senghor and M. Lamine Gueye have played their part in this development, as have those between M. Houphouet and M. D'Arboussier in those just described. But the account given by the party emphasizes rather the rejection of the Marxist rigidities of the French Socialist party as inappropriate to the actual circumstances of Africa, its concentration on practical politics, especially economic and social development, and its strongly expressed hostility to the corruption and organized spoils system which it alleges have characterized the Socialist party domination in Senegal.

The B.D.S. has emphasized the importance of organizations and groups based on tribal and customary association, but it also stresses the need, while recognizing their legitimate claims and seeking to insure their effective integration in the party organization, to work for "l'unité du pays par l'unité du parti." It has also stressed the importance, as the basis of social and economic development, of trade-union organization, but it looks to an enlarged conception of the scope of such organizations and to their development to protect the interests of the peasant cultivator and the small producer and not merely those of wage-earners. Finally, it has placed great stress on the development of co-operatives "instrument de socialisation par excellence" and has advocated the creation of pilot co-operatives which, it suggests, might form the bridge between the government-controlled "provident societies"[54] and true co-operatives. The party statements place considerable emphasis on the development of a truly African culture as well as on practical social and economic issues.

Some details of its local organization in 1950–51 may be of interest.[55] It is based on local "sections" and holds an annual territorial conference. The local section of Tattaguine in the *cercle* of Kaolack had twelve honorary presidents, seven of whom were marabouts, three "notables," and one businessman.

54. See *Condition humaine* (the B.D.S. newspaper), June 10, 1952. For the provident societies see K. E. Robinson, "Les Sociétés de prévoyance in French West Africa," in *Journal of African Administration*, October, 1950.

55. I am indebted for these details to my pupil, Mr. A. L. H. Weller, of the Colonial Administrative Service.

In addition to the officers, of whom there were six, there was a commission for resolving disputes consisting of ten members, including a village chief, four notables, a tailor, a butcher, and three whose occupations were not stated. Apart from the office-holders, there were only thirty-seven members. The section of Ziguinchor, a *cercle* headquarters and a *commune mixte* with a population of 14,000, has no honorary presidents. It had the same officers (secretary-general, treasurer, and accountant) as Tattaguine. There was a propaganda commission, including two tailors, a businessmen, an employee in commerce, a boat-owner, a tinsmith, a painter, a blacksmith, a teacher, and a notable. There was also, besides the commission for the resolving of disputes, an administrative commission of forty-one members, without any persons described as notables. This may be cumbrous, but the general impression is of a broad basis in local society. The administrative commission included a municipal councilor, an accountant, a military orderly, and several small boat-owners. At Rufisque there was a section in each *quartier* of the town, as well as a central section, including a secretary-general who was a schoolteacher, a treasurer who was a cabinet-maker, two auditors (both teachers), a director-general for propaganda with an assistant (also a teacher), and a commission for audit, containing one notable, a dispatch clerk, a chauffeur, a Shell company agent, and another business manager. Attached to this section were six delegates representing the *quartiers;* they included a cabinetmaker, a mason, a business-man, and a property owner. The Bloc Démocratique Sénégalais is, like the Union pour la Défense des Intérêts de la Haute Volta, a constituent party of M. Senghor's Mouvement des Indépendants d'Outre Mer, founded in 1948. The declaration issued by this group in 1948 emphasized that the political, economic, and social problems of the overseas territories were very different from those of the metropole:

Ce n'est pas uniquement avec les méthodes applicables à la France que l'on pourra trouver rapidement des solutions à ces problèmes: réaliser une organisation politique et administrative entièrement nouvelle, adaptée à la situation présente des Territoires d'Outre-mer, et capable de favoriser leur évolution au lieu de la freiner.[56]

56. *Journées d'études des Indépendants d'Outre Mer*, July, 1950.

From the beginning it has stressed the interdependence of the modern world and the need to develop the French Union in a federal direction. It has consistently rejected the notion that either the regime of overseas departments or that of associated states was a satisfactory political objective for the overseas territories. More recently it has moved a little further in the direction of a larger measure of autonomy within a federation of "integrated states."[57] This conception is not very precisely defined, but it is unquestionably a move away from any acceptance of assimilation in the classical form of overseas departments. The rest of the program of the I.O.M. is essentially evolutionary and concentrates on immediate social and economic problems.

The elections of 1951 marked, in French West Africa, as in France, a move away from the radical ideas of the Resistance and of the constitution-making period and registered the tendencies previously exhibited in both the R.D.A. and the I.O.M. parties in French West Africa toward a more center party position and a more opportunist policy. Of the twenty seats, the R.D.A. (now affiliated to the U.D.S.R.) held two, one in the Ivory Coast and one in the Sudan. In Upper Volta and Senegal, parties affiliated to the I.O.M. carried six seats, as well as one in Dahomey and one in Guinea, where the remaining two seats were held by Socialists, as were three of the Sudan seats. The totals for French West Africa were: I.O.M., eight; U.D.S.R., four; S.F.I.O., five; R.P.F., one; Independants, two. This move away from revolutionary toward more moderate policies, more limited ends, in return for practical gains, has its parallels in the British territories in West Africa. "The interesting question is how long the present equilibrium is likely to continue."[58]

Up until now, nationalist movements, in the sense of movements demanding political autonomy or independence and comparable with Nkrumah's Convention People's party in the Gold Coast, or Awolowo's Action Group, or Azikwe's National Council of Nigeria and the Cameroons in Nigeria, have not made an effective appearance in French West Africa. Demands for "na-

57. Congrès des Indépendants d'Outre Mer de Bobo Dioulasso, 1953.
58. Hodgkin, op. cit., p. 16.

tional" independence have there been replaced by demands for political, economic, and social equality—demands, for instance, for the abolition of the double college system in elections and of special allowances for civil servants recruited in the metropole. These demands for equality probably fulfil a similar role, psychologically, to that of earlier "nationalist" movements in British territories. They are, moreover, realizable, at any rate in principle, within the political structure established by the French; formally, at least, they involve only modifications or amendments to that structure, not its replacement by an altogether different one, though the large and continuing influx of non-African immigrants into French West Africa since the war may eventually make such modifications difficult to achieve. It has, however, been explained above that even the existing moderate parties have recently shown signs of a shift toward demands of a more "autonomist" character, though still within the framework not merely of a French Union but of a federal association with metropolitan France. Observation of West African students in France and of other younger elements suggest that this tendency may be expected to increase in future. If economic and social change continues at any accelerated pace, such tendencies will inevitably be reinforced, as they will be by the emergence of independent, or near-independent, governments in the Gold Coast and Nigeria.

Yet is does not seem that there are, as yet, in French West Africa, interests and forces which would make changes in the political structure in the direction of such greater territorial autonomy impossible without a more or less revolutionary upheaval. Adjustment of this structure in this direction would, however, involve major changes in the political structure of France itself (for example, in the composition and functions of metropolitan assemblies) which, in the present tragically divided state of France, seem unlikely to be practicable. Such changes would also call for very considerable changes in the habits of mind and assumptions both of politicians and of bureaucrats. Moreover, the failure of the initial conception of an associated state to secure acceptance in Indochina, and the consequent removal from it of that practical recognition of the interests of the Union as a whole, which was expected to be its main attraction, combined with the dangers in North Africa of any political formulas which seem likely to end in "independence," may well result in an unyielding opposition to proposals in Black Africa for "autonomous states" within a federal association with France which, however different in intention, could be represented as the "thin end of the wedge." Unless, however, there are some developments in the direction of a larger transfer of effective power from Paris to West Africa, as, for example, by an increase in the powers and revenues of territorial assemblies, it seems inevitable that the future should see a substantial shift in the pattern of political demands toward a more strictly "nationalist" form. It is doubtful whether, even in French West Africa, where their prospects are better than in certain other French overseas territories, changes in the political structure on more traditional "assimilationist" lines would prevent such developments.

# POLITICAL DEVELOPMENTS IN
# EAST AFRICA

JOHN A. NOON

*United States Information Service*

DURING World War II partnership was formulated as a principle of colonial policy to define a more dynamic relationship between dependent areas and the metropole within the framework of the British Commonwealth.[1] When employed to describe the goal of political evolution in East Africa, partnership appears to refer to the creation of a political community wherein the ethnic components will enjoy equal rights, privileges, and duties.

The above description of partnership emphasizes two major points: (1) communalism is the basis for the structuring of political institutions and (2) the principal task of the governing power is to evolve a formula which will give satisfactory expression to the principle of communal equality.[2] A third point is probably implicit—this is the rejection of partition as the solution to intercommunal tensions.[3]

Although communal partnership provides the framework for current political developments, there are alternate goals which East Africa could pursue. These appear to be (1) the partitioning of the region into ethnic states united in a federation and (2) the adoption of a new basis for partnership probably utilizing Rhodes's doctrine of "equal rights for all civilized men."

The first alternative is readily recognized as apartheid or

1. The term was employed in this sense by Undersecretary for Colonial Affairs Harold McMillan in 1942, and by Colonel Oliver Stanley, the Colonial Secretary in 1943 (cf. S. Gore-Browne, Rita Hinden, C. W. Greenidge, and E. E. Dodd, *Four Colonial Questions: How Should Britain Act?* ["Fabian Research Series," No. 88 (London, 1945)]).

2. The solution of this problem does not supplant the goal of preparing colonial. peoples for self-rule. However, in a plural society, communal equality is a condition prerequisite to granting responsible government.

3. Proposals for partitioning East Africa into ethnic states are basically nationalistic, although they may involve a limited sphere of communal co-operation.

[ 182 ]

POLITICAL DEVELOPMENTS IN EAST AFRICA

parallel development. Separatism gives recognition to the sharpening conflict between African and European nationalism. As a recent Hansard Society report stated:

It is well to remember that political developments in plural societies take place within the framework of the larger world. The African in Kenya has one eye on Accra and Lagos and the other on Capetown and Pretoria. The Indian tends to look to Delhi, the Pakistani to Karachi, the British settler to London [and, might we add, to Salisbury and Pretoria].[4]

Those who have sought a basis for partnership other than communalism frequently quote Rhodes's advocacy of "equal rights for all civilized men." The East Africa Asian community has long been critical of communalism. During the 1920–24 controversy over the Indian question, they demanded, among other proposals, a joint electoral roll with Europeans based on educational and property qualifications. The Colonial Office, under pressure from the India Office, provisionally accepted the common roll in the Wood-Winterton Agreement of 1922.[5]

Europeans vigorously opposed this application of the Rhodes principle, and the common roll was deleted from the final settlement.[6] Aside from continued Asian opposition, interest in exploring bases for partnership other than communalism appears to have lagged. Recently, Mr. Blundell, leader of the Europeans, made reference to the Rhodes principle in addressing the European constituency of the Nairobi area. Both the audience and the local press seemed to overlook this section of the address, and it is doubtful if its inclusion indicates that Europeans are giving this principle serious consideration.

RECENT CONSTITUTIONAL CHANGES IN EAST AFRICA

A brief review of the constitutional revisions which recently have taken place in the three East African territories will serve

4. Hansard Society, *Problems of Parliamentary Government in the Colonies* (London, 1953), p. 77.

5. The inclusion of educated Africans does not appear to have been contemplated. However, Mr. Churchill, then Colonial Secretary, did mention Africans when addressing the East Africa Dinner in London (January, 1922): "We shall apply broadly and comprehensively Mr. Rhodes' Principle of equal rights for all civilized men. That means natives and Indians alike who reach and conform to well-marked European standards shall not be denied the fullest exercise and enjoyment of civic and political rights."

6. Colonial Office, Cmd. 1922 of 1923.

[ 183 ]

both to outline the present system of government and to provide data for discerning trends in political development.

A. UGANDA

The Legislative Council of the Uganda Protectorate as constituted in 1950 consisted of sixteen official members and an equal number of unofficials, of whom eight were African and four each represent the Asian and European communities. The governor is president of the council, holding both an original and a casting vote. The major change in this over the preceding council of twenty members was the increased size of the body. There was no alteration in either the proportionate representation of the communities or the official majority.

In July, 1952, unofficial participation in the executive or policy-making branch of the government was increased by doubling the number of unofficials on the Executive Council (from three to six), and the unofficial representation of all communities was equalized by the appointment of two African members.

In 1953 further constitutional changes affecting the Legislative Council were announced. Effective January, 1954, the council's membership will be increased from thirty-two to fifty-six members and a cross-bench will be introduced on the official side which is renamed the "government" side.[7] Numbering approximately half of the twenty government-nominated members, this bench is expected to include one or more chairmen of statutory boards and prominent members of the public. Members will be free to speak except on an issue which the government considers a matter of confidence. Representation on the government side will be completed by eight ex officio and ten nominated members[8]—all officials of the administration. Left unchanged are the proportionate representation of the communities, the relative size of the government and unofficial sides, as well as the existing voting powers of the governor. To safe-

7. Uganda Government, *Correspondence Relating to the Composition of the Legislative Council in Uganda* (Entebbe, 1953).

8. Provisionally, the commissioners for labor, co-operative development and commerce, the land officer, the resident of Buganda and the three provincial commissioners, the solicitor-general, and the deputy financial secretary.

guard the position of the government against defections in support from the cross-bench, the governor is granted reserve legislative powers.

By increasing the number of unofficials, it is hoped to make the membership more representative geographically. On this point the governor noted: "Because of the very small number of seats available, it has been necessary to appoint only the most experienced men." As a result, Asian and European membership has been exclusively from Kampala and Jinja, leaving large areas of the country or whole groups of constituents not linked to a member.

Heretofore, outside of Buganda, African representation has been on a provincial basis, frequently placing under a single representative constituents whose interests were incompatible. Owing to the increased number of seats, it will be possible to switch from provincial to district members, thereby making this more vital political unit the basis of African representation. In addition, all council appointments will be made for four years, eliminating the present necessity for a two-year term in order to rotate representation among the various districts of the province.

The introduction of a cross-bench was considered preferable to creating an unofficial majority, since the latter might weaken the government's ability to provide firm and bold leadership. It is also consistent with the policy of "gradually increasing participation of representatives of the public in the . . . government"—by unofficials and by the addition of a cross-bench on the opposite side.

Direct elections were rejected as the method of selecting council members from all communities. For African representatives it was recommended that, outside Buganda, the district councils replace the provincial councils in choosing candidates for nomination. In Buganda it was to be hoped that the Great Lukiko (central legislature) would agree to make the selections —otherwise the present system of nominating candidates put forward by the Kabaka would be continued.

In addition to constitutional changes involving the structure of the protectorate, attention has also been given to (1) the relationship between the protectorate and the native states and (2) the strengthening of local government institutions.

Unlike other territories of East Africa, much of Uganda was governed in precontact times by well-developed native states.[9] Relations between the protectorate and the native states are regulated by agreements; the first was made with the Buganda in 1900. Hailey describes the position of the Buganda government under this agreement:

> The agreement . . . contemplated that the Kabaka should . . . exercise direct control over the natives of Buganda. Given the circumstances existing in 1900, that provision clearly applied primarily to requirements such as the maintenance of law and order or the administration of justice. But there have arisen since 1900 a number of other requirements, vital to the social and economic life of the people. . . .
>
> As the picture presents itself today, the Native Government provides a large part of the machinery for the administration of law and order and justice while the Protectorate Government provides the greater part of the services ministering to the social and economic needs of the Province.[10]

While the recognition of the agreement governments protected African political institutions, it served to perpetuate tribal nationalism and the ancient animosities between the Hima states. Ankole, Toro, and Bunyoro, by sending representatives to the Legislative Council, in a measure recognized the status of component units in the protectorate. The Great Lukiko of Buganda, however, declined direct representation, "since they prefer[ed] to regard their relations with the Protectorate Government as being of a political character, and feel that their interests can best be secured by negotiation with the Protectorate."[11] That confusion continues to prevail as to the position of the native states vis-à-vis the protectorate was noted by Wallis during an inquiry conducted in 1952.[12]

A third problem on the provincial and local government level

9. These were conquest states created by the subjugation of the Bantu agricultural tribes by the invading Hima pastoralists of Hamitic or Nilotic origin. Buganda, the most important native state, comprises one of the four major administrative units of the protectorate. Bunyoro, Tor, and Ankole are in the Western Province.

10. Lord Hailey, *Native Administration in the British African Territories*, Part I: *East Africa—Uganda, Kenya, Tanganyika* (London, 1950), p. 8.

11. Report to Colonial Office, 1940, quoted by Hailey, *op. cit.*, p. 80.

12. C. A. G. Wallis, *Report of an Inquiry into African Local Government in the Uganda Protectorate* (Entebbe, 1953).

arose from the fact that native states were organized on feudal lines with power concentrated in a landed aristocracy. In order for the new elite (created by Western education and cash-crop agriculture) to participate in local government, it was necessary to broaden the basis of representation in the native authorities and, where possible, to modernize their procedures.

These three problems are interrelated and require unified treatment. In 1947 Sir John Hall, the governor, announced that Uganda was to be regarded as a unified state with the native states as component units at the provincial and district levels.[13] As to the method to be adopted (later formalized in the African Local Governments Ordinance No. 2 of 1949), the governor stated: "The Uganda Government hopes to find this unifying process in a progressive development, both in executive responsibility and in their representative character of the system of the Councils, with official and elected members at the level of province, district, parish and village."[14] The creation of councils together with the devolution of functions previously under the sole control of the central government was applied to all parts of the protectorate except Buganda.

Another review of Uganda local government is now in process. The commissioner of inquiry has submitted his findings, and the government has commented on his report. After the question is debated in the Legislative Council, a new local government ordinance is expected which will probably be confined to extending the principles laid down in the 1949 ordinance.[15]

Early in 1953 the governor initiated conversations with the Kabaka of Buganda regarding changes in his government which would bring the kingdom more into conformity with Sir John

13. "It is a matter of prime importance to devise some unifying process, which over a period of years will tend to produce a sense of common interest, common purpose—and later, it is hoped of common nationality—and at the same time to encourage and not impede the growth and development of indigenous political institutions" (dispatch of Sir John Hall to the Secretary of State for the Colonies, August 29, 1947; quoted by Wallis, *op. cit.*, p. 9).

14. Speaking of these bodies, Sir John Hall added: "These Councils will be of little value as an educative factor or as an outlet for political aspirations unless they are given . . . real financial and executive responsibility" (*ibid.*).

15. Wallis, *op. cit.*; Uganda Government, *Government Memorandum on the Report by Mr. C. A. G. Wallis of an Inquiry into African Local Government in the Uganda Protectorate* (Entebbe, 1953).

Hall's concept of a unitary state.[16] In essence the proposals agreed upon transform the government on which will devolve responsibility for certain departmental services transferred from the protectorate government. To discharge these additional responsibilities, the number of senior officers of the Buganda government will be increased. A further broadening of the representative character of the legislature (Great Lukiko) will be effected by an increase in the number of elected members. Lastly, the Kabaka will make proposals to the Lukiko for the establishment of local government at the *saza* (county) level, to which the Buganda government will devolve certain functions.

Underlying the developments in both central and local governments is the attempt to increase the number of citizens actively participating in government. The minimum advantages likely are (1) to broaden support for the government and (2) to educate the citizenry in the arts of government. Of the two, the second may be the more important. Most African territories suffer a scarcity of the politically competent. Although this is in part due to limited facilities for higher education (a difficulty which is being remedied by colonial university colleges), it is also attributable to the paucity of opportunities for securing experience in government. The development of closer ties between the Legislative Council and the districts, which are the functionally active local units, should materially assist in bringing the central government closer to the public.

While the increase in unofficial members on the executive council provides non-civil servants with experience in policy-making, comparable opportunity for training in public administration has not been furnished. Such experience will be required when responsible government is established and the heads of executive departments sit on the opposite side of the council. One such device currently employed in Kenya is to have unofficials join the government bench as holders of portfolios.

Developments in local government are indicative of the po-

16. Uganda Government, *Memorandum on Constitutional Development and Reform in Buganda* (Entebbe, 1953).

litical maturing of the Uganda population. So long as institutions of local government were agencies of the central government, they were imposed from the power center. As autonomous bodies, local governments acquired grass roots to become self-generating, peripheral power centers balancing the central power concentration.

The insistence that local government institutions be vested with authority should provide a larger measure of support for local government. The members both of advisory bodies and of those vested with authority, but subject to a veto over their decisions, are likely to be frustrated by the failure to see their decisions put to the test. In other words, the administering power must be willing to have its colonials learn by their failures as well as by their successes.

It is to be hoped that the continued addition of elected representatives will attract the new elite to participate in government, avoiding the situation in which members of this group, denied opportunities for government service, direct their political aspirations to the formation of political associations. Not being a part of government, they frequently consider opposition to it as their *raison d'être*.

B. KENYA

Kenya Colony and Protectorate is perennially the political storm center of East Africa. Its larger intrusive communities,[17] the political aggressiveness of Europeans and Asians, and the inability to resolve fundamental differences in the policies advocated by the communities appear to affect adversely the maintenance of stability. Since October, 1952, Asians, Europeans, and that faction of the African community which seeks to advance its interests through constitutional channels have been bitterly combating the terrorist activities of a tribal-nationalist association, the Mau Mau. This threat to order, authority, peace, and security is the most costly in terms of money and manpower and in destruction of life and property which has hitherto befallen the colony.

Probably owing to European pressure for increased self-rule,

17. Europeans number approximately 40,000; Asians, including Arabs, 158,000.

the Kenya government, over all, is structurally more advanced than the two neighboring territories. Thus, its Legislative Council has an unofficial majority (1948), is presided over by a speaker who has a casting but not an original vote, and has elected European, Hindu, and Moslem members.

Post–World War II changes in the composition of the Legislative Council have enlarged its membership and introduced Africans to represent the affairs of this community (1945). On the unofficial side, all delegations were increased in 1952, the European from eleven to fourteen, the Asian from five to six, and the African from two to six. Unofficial non-European representation has made a small proportional gain. Asian membership is now divided three ways (1952). The two Moslem and four non-Moslem members are elected by separate franchise,[18] while the two Arab representatives . re nominated.

The practice of associating unofficial members with the official side (the latter consists of eight ex officio, eight nominated official, and ten nominated unofficial members) was begun in 1945, when a European unofficial resigned his seat to become Member for Agriculture. In 1950 another unofficial member assumed the portfolio for Local Government and Education.[19] This practice, plus that of consulting with unofficial members before legislation is introduced, has led to what is termed "government by agreement."

The principal change in the Executive Council has been the replacement of the European representing native affairs by an African (1952). Ex officio members (eight) are double the number of unofficials who are the European leader, and deputy leader, and the African and Asian (Hindu) members in like position. Further constitutional changes have been halted by the state of emergency declared on October 21, 1952. A round table

18. The division of the Indian electorate is an example of the continually boiling political cauldron. This change was instigated by Moslems, who professed fears of being overwhelmed by the numerically superior Hindu-Asians. The Indian National Congress was opposed, viewing the move as a serious blow to their demand for a common Asian-European franchise. Affronted by European and Colonial Office acceptance, Hindu members took the oath of office but refused to assume their seats on the fourth day of each session.

19. At present three non-civil servants are ex officio members—all Europeans.

on constitutional revision was to have convened in Nairobi in May, 1953.[20]

Local government in Kenya was established as a dual system recognizing the distinction between native and settled (principally European) areas. In the former, local government institutions were based on appointed (direct rule) rather than traditional authorities.[21] Thus, Lord Hailey notes that Kenya "anticipated by some years steps now being taken in other territories of East and Central Africa to secure popular representation on District Councils or equivalent bodies. There is no doubt that the procedure adopted . . . has resulted in providing representation from the more progressive and intelligent members of the local African community."[22]

The non-native or settled areas were organized as districts, townships, and municipalities, the latter two being exclusive of the districts in which they are located. Only the municipalities are corporate bodies, and only those governed by municipal councils (Nairobi and Nakuru) are empowered to elect their own mayors and appoint their own officers. At the other end of the scale are Grade B townships directly administered by the district commissioner without advice of councils.

Under the County Councils Ordinance of 1952 provision is made for linking urban and adjoining rural communities. The separation appears to have arisen from the reluctance of Europeans to accept non-European representation in rural councils.[23] The ordinance creates a two-tier system—the upper, the county councils; the lower, the county district councils, whose jurisdiction may be either an urban or a rural area or a municipality that elects to become a part of the system.

County district councils will deal with local matters corre-

20. Statement to the House of Commons by the Colonial Secretary, Mr. James Griffiths, on May 31, 1951.

21. Rita Hinden (ed.), *Local Government and the Colonies: A Report to the Fabian Colonial Bureau* (London, 1950), p. 128. The first councils were termed "local native councils," but in 1948 the Native District Councils Ordinance increased the jurisdiction of the councils, making them comparable to that of councils in settled areas.

22. *Op. cit.*, p. 95.

23. The districts or rural areas were, except in Nyanza, exclusively European, while non-Europeans predominated in urban areas.

sponding to responsibilities now assumed by municipalities (sanitation, housing, water, etc.), while the powers of the county council will include finance, roads, town and country planning, etc.—functions best carried out on a county-wide basis. Although the majority sitting on either a county or a county district council is expected to be European, at least minimum participation by non-Europeans is guaranteed through the power of the Member for Local Government to appoint up to three members of any council.

Despite the grant of many of the forms of responsible government, Kenya probably has failed to advance so far in this direction as appearances suggest. Wight has noted that constitutional advance is difficult to achieve in plural societies, since "in homogenous societies progress comes through pressure by the community on the government; in a plural society such pressure tends to be dissipated between different sections [or communities]."[24] The rare instances in which the communal contingents comprising the unofficial majority are able to unite and outvote the official bench illustrates Wight's observation and points to the futility of creating forms which are certain to be meaningless in the absence of intercommunal co-operation.

Communal rivalries act as a brake upon constitutional reform. The weaker Asian and African communities, finding that their interests are best safeguarded by the continuation of Colonial Administration control, endeavor to thwart European demands for increased self-government. Therein lies the possibility that the dominant community will find itself on the horns of a dilemma. In order to overcome this opposition, they must accede to African and Asian demands which are, at the minimum, parity in council representation. But, by accepting, Europeans lose the ability to dominate.

As previously noted, Kenya has succeeded in installing a comparatively advanced system of local government. However, this achievement is to a large measure offset by the failure of these institutions to win popular support. Instead, political associations are, for many Africans, the focus of political activity.

24. Martin Wight, *The Development of the Legislative Council, 1606–1945* ("Studies in Colonial Legislatures," Vol. I [London, 1946]).

In turn, these associations may gain considerable control over the composition of local government bodies, with the result that attention is diverted from the work of local government to political objectives, and these may frequently have an anti-government bias.[25] In the end the administration may merely have succeeded in creating the instrument whereby its program and even its existence is subverted.

The causes responsible for the anemic condition of local governments are complex and subtle. Very frequently the functions which the district councils and similar bodies discharge are alien to African cultural patterns. Efforts to offset the lack of grass-roots support by more vigorous leadership by the district administration is a doubtful remedy. Also, sooner or later an African tribe falls prey to factionalism. Individuals react variously to innovations and to attempts to eradicate customs believed harmful (female circumcision) or immoral (polygamy). Eventually the group splinters into the progressives, the conservatives, and the reactionaries, so that local government bodies are rendered impotent by wrangling and discord, while more extreme elements withdraw from the organization. Lastly, the administration is often oversolicitous in its desire to prevent the council from acting in a manner which appears ill advised. Thus, one African leader suggested, remove the district commissioner's veto, and life will spring into the district council.

C. TANGANYIKA

Tanganyika shares many of the characteristics of other East African territories, favoring Kenya in some respects and Uganda in others. Like the former, parts of the area are suitable to European settlement. However, this community numbers roughly but one-fourth that of Kenya, while Asian residents are only a third. While its African tribes do not possess such highly developed political institutions as the Buganda and other agreement states, traditional authorities have in general been employed as the basis for local government. Hence the Tanganyika system more closely parallels that of Uganda. Unlike its East African neighbors, its administration has been under interna-

25. Hailey, *op. cit.*, pp. 93–94.

tional supervision since coming under British rule. Formerly a mandate of the League of Nations, it is now a United Nations trust territory.

Late in 1949 the governor appointed a committee on constitutional development. Its inquiries covered all fields from the central administration to local government and included an extensive consideration to the problem of decentralization. A few of the committee's recommendations have been implemented, while others, after review by a special commissioner of investigation,[26] are being contemplated.

Changes in the composition of the central government parallel those which occurred elsewhere in East Africa. An African member has been added to the executive council (1952), and the proposal to increase the number of Africans in the legislative council to parity with Europeans and Asians has been accepted in principle.

In discussing the recommended addition of three African and four Asian members, the committee members admitted that "we have found it impossible either on the basis of numbers, financial interests, or political maturity to make any assessment of the relative claims to representation by the three races."[27] When justifying their proposal, they said: "We are convinced that the only solution which is equitable and capable of obviating feelings of distrust and lack of confidence, and of laying a sound foundation for the political development of the Territory is the equal distribution of unofficial seats on the Legislative Council."[28]

Recommendations for the devolution of central government functions parallel in principle and purpose, if not in detail, those advocated for Uganda. The introduction of the county council system has already been encountered in Kenya. It is planned to

26. Tanganyika Government, *Report of the Special Commissioner Appointed To Examine Matters Arising Out of the Report of the Committee on Constitutional Development* (Dar-es-Salaam, 1953).

27. Tanganyika Government, *Report of the Committee on Constitutional Development 1951 and Despatch of 22nd March 1951 from H.E. the Governor to the Secretary of State for the Colonies and Despatch of 25th July 1951 from the Secretary of State for the Colonies to H.E. the Acting Governor* (Dar-es-Salaam, 1952). The committee also noted that the views of the three races were irreconcilable (*ibid.*, p. 18).

28. *Ibid.*, p. 19.

make more extensive use of the elective principle than has been contemplated for Uganda and, if put into effect, will bring Tanganyika more in line with current practice in Kenya.

Parity in council representation will make possible the creation of seven legislative districts each having an Asian, European, and African member representing different constituencies but the same geographical area. This development could promote among Africans, Asians, and Europeans the recognition of a common body of interests. Other recommendations having merit pertain to the creation of joint electoral qualifications and to instituting a common franchise in certain areas (Dar-es-Salaam and Tanga Province).

While Tanganyika has made fewer postwar changes in its constitution than other territories, the program mapped in broad outlines by the committee and spelled out in considerable detail by the special commissioner provides a comprehensive and co-ordinated plan whose implementation could materially advance communal partnership. Given a situation which appears to be less inhibited by the intercommunal tensions which bedevil Kenya, it might be advisable to seize time by the forelock and get on with the job. Despite the soundness of British objectives and procedures for their realization, there is often a startling lack of appreciation for timing. An innovation such as representational parity, which, appearing as a bold new venture, captivates the imagination, has added power for reducing tensions and promoting harmony. But, if its implementation is delayed, anxieties arise to rob the change of its full effectiveness. Many observers acquire a feeling which they can best phrase as "the time is running out." If this has validity, then a new sense of urgency is given to the rate at which changes are introduced.

### D. THE EAST AFRICA HIGH COMMISSION

Developing from diverse origins, the East Africa High Commission was created in 1948.[29] As early as 1904 there was co-operation between Kenya and Uganda in matters of tariffs, transport, and the use of a common currency. Kenya Europeans

29. East Africa (High Commission) Order in Council, December 19, 1947.

have long advocated closer union between East African territories. When Tanganyika passed from German control, the question became a live issue, and two commissions studied the problems involved.[30] From 1919 on the governors of the three territories met from time to time, and from 1926 the meetings were formalized as the "Governors' Conference." Proposals for a commissioner and a central legislature date from 1927. The second World War gave rise to a number of regional boards and demonstrated the practicality of dealing with problems on a regional basis. In 1947 interterritorial co-operation was formalized by an order in council providing for an East Africa high commission consisting of the three governors, the appointment of a high commissioner, a central legislative council, and departmental advisory councils.

THE FUTURE OF COMMUNAL PARTNERSHIP

It would appear that communal partnership is not the central issue in Uganda. Postwar constitutional changes point to the development of the protectorate as an African state, and it is within this framework that the numerically insignificant intrusive communities will have to define their role in the political and economic life of the territory.[31] Instead, the major question revolves around the creation of a unitary state supported by a national consciousness transcending loyalty to the tribe or native kingdom.

While the alterations in the structure and functions of the Buganda government agreed upon by the Kabaka and the governor are directly related to this problem, the recommendations for decentralizing the functions of the central government and adding to the powers of the provincial and district authorities contribute to securing this objective. Thus far, the Buganda offer the only considerable opposition to reconstituting the native kingdoms as provincial or district components of the protectorate.

30. The Ormsby-Gore Commission (1924) and the Hilton Young Commission (1927).

31. However, it is difficult to dispel fears of European dominance. Concern is expressed that the Owen's Falls hydroelectric development and the industrialization program in Jinja will, by increasing the size of the European community, enlarge its influence. Also indicative is African opposition to East African federation.

Communal partnership remains a primary issue in Kenya and Tanganyika, and it is here that its future in East Africa will be decided. Without reference to the specific situation in these territories, mention is made of certain difficulties inherent in this principle of social organization.

There is broad agreement that communalism is a valid basis for social differentiation at the time of initial contact between peoples markedly different in race, culture, and level of development (civilization). However, if communal groupings are perpetuated after readily demonstrable distinctions (racial differences excepted) have been eliminated, then the functioning of more advanced principles of social organization is inhibited, since the groups (economic, educational, and occupational interest groups) through which these principles operated continue to be fractured along communal lines.

In both Tanganyika and Kenya, progress in various fields is slowed and at times stalled because communal organization, although it has outlived its usefulness, is still the basic structural principle. Solution of economic problems is complicated by separate Asian and European chambers of commerce. Effective unity among persons of like political opinion is hampered by the more fundamental loyalty to their respective communities. On top of these disadvantages is the wasteful practice of creating and maintaining parallel facilities for each community.

A second difficulty is devising a formula for weighting the participation of the different communities in various activities. Solutions are *ad hoc* and artificial, and Table 1, which shows the relation between population and Legislative Council representation, reveals that there is little possibility of finding a means for objectively weighing the claims of various communities.

The time has arrived when communalism should become a minor instead of a major principle of social organization in East African society. In promoting this change, effective communal partnership plays a fundamental role. By broadening and intensifying intercommunal reaction patterns, the unimportance of communal differences relative to economic, educational, and professional interests will be recognized.

Tanganyika may hold certain advantages over Kenya in developing communal partnership. First, its intrusive communities are smaller. Second, owing to the uprooting of the Germans, mainly in the first but also during the second World War, the European community is less firmly intrenched. Third, supervision by the Trusteeship Council of the United Nations serves as a check upon the political aggressiveness of Europeans. Lastly, the comparatively long history of intercommunal strife in

TABLE 1

RELATION BETWEEN POPULATION AND LEGISLATIVE
COUNCIL REPRESENTATION

| TERRITORY | EUROPEAN | | ASIAN | | AFRICAN | |
|---|---|---|---|---|---|---|
| | Population | Legislative Council Representation | Population | Legislative Council Representation | Population | Legislative Council Representation |
| Uganda....... | 5,000 | 7 | 35,000 | 7 | 5,000,000 | 14 |
| Kenya........ | 40,000 | 14 | 158,000 | 6 | 5,500,000 | 6 |
| Tanganyika.... | 15,000 | 7* | 55,000 | 7* | 7,000,000 | 7* |

* Recommended.

Kenya has fixed opposition rather than co-operation as the traditional reaction pattern.

### NATIONALISM IN EAST AFRICA[32]

All regions of Africa, regardless of the policy governing their development, are increasingly subject to nationalist influence. Such movements assume various forms. In some areas (i.e., the Gold Coast) nationalism aims at overthrowing colonial rule and creating an autonomous nation in the Western sense. For other African peoples (i.e., the Buganda and the tribes of Northern Nigeria) nationalism is essentially synonymous with tribalism and seeks to re-establish the position of the tribe which existed prior to European overlordship. Where there are plural societies (East and Central Africa and the Union of South Africa), nationalism is polarized on the basis of race. As differences of this nature are interpreted as being fundamental and eradicable,

32. This section is confined to Kenya.

parallel development of the communities is deemed necessary in order to assure that each can fulfil its destiny.

In Kenya nationalism first appeared among Europeans. Organizations for promoting their interests and protecting their territory (the "White Highlands") date from the Farmers and Planters Association of 1903. Four years later the Colonists Association was formed, and in 1911 it was followed by the Convention of Associations. The Electors Union, the present European association, was established in 1944.

The Kenya settler realizes that he is a controversial figure[33] but wonders that he should be so considered. He feels that his presence in Kenya is justified[34] and that, after being endowed with a mission, the colonial government has placed innumerable obstacles in the way of its fulfilment.[35] On several occasions situations have arisen which created a sense of insecurity[36] and in part his aggressiveness can be attributed to this cause. Another cause is the frustrating fluctuations in British colonial policy which settlers take pains to document.[37] Finally, he believes that the affairs of the colony frequently are not settled on their merits but are treated as political pawns in empire or commonwealth affairs or in United Kingdom politics.[38] In all these contentions there is an element of fact providing a plausible basis for constructing a persecution complex.

33. Two contrasting views of the settler community are provided by Elspeth Huxley, *White Man's Country: Lord Delamere and the Making of Kenya* (2 vols.; London, 1935), and W. McGregor Ross, *Kenya from Within* (London, 1927).

34. The decision to open Kenya to white settlement was made by Sir Charles Eliot, the first commissioner for the East African protectorate (1901–4), in order to put the railway on a paying basis. The idea appears to have been advanced by Lugard in 1893.

35. The settler considers his task to be the development of the territory and to act as one of the agencies for training Africans in the arts of civilization. To succeed in the former, it was necessary to acquire land; to both labor was essential. On the first count he is accused of robbing the native, and on the second he has been charged with exploitation. In addition, the government frequently refuses to co-operate in securing labor on the grounds that native rights must be protected.

36. In the early days of the protectorate some thought was given to making East Africa a colony of India. Later a Polish-Russian refugee settlement was projected. Another example is the native paramountcy pronouncement of 1923.

37. The Voice of Kenya, *A General Survey* (Nairobi, 1954), pp. 6–7.

38. The role of India in the 1920–24 controversy, Labour party sympathy for Africans during the present emergency, and statements by Mr. Nehru on present disturbances are examples.

More closely conforming to fact is that the European's ability to organize, to publicize his side of the question, and to exert pressure in political circles at home and abroad has repeatedly paid off. Were it not that Europeans always have won over 50 per cent of their demands, they probably would have acquired a greater willingness to arbitrate.

Other unfortunate aspects of European nationalist movements have been (1) their leaders' proclivity for irresponsible and inflammatory statements and (2) their willingness to consider resort to direct action.[39] In these instances the community frequently loses the sympathy of world opinion and provides the non-European communities with dangerous precedents.

The program of European nationalism generally involves more than the partition of East Africa into European and African states—the European population of the area is believed to be too small for this to prove a workable solution. Instead, Europeans look to joining forces with whites in Central Africa and, before the advent of the Nationalist government, more vaguely with the Union of South Africa.[40] Proposals of this nature continue to be put forward.[41]

The difficulties involved in so comprehensive a union, plus the recent decision establishing the Central African Federation, reduce the practicality of the nationalist program to the point where it does not constitute a present threat to partnership. Were Europeans to reduce their demands to embrace only Kenya, then the nationalist solution might be taken more seriously.[42]

Leadership in African nationalist associations as well as the

39. Extensive preparations for rebellion were made during the 1920–24 Indian controversy. The march on Government House during the current emergency is another example.

40. A community of interest with Europeans in other parts of Africa has long existed. The deputation sent to England to fight the Indian question (1922) sought an interview with General Smuts when passing through Cape Town. Later the General advised the Europeans to accept the settlement of the question set forth in Colonial Office, Cmd. 1922 of 1923. Lord Delamere sponsored unofficial conferences on federation, bringing together East and Central African leaders during the 1926–29 agitation over federation.

41. *Comment*, October 1, 1953, pp. 5 and 6.

42. Sugestions along this line were put forward by Lord Lugard (cf. Elspeth Huxley and Margery Perham, *Race and Politics in Kenya* [London, 1944], pp. 9–12, 177–90).

majority of the membership has been supplied by the Kikuyu. Such movements date from the close of World War I, and the first appears to have been the Young Kikuyu Association led by Harry Thuku, which was active in protesting against reductions in native wages during the 1921 recession. In 1929 the Kikuyu Central Organization was formed with Thuku as president. Jomo Kenyatta was for a time the secretary-general. This organization was proscribed in 1940.

When the Kenya African Union was founded in 1944, an attempt was made to extend membership to other tribes. Success was greatest among the Luo—but, in the main, the K.A.U. was largely a tribal nationalist movement. After Mr. Kenyatta and members of the executive committee were detained in October, 1952, the K.A.U. continued to function under temporary officers until allegations of connection with Mau Mau led the government to proscribe the organization in April, 1953.

African nationalism has displayed certain characteristics of its European counterpart. Like the settler organizations, the K.A.U. has been critical of the Kenya administration. When it has resorted to direct action, as in its frequent programs of non-co-operation, the movement showed finesse in circumventing the government. In stating the African point of view, it has frequently made excessive demands, such as in its proposals to the Carter Commission. The public utterances of K.A.U. leaders have been inflammatory and provocative of intercommunity friction. Thus, both African and European nationalism appears antagonistic to operating within the framework of partnership.

The Mau Mau is not a nationalist-type organization. Following a recent analysis of African nationalism,[43] Mau Mau is described as a nativistic movement, and, according to Coleman's definition, these are "usually of a magico-religious character—which are psychological or emotional outlets for tensions produced by the confusions, frustrations, or socio-economic inequalities of alien rule."[44]

Their program seeks to eliminate frustrations by striking directly at their root—in the case of the Mau Mau, the presence

43. James S. Coleman, "Nationalism in Africa" (unpublished MS, 1953), pp. 3–4.
44. Ibid., p. 4.

of the Europeans in Kenya. If successful, the clock would be turned back and the golden age of precontact African society would be re-established. The first obstacle the Mau Mau encountered was the tribal factionalism produced by the penetration of intrusive cultures. Therefore, the initial effect of the movement was to restore communal solidarity. Thus far, it would appear that Mau Mau operations have been principally occupied with this phase of the program, and, if it had been possible to strengthen the so-called "loyal Kikuyu" more rapidly and more effectively, the Mau Mau movement might have been dealt with speedily. The limited terrorism directed against Europeans is either related to achieving solidarity by proving to waverers what Mau Mau can accomplish or to driving Europeans from the colony.

Although Mau Mau is not a nationalist movement, there appears to be convincing evidence that K.A.U. was willing to use it for the advancement of nationalist objectives. That such has been the case would seem to cap definitely the earlier suggestion that nationalism and partnership are fundamentally incompatible.

Asian policy gives little indication of pursuing nationalist aspirations. Standing between Europeans and Africans, this group has displayed greater interest in developing working arrangements with these communities. In the earlier years the approach was to the European community. But, following the Indian controversy of 1920–24, Asians have directed their attention to the African community, while leaving the door open to co-operation with Europeans.

A NEW BASIS FOR PARTNERSHIP

As pointed out in the Introduction, those who reject communalism generally grasp the Rhodes principle of "equal rights for all civilized men" as furnishing a lead for reworking the policy of partnership. Thus far, it has been employed largely as a catch phrase, and serious consideration has not been given to its implications either for remaking East African society or to drafting a program for its implementation. At the outset its proponents probably would have to agree that, to employ the principle successfully, its application could not be restricted to the political sphere. Communalism is so deeply ingrained in all the major social institutions, and all institutions are so inter-related, that the principle must operate throughout the society.

Second, it would be necessary to so frame the qualifications on which the society of civilized men was to be constituted in a fashion (1) to avoid giving any group a membership so small that their participation is ineffectual and (2) to prevent the numerically superior group swamping the minorities.[45] Admittedly, this is a difficult task.

Third, any organization constituted on this principle would, under existing constitutional arrangements, be denied channels for effective political action, and it would be relatively simple to crush the organization by failing to amend the constitution.

Presuming that the first three difficulties are not insurmountable, it then becomes important to see that, in drafting a program, the organization first tackles the easier problems and avoids those so difficult that it is doubtful if a workable solution is immediately possible. A series of quick successes might go a long way in winning public support. Suggestions along this line are (1) the abolition of pay differentials; (2) the opening of upper-level civil service positions, including ministerial portfolios, to all communities; and (3) the elimination of residential segregation in urban areas.

As yet there is little if any evidence that a revision of communal partnership along lines of the Rhodes principle is likely to occur in Kenya. It seems reasonable to expect that, as the duration of the emergency lengthens, the chance of communal partnership surviving becomes less. Choice of a policy to succeed probably lies between nationalism and partnership on a noncommunal basis.

45. An example of the first difficulty occurs in Southern Rhodesia, where the presence of five hundred Africans on the common roll virtually disenfranchises this community. Any threat of majority domination would play to the basic fear of Europeans.

# THE FORMER ITALIAN COLONIES AND ETHIOPIA: TRENDS AND PROSPECTS

ROBERT D. BAUM

*American University, Washington, D.C.*

PROBABLY nothing since the Italian occupation has affected the course of political events in the former Italian colonies and Ethiopia so profoundly as the decisions of the United Nations General Assembly in 1949 and 1950 with respect to the disposition of Libya, Eritrea, and Somaliland. As a result, Libya achieved independence in 1951; Eritrea in 1952 became an autonomous unit federated with Ethiopia under the sovereignty of the Ethiopian crown; and Somaliland will become independent in 1960.

The General Assembly assumed this responsibility in accordance with the Italian Peace Treaty of 1947 after the Council of Foreign Ministers (France, the United Kingdom, the United States, and Soviet Russia) had failed to agree on this question within a year after the peace treaty came into effect. The task of finding a formula acceptable to a two-thirds majority of the Assembly proved exceedingly difficult and was accomplished only by compromises, some of which, however inevitable, may not in the long run prove to be the most suitable for the particular area affected.

The role of the United Nations has not been limited simply to reaching these broader decisions but has also included guidance during the transitional periods and a continuing interest through technical assistance in the social and economic advancement of these territories. United Nations commissioners in Libya and in Eritrea aided the inhabitants in drafting their constitutions and in preparing themselves in other respects for independence or self-government; and a United Nations advisory council is assisting the Italian administering authorities in Somaliland throughout the period of the trusteeship. A United Nations tribunal in Libya and Eritrea is authorized to decide questions relating to Italian property. The specialized agencies of the United Nations (e.g., WHO, FAO, and UNESCO) have rendered valuable services to Libya and Somaliland through the United Nations expanded program of technical assistance. Libya is now receiving more aid per capita from the United Nations than is any other country.

All these territories face the common challenge, so familiar elsewhere in Africa, of developing backward economies, raising low standards of living, and providing increased facilities for education and health. In addition, all are seeking to prepare their inhabitants for more effective participation in government and to strengthen their sense of national solidarity. It is to these problems that we shall now turn as we examine separately the trends and prospects in Libya, Somaliland, and Ethiopia-Eritrea.

## LIBYA

The establishment of the United Kingdom of Libya on December 24, 1951, marked the end of centuries of foreign occupation and control and the birth of a constitutional monarchy federal in nature and faced with innumerable problems of policy and administration. Four of these problems in particular pose serious and basic questions for the West because of Libya's strategic position in northeastern Africa. First, how can a state with obviously limited economic resources and technical skills develop a viable economy? Second, how can a strong sense of national unity be generated to overcome separatist tendencies latent in the history and diverse characteristics of the three component provinces—Tripolitania, Cyrenaica, and Fezzan? Third, how can a Western-type constitution and a modern governmental bureaucracy best be adapted to the political dynamics and social and economic institutions of this Arab state? Fourth, how can a foreign policy be formulated which will permit Libya to remain on good terms simultaneously with the Great Powers of the West and with its sister Arab states, some of which see "imperialist" motives in Western policies toward Libya?

*Economic and technical assistance.*—Libya is a poor country, almost totally lacking in valuable known mineral resources or

fuel; its precarious agricultural and pastoral economy is subject
·to inadequate rainfall, often resulting in drought, and to dam-
age of crops from searing desert winds, flash floods, and pests.
Coastal fishing and simple manufacturing supplement the fluc-
tuating returns from agriculture. Nevertheless, based on a
United Nations estimate, economic benefits equal to more than
half of Libya's national income are derived from foreign expenditures relating to military facilities and the contributions of
foreign governments to meet budget deficits and further economic development.

Without this external assistance, it is clear that Libya today
could maintain neither its present standards of living (however
low), nor the average annual cash income of its people (estimated at only about $35 per capita), nor its present level of imports
(most of which consist of essential consumers' goods such as
food and clothing and only half of which it can pay for through
exports), nor its present low level of government services. The
country incurs a budget deficit of 35 per cent, which is balanced
only through the direct contributions of France and particularly of the United Kingdom.

Many years of concentrated effort to overcome its economic
and technical deficiencies lie ahead if Libya is gradually to dis-
pense with the foreign props which now support its economy. A
long-term program for improvements in such fields as education,
agriculture, health, and development of natural resources is
supported by technical assistance from the United States
(amounting to $2.8 million in 1951 and 1952) and the United
Nations (about $2.5 million for the same period).[1] In addition,
with the financial help of the United Kingdom, France, and
Italy, Libya has established a development and stabilization
agency to execute public capital improvements and mitigate the
effects of drought and a finance corporation to provide long-
term low-interest loans for agricultural, industrial, and commercial projects.

In June, 1953, the Libyan government submitted a memo-

1. In September, 1954, the Libyan government signed a twenty-year agreement
with the United States whereby the latter was permitted to operate air bases in Libya.
Financial aid amounting to $40 million is also being provided during the same period.

randum to the United Nations Economic and Social Council on the additional technical and financial assistance required to meet its urgent development needs. A five-year capital development program was outlined, calling for the expenditure of almost $18 million, in addition to the maintenance of a drought-relief fund of $2.8 million. Much of the needed aid became available as the result of a financial agreement with the United Kingdom signed in July, 1953, along with a treaty of friendship and alliance. Under its terms, Libya receives annually for five years $2.8 million for economic development and about $7.7 million for budgetary purposes. The ECOSOC proposed in August, 1953, that the General Assembly invite all governments in a position to do so to provide financial and technical aid to Libya and recommended that the United Nations and its specialized agencies give due consideration to Libya's specific development needs, if and when further means become available for assisting underdeveloped areas.

*National unity.*—With the establishment of a Libyan state, there were those who feared that the centrifugal forces of regional separatism would prevent the development of strong national unity. They pointed, among other things, to (1) the wide differences in population among Tripolitania's 800,000 inhabitants, Cyrenaica's 300,000, and the 50,000 of Fezzan and to the determination of the two latter areas to avoid interference in their own affairs by Tripolitania; (2) the great stretches of desert separating these three "islands" and the resulting difficulties of rapid or extensive intercommunication; and (3) the differences in outlook arising from separate local histories, degree of contact with foreigners, and structures of society. Cyrenaica contains the most homogeneous, closely knit tribal nomadic and seminomadic peoples; Tripolitania, a population more Westernized, detribalized, and less ethnically or politically cohesive; and Fezzan, largely sedentary groups of politically untutored oasis dwellers.

The period since Libyan independence is indeed too short to permit fair judgment on the future prospects for national unity, but it is well to bear in mind some of the chief elements which are working to overcome this problem with even chances of success. Aside from the unifying effects of language, religion, and culture, they include (1) the central position of the king, Idris I, as a symbol of the united allegiance of all parts of Libya and as a force for emphasizing the overriding importance of national over provincial interests; (2) the federal nature of the constitution, which, while allaying the provinces' fears of being dominated by one another, nevertheless provides the framework for a strong central government in control of the major sources of revenue; and (3) the sense of national consciousness derived not only from sheer existence as an independent state but also from the slowly growing realization of Libya's citizens—especially in parliament and in the urban centers—that they share common domestic and foreign problems.

*Adaptation to Western institutions.*—Given the political and social patterns which have long characterized Libyan society, it would be surprising if custom and usage did not result in special adaptation of the Western form of responsible government provided in the constitution to the peculiarities of the Libyan environment. Thus, political power is likely to remain for some time in the hands of a few prominent families and traditional leaders supplemented by a small but growing educated urban elite. Submission of the individual to the group and acceptance of decisions made by traditional leaders with higher social status have long been the rule. To most Libyans—inexperienced in self-government beyond the tribe or village and accustomed to associating central and regional government with foreign domination—loyalty to the state and direct participation in government are still innovations. While these attitudes are changing, especially in the urban centers and coastal Tripolitania, they remain significant limitations to any rapid or drastic changes in the traditional social system.

The Libyan constitution affords considerable latitude in this respect for a gradual transformation toward more modern practice. The framework for responsible government in the Western sense is clearly provided through direct responsibility of the council of ministers to a popularly elected lower house, exemption of the king from all responsibility, and the required countersignature of his ministers to all his acts of state. Despite these limitations on the king, the constitution enables him to take control if an emergency so demands. Thus, he may exercise a suspensive veto on legislation and dissolve the lower house or adjourn both houses of parliament, and today, when legislators tend to follow his lead, he may appoint and remove his ministers virtually as he pleases.

In the early years national stability was fostered by the able leadership of Prime Minister Mahmud Muntasser, but, in trying to reconcile his responsibility to both king and parliament, he occasionally was placed in a difficult and ineffective position. His resignation because of illness left few other Libyans with known comparable qualifications to succeed him.[1] A similar uncertainty surrounds the question of the royal succession, which the constitution leaves for determination by the present king, a man without issue and frail in health.

*Foreign policy.*—Libya desires the friendship both of the Arab states and of the Great Powers of the West; yet, so long as strained relations exist between certain members of both groups, Libya's middle position could be misunderstood by either side. On the other hand, Libya might serve as a bridge in bringing the two closer together. Libya is tied to the Arab world not only by religion, culture, and a similar history of recent foreign domination but also by membership in the Arab League. At the same time, by permitting the United Kingdom, the United States, and France to maintain military facilities on Libyan soil and by recently concluding a treaty of friendship and alliance with the United Kingdom, the Libyan government has shown its readiness to be associated closely with the Western powers. This treaty specifically stipulates that nothing therein is to prejudice Libya's obligations under the Covenant of the Arab League and thus places Libya in a position similar to that of Iraq and Jordan in being linked both to the Arab League and to the United Kingdom by a treaty of alliance.

## SOMALILAND

Many of the problems faced by Libya in mastering the art of self-government and establishing its economy on a firm and

1. Prime Minister Mahmud Muntasser resigned on February 15, 1954, and his successor, Mohammed Saquezli, resigned on April 8, 1954, to be followed by Mustapha ben Halim.

solvent basis are present in even more serious form in the Trust Territory of Somaliland under Italian administration. The handicaps to be overcome before December 2, 1960, when, in accordance with the decision of the United Nations General Assembly, Somaliland is to become independent, are truly formidable if independence is not to be premature.

The difficulties, both human and physical, present a challenge which can be met only by time, persistent application, adequate financial resources, and human ingenuity. Somaliland's inhabitants (1,275,000) are predominantly pastoral nomads eking out a precarious existence in a semibarren land, illiterate, untrained in modern skills, and unprepared to exercise the modern institutional techniques of national self-government.

The Italian administering authority, under general guidance of the United Nations Trusteeship Council, is endeavoring to raise the standards of education and health, organize representative and democratic institutions, and increase the productivity needed to approach economic self-sufficiency. Educational and technical training has made a good beginning, handicapped as it is by nomadism, the necessity of using foreign languages in instruction, shortage of teachers and funds, and the pressure of time. A representative territorial assembly has been established and, on lower levels, residency and municipal councils. These bodies are advisory at the moment, but, as they gain greater knowledge of parliamentary procedure and appreciation of the need for considering public problems on a broader basis than the traditional kinship group or tribe, they will be granted fuller legislative authority. Members of the younger, educated, urban Somali elite have sought with some success to break down tribalism through emphasis on modern education and political organization (notably the Somali Youth League). Their effectiveness has been limited, however, not only by the sheer magnitude of the problem but also by their difficulties in bringing themselves to co-operate with the Italian authorities, whose return they had bitterly opposed.

Somaliland faces staggering problems in achieving economic independence, given its meager natural resources, its perennial budget deficits (amounting to roughly one-half of expenditures), and its adverse balance of trade. Its exports (chiefly bananas, cotton, and hides and skins) pay for only about 40 per cent of its imports. Short of promising discoveries of oil, not yet achieved but being sought, or of some other valuable resource, Somaliland will find itself heavily dependent on external financial and technical aid after independence. There are possibilities, however, for improvements which could reduce this need. Studies (some of them undertaken by the United Nations and its specialized agencies), plans, and programs are already under way to expand the small agricultural potential, coastal fishing, and the processing of raw materials.

### ETHIOPIA-ERITREA

Ethiopia's postwar years have been marked by great progress in modernization, federation, and increasingly active participation in world affairs.

*Modernization.*—For centuries Ethipia was isolated from the rest of the civilized world primarily because of geographic inaccessibility—the rugged interior of the country, fringed by desert, the absence of adequate all-weather roads, and the lack of a direct outlet to the sea. Its peoples, mostly peasants and herdsmen of many strains and tongues, have lived in a tribal and semifeudal society strongly resistant to innovation and, not without reason, suspicious of outsiders. Long ruled by a "King of Kings," whose theoretically absolute power fluctuated in strength from one century to another with the tides of internal warfare, Ethiopia has made its greatest strides toward adoption of Western institutions during the past quarter-century under its present emperor, Haile Selassie I. So rapid have been the changes that, under a less wise ruler, the strain of adjustment would have taxed sorely the loyalty of the traditional, conservative lesser ruling class. Economically the country remains relatively undeveloped, and the impact of new ideas and methods still has affected directly only a comparatively small proportion of the entire population of 16,000,000. But the seeds have been sown for much wider advancement in future generations.

The most notable changes are visible in the fields of education, government administration, and economic development.

Despite the serious decimation of the Ethiopian intelligentsia during the Italian occupation, the government has pushed energetically ahead since its return in 1941 toward the goal of education for the masses. Education is of major concern to the emperor and is allotted over 10 per cent of the national budget. Student enrolment in public schools rose from 19,000 in 1943 to over 60,000 in 1952, including more than 6,000 girls. The number of government schools—most of them with only four or five grades and only four of them secondary—increased from 120 to over 500. Ethiopian teachers, most of whom have had only a few years of schooling, now number over 2,000 in contrast to one-tenth that amount before the war; and foreign teachers, over 300 instead of about 40. To the various specialized post-primary schools already in existence was added, in 1951, a university college of arts, sciences, and law. An agricultural college and other agricultural and technical schools are now being planned. Despite these steps, there is wide room for improvement, as the Ethiopian government is well aware, in such matters as teacher-training, expanded schooling, and a more varied and practical curriculum.

The structure of government was reorganized after 1941 with much greater centralization and unification of control and the adoption of such innovations as a budget, centralized accounting, and a more modern system of taxation and currency. There are still too few persons qualified to handle the governmental work load, a corresponding reluctance of ministers to delegate responsibility to subordinates, and—as in all governments—problems of bureaucratic jurisdiction. The great need for technically trained personnel will continue for many years despite the increasing availability of Ethiopians with higher education. Foreign advisers still play an important role in certain of the ministries.

The Ethiopian economy, based primarily on the export of coffee, hides and skins, cereals, pulses, and oilseeds, has enjoyed a postwar prosperity reflected in balanced budgets and favorable balances of trade. Long handicapped in further economic expansion by its limited communication facilities, Ethiopia is now beginning to reap the benefits of loans from the International Bank for Reconstruction and Development, which, together with its own expenditures, are now being used to improve roads and telecommunications as well as to finance the operations of a development bank. The country is now raising sugar cane for the first time in quantities which in the near future should be enough for its own domestic requirements. Similar production plans are under consideration to end the need for imports of raw cotton. With the help of technical assistance from the United States and specialized agencies of the United Nations, many other improvements are under way in agriculture as well as in education and health. Thus, a cattle rinderpest control program is part of a wider scheme to use more fully the potentialities of Ethiopia's large livestock population. Other promising signs of economic activity include the successful operations of the Ethiopian Airlines, Inc.; the search for oil, thus far without discovery; and the continued interest of foreign investors in possible opportunities within the country. While the government officially welcomes investors, it has not often thus far taken prompt action to facilitate their plans.

*Federation.*—The federation, as a result of United Nations decision, of Eritrea with Ethiopia under the crown of the emperor in September, 1952, assured Ethiopia a long-sought direct access to the sea, an enlarged free-trade zone, and more diversified labor skills. It also removed Ethiopia's anxiety that Eritrea might be occupied by a future aggressor, and it brought into closer contact peoples with some common geographic, historic, and ethnic ties. At the same time Eritrea was assured by the United Nations resolution, among other things, of an opportunity for local self-government, protection by the federal government against possible external aggression, and the removal of the few existing impediments to the free flow of trade with Ethiopia, its chief source of grain supply.

Great tact and flexibility will be essential on the part of both Ethiopians and Eritreans if the new federation is to function harmoniously. While the trend in recent years within Ethiopia has been toward the strengthening of the central government's authority over the provinces, the separate autonomy of Eritrea may stimulate desires in some of the Ethiopian provinces for similar status and privileges. The urban inhabitants of Eritrea have been disturbed by the rise in the cost of living immediately after federation as a result of higher customs and other duties. Ethiopia, however, has assured the United Nations that it will respect Eritrean autonomy and grant Eritrea all necessary economic assistance.

*Role in international affairs.*—The emergence of Ethiopia from its centuries of isolation to active participation in affairs of the outside world reflects the trends toward modernization already noted within the country as well as the political sophistication of its emperor. Represented abroad today by at least twenty-six diplomatic and consular posts, Ethiopia has joined fully in postwar international activities since the San Francisco Conference in 1945. Despite its failure in 1935 to receive effective aid from the League of Nations against Fascist aggression, Ethiopia's subsequent sufferings have if anything reinforced its advocacy of the principle of collective security. Striking evidence of this position was Ethiopia's sending of troops, who gained a high reputation for valor, to join the United Nations military effort in Korea.

In December, 1952, the emperor declared in a press interview not only that Ethiopia would do its utmost to join a Middle East Defense Organization if one were established but also that he would welcome an American military mission to help modernize his forces. The United States and Ethiopia in May, 1953, concluded a Mutual Defense Assistance Agreement under which the United States will supply military aid and training assistance and thus enable Ethiopia to strengthen its own internal defense and capabilities for joining in the collective defense of this part of the free world. In determining that Ethiopia was eligible for grant aid under the Mutual Security Act, President Eisenhower took into consideration Ethiopia's strategic position in the Near East and Red Sea area and the importance of Ethiopia's defensive strength to the security of the United States.

From the foregoing discussion it should be clear that the former Italian colonies and Ethiopia have made steady progress since the war toward modern self-government and, in certain territories, toward economic viability. These accomplishments are magnified in the light of the physical and human handicaps under which they have been achieved. While these difficulties are similar to those found elsewhere in colonial Africa, they appear greater in some respects, given the new or promised independence of some of these territories and their limited resources.

# BELGIAN CONGO AND THE UNITED STATES
# POLICIES AND RELATIONSHIPS

GEORGE W. CARPENTER

*Executive Secretary, Africa Committee of the Division of Foreign Missions, National Council of the Churches of Christ in the United States of America*

SIR WINSTON CHURCHILL once remarked that there are two things which can be done with an egg: it can be heated slowly for a long time and produce a chicken, or it can be heated strongly for a short time and become hard-boiled. Either process unfits the egg for the other. There is a sense in which it may well be asked whether colonial development in Africa does not resemble the egg. Must there be a choice of objectives of whether to make the primary concern the rapid development of Africa's material wealth for the benefit of non-African interests, or whether to give primacy to the development of the peoples of Africa, leading them as quickly as possible toward full autonomy? In other words, can there be the desired economic exploitation without a simultaneous and most undesired human exploitation?

This is a question which confronts one at every turn in Africa, but it is not one which can be easily answered in categorical terms. On the one hand, it is perfectly clear that no adequate human development of Africa is possible *without* concurrent economic development. Ethiopia prior to 1935 and Liberia prior to 1944 sufficiently illustrate the difficulty confronting independent African countries when left largely to their own resources, cut off from outside capital, from the skills and techniques of the Western world, and from international commercial intercourse. Their experience demonstrates the economic and cultural interdependence which is a primary factor in African advance. On the other hand, the incursion of foreign economic interests has too often meant the dispossession of the African peoples from the land of their fathers, their reduction to a subordinate position, and the denial to them of any voice in determining their own future state or status. Can the evils of these two extremes be avoided by the intelligent choice of some middle way?

The authorities of the Belgian Congo believe that such a choice is possible, and they are intent upon the task of working it out. Their success in doing so is a matter of the most vital interest to the United States, since this country has inescapable commitments with respect both to the economic and to the human development of that colony. Urgent political and military considerations demand the rapid and effective exploitation of the Congo's mineral wealth. Uranium, industrial diamonds, and cobalt are three materials of the highest strategic importance for which we are dependent largely on the production of the Congo. There are others of somewhat less importance. Under present conditions the urgency of maintaining and perhaps of increasing their availability cannot be overstated. Their production forms a part of the great industrial complex which is developing in Central Africa and which inevitably changes the whole fabric of life for millions of Africans. Being thus partly responsible for that change, we cannot turn our backs upon the African people and say that what happens to them is no concern of ours.

In point of fact our concern for the human development of the Congo was deep and active long before the present crisis. It was nonetheless real for being expressed through private agencies rather than through government. American missionaries today are carrying on a work in the Congo which goes back more than seventy years to the very earliest days of penetration into the Congo from the West prior to the formation of the Congo Free State. Thus it antedates Belgian occupation of the colony. The large majority of American residents in the Congo have always been Christian missionaries. Their aim has not been economic betterment for themselves, or even primarily economic betterment for the African, though their work has often provided him with knowledge, skills, and tools tending to that end. Their concern has been primarily with the upbuilding of African men and women as people, and it will be stultified if in the long run the African peoples are not assured of the equality of rights, privileges, and opportunities which are their natural heritage as human beings.

This concern for the peoples of Africa is in harmony with the deepest and most cherished traditions of our nation. Freedom for all men is an ideal to which we Americans respond with passionate devotion. For that reason perhaps we are essentially anticolonialist in viewpoint. This anticolonialism tends, however, to be an emotional reaction, an attitude often assumed without adequate knowledge or understanding of the facts in a given situation. In our ignorance we become impatient. We demand the early political emancipation of subject peoples without pausing to inquire whether those peoples are yet equipped to govern themselves or even desirous of doing so. We fail to recognize the immensity of the tasks of education and of economic development which are needed to prepare the way to effective nationhood; and we often fail to give proper credit to those who are carrying out these laborious and essential tasks. The development of a more balanced view in regard to the problem of colonial development on our part is most urgently needed.

It is therefore appropriate that we should look carefully and in some detail at the effort which Belgium is making to combine the two objectives of economic development and human development in the Congo.

The most comprehensive and authoritative summary of accomplishments and projected lines of development is contained in the "Ten-Year Plan for Economic and Social Development of Belgian Congo" issued by the Minister of Colonies in 1949. This plan was the result of a long series of discussions presided over by the governor-general at Leopoldville and subsequently by the Minister of Colonies in Brussels. While it is basically economic in character and aims to foresee and to provide for the principal needs of the colony in respect to economic development and expansion during a ten-year period, concern for the development of the African peoples is not limited to economic considerations. As the plan itself remarks:

It is essentially economic . . . but we have many other preoccupations also. How can we bring into the economic circuit, into the current of progress, all these rural populations which continue to stagnate in their ancestral mode of life? Are we certain that the execution of the plan will assure, with priority, a substantial improvement in the level of Native life? Will there be an equilibrium between industry and agriculture, between consumers and producers of food? Will this economy be more stable than today, better balanced, and will it better withstand external economic variations? . . .

Nor must the idea of economics be unduly restricted. There is not only production, distribution, and consumption of goods. There are related problems which must be examined together. It would be impossible, for instance, to execute an economic program without concerning one's self with its social repercussions. Government proposals in the field of social legislation, though numerous and important, are not included in this study; but one will find here salary policies on which depend both the purchasing power, the will to produce, and welfare; questions of hygiene, nutrition, lodging, and urbanism are examined; whole chapters are devoted to public health and to education. So true it is that even from the economic point of view, apart from his inherent dignity, the most precious wealth in the world is man himself.[1]

The plan includes detailed studies of needs and projects in such fields as population and working force, both black and white; transportation by rail, road, water, and air; government research in urbanization and construction, in conservation and storage of products, in cartography and geodesy, in geology, hydrology, and meteorology, and in telecommunications; the provisions of fuels and electricity; soil conservation; forestry; agriculture; animal husbandry; fisheries; mineral and industrial development; etc.

The whole plan projected an expenditure of public funds amounting to approximately a half-billion dollars and estimated that at least an equal sum, perhaps more, would simultaneously be invested by private interests on their own initiative. While it is not expected that the entire plan will be realized within a decade, the government is proceeding energetically to put it into effect as rapidly as possible and of course constantly revising it at the same time in the light of experience. Actually it is quite evident that the investment required, both public and private, will greatly exceed the estimates made in 1949. Belgian private investment in the Congo is currently estimated at $70,000,000 per annum. Results are already evident, not only in the tangible form of roads, harbors, machines, and a quickened pace of economic development, but also in rising wage and salary scales for Africans, in rapidly growing school enrolments,

1. *Plan décennal*, I, xiii. (My translation.)

in a still more rapid movement of population from the villages to the cities and centers of enterprise, and in the sense of life, vigor, movement, and hope which is apt to impress the visitor to the cities of the Congo.

There can be little doubt that this effort to co-ordinate the economic and social development of the colony within an over-all plan rather than leaving it to an unplanned growth guided by chance alone is a wise and timely measure. The high level of economic development, of which the plan is the expression, has however had other effects which were hardly foreseen, and to this internal influence has been added the rising national con-sciousness of the peoples of British West Africa and other ex-ternal factors.

Both government and private enterprise in the Belgian Congo have been exceedingly paternalistic toward the African. The view has been almost universally held that the African is still a child, to be guided and controlled in his own best interest by the superior wisdom of those Europeans who have responsibility for his welfare and advancement. It has been hoped and believed that such measures as good wages, free hospitalization, ade-quate housing, and provision for normal family life at industrial centers, sports, maternity centers, study circles, and company unions would satisfy the aspirations of the native peoples of the Congo of this generation at least. As compared with certain other colonies, the Congo was notably backward in education beyond the elementary level, in provision for any active par-ticipation by the African at the managerial level in private en-terprise, or in government above the level of the local chief or judge in an African tribunal.

On the latter point it may be remarked that the European in the Congo is as completely disfranchised as the African; the policy has always been to reserve the legislative power to the Belgian government for fear that white colonials in the Congo might exert a preponderant influence and thus jeopardize the welfare of the African peoples. It may perhaps be asked whether the actual result of this policy has not been to subordinate the interests of all the residents of the Congo, white and black alike, to those of certain Belgian financial powers, notably the Société

Générale, which controls a major part of the mining and industrial activity in the Congo. It is obvious that the Société Générale and a few other large-scale economic interests are in a position to exert great pressure on the government, and there is no way in which the public can inform itself authoritatively as to the effect of such influence on public policy or exert any countervailing influence of like magnitude.

It is clear that, as long as the people remain quiescent under a paternalistic regime which makes no provision for their progressive training in the direction of autonomy, while at the same time the economy of the colony becomes increasingly complex, demanding ever higher levels of managerial ability and skill, the gap between proved African competence and the demands of high-level leadership continues to widen rather than become less. There was until recently hardly any real thought of transferring effective responsibility from European to African shoulders. It was believed that the present pattern of relationships might continue more or less unchanged for a century or more.

This paternalistic viewpoint was evident in educational policy and in social organization. Educational policy was directed toward the provision of elementary schooling designed to make the African a useful artisan, laborer, or clerk in the lower levels of employment, with hardly any provision for secondary education, and none at all for training at the university level. It was contrary to accepted policy to send students abroad for such training. Only the Roman Catholic church broke this taboo, sending its seminarians to Rome in preparation for the priesthood, with the result that this church has been able to consecrate Congolese bishops before any African laymen with comparable preparation were ready for civil employment or government service.

Thus, while there was no legal color bar limiting freedom of employment in the Congo, there was a generally accepted distinction of function and status in the economic order. Posts of leadership were automatically reserved for Europeans; Africans were not expected to be competent to hold such posts and consequently had no opportunity to apply for them. This pattern of segregation is reflected in the organization of the cities of the Congo. There is a European quarter and an African quarter; Africans may reside in the European quarter only as resident servants in the households of their employers. Up to the present, economic status has, by and large, been sufficient to maintain the distinction, and considerations of public health have been invoked to enforce it so that questions of race did not arise in overt form. How long these devices will remain effective remains to be seen.

The postwar period has brought the inadequacies and dangers of these policies sharply into focus. Across the river from Leopoldville, capital of the Belgian Congo, lies Brazzaville, capital of French Equatorial Africa. Since 1946 the people of French Equatorial Africa have had the status of citizens of the French Union. They vote and send their deputies to Paris. Political parties exist and compete for popular support. The external manifestations of democratic political procedure are much in evidence. All this is not lost upon the Congolese.

Less immediate but perhaps, in the long run, even more influential is the rise of autonomous self-government in British West Africa. In the highly centralized French system authority remains largely in Paris despite recent developments; but in the Gold Coast and Nigeria real autonomy is developing, with African leaders holding key positions of responsible authority. The people of the Congo, white and black alike, are watching with the deepest interest the outcome of this experiment. The evident stature and capacity of the West African leaders opens a whole new dimension to their eyes as they think of the future of the Congo. If such resources of leadership exist in West Africa, can they be absent from the Congo? If they are there, why are they not being recognized, developed, and used? Can the Congo keep pace with West Africa unless urgent attention is given to the development of African leadership? While such questions are only beginning to be formulated by more than a very few Africans in the Congo, they represent a viewpoint which can no longer be neglected. It is urgent that the white leaders in the Congo should also ask them and act upon them before the Africans become impatient and restive.

Belgian publicists are apt to blame "outside interference," especially through the United Nations, for the mounting pressure to move toward greater political and social autonomy in the Congo. They fail to realize that such pressure is simply the expression of the inexorable movement of history and that the old patterns of paternalism and authoritarianism are no longer serviceable.

Another factor in this ferment of unrest is the new class of *évolués* which has become significant within the last decade. These are the intelligent and advanced young people, habituated to city life, who most urgently desire to advance into full participation in the European culture patterns practiced by white people with whom they come in contact. A few years ago an ill-conceived project endeavored to legislate a special legal status for this class as a distinct element in the population. This would have had the effect of fixing in static terms what should continue to be a process of dynamic growth and change. It would have led this group to find satisfaction in the enjoyment of its own special status rather than devoting its energies to its own further development and to helping others who had not yet come so far. So the project was dropped.

Instead, the government is trying to devise measures which will make accession in status a continuing incentive operating at a number of levels. At the same time it is recognized that complete assimilation to the European manner of life is not a necessary or even a desirable goal for the vast majority of the people of the Congo. New types of society must be projected in which both African and European cultural elements will be functionally blended in a way which cannot be fully foreseen. No one expects any more that this new society can be planned, legislated, and imposed from outside in the wisdom of the European. It must rather develop on the basis of experience, utilizing to the full the intuitive social wisdom of the peoples of the Congo themselves. For the next generation at least it appears that the government expects the African society to undergo a process of plastic change, and it aims to encourage that process.

Similar processes of change and development are envisaged in the relation between the races and in provision for African advancement into growing responsibilities. Secondary schools heretofore provided on a segregated basis and with few exceptions reserved to white children will now be open to all on an interracial basis. A university foundation related to Louvain University in Belgium and to the Roman Catholic mission at Kisantu in the Congo is being established at government expense and was expected to open in 1954. A second university, nonconfessional in character, is projected for Ruanda-Urundi some years hence.

Eight African members have been named to the governor-general's advisory council, and similar appointments to the lower levels of administrative councils are being made. Higher posts in the government civil service and in some of the companies are gradually being opened to Africans. As a result of past policies, the major difficulty in this field is naturally the lack of educated men to fill such posts.

Steps are being taken to end segregation in hotels and on the boats and railways. Much remains to be done in these fields, and the vast mass of the African traveling public is still compelled by poverty to use the cheapest class of accommodations even if it means severe crowding and discomfort. And in the matter of social relations there are of course many Europeans whose viewpoint remains unchanged, who maintain a paternalistic and authoritarian attitude which is becoming increasingly obnoxious to the African, and who have nothing but criticism for the efforts of the government to achieve more equitable and harmonious relationships between the races.

White settlers in the Congo are relatively few in number and are concentrated for the most part in the higher regions in the eastern parts of the colony. There is an active movement among them, related to similar movements in British territories, which seeks to safeguard the special interests of this group. While some of them are conscious of the need to build a multiracial society and have even taken the initiative in breaking down racial barriers, their presence constitutes a major problem for the government as it seeks to promote the advancement of the African peoples.

It is still too early to judge whether the new policies of the government have been adopted in time and whether they can be implemented fast enough to satisfy the aspirations of the people. There is at least a chance that dangerous social tensions will be averted. In that case a growing co-operation between the races may provide a firm social basis not only for efficient economic development but also for growing African autonomy and self-realization in every sphere. On the other hand, social pressure from within may force the pace beyond the rate at which the government can effect orderly change.

To revert for a moment to the egg, it is clear that the parable is inadequate in two respects. First, the people of the Congo are not, like the egg, an inert body without a will to influence their own destinies. Colonial governments can effect their purposes only in the degree to which they can enlist the co-operation of the African. The will of the people is ultimately decisive. Second, when the human element and the time factors are taken into account, the choices before Africa cease to be simple cases of either-or and become questions of priorities—of doing in due order and proportion *all* the things that are requisite to African advance.

Since our national interest and security are so deeply involved in all of this, it is appropriate for us to consider how the United States can relate itself most constructively to the development of the Belgian Congo. There are several agencies or channels through which American interests in the Congo may be expressed, of which government is only one and not necessarily the most important. It may be useful to suggest some of the ways in which these different channels may serve.

### AMERICAN PUBLIC AWARENESS AND CONCERN

For the most part America is still woefully ignorant of the Congo and of Africa as a whole. Interest and concern are rising but are often poorly based in factual knowledge. The increasing news coverage on Africa in some of the leading American papers is encouraging, as in the sending to Africa of a growing number of competent and experienced reporters. Every effort should be made to provide the American public with a more balanced understanding of the true situation in colonial areas and of the degree to which the responsible powers are solving their problems effectively. Such understanding would go far to broaden the perspective of those who are impatient because of supposed lack of progress.

Second, the Congo and all of Africa will be greatly helped by every American advance in achieving better race relations here. We are not in a position to make effective protest in regard to segregation or human exploitation in Africa as long as similar conditions exist unchecked in our midst. "Those who live in glass houses must not throw stones." But to the extent that we have solved and are solving these very real problems here we may be able to help others find the solution to their problems also.

In all relations between the public of America and those of the Congo or other countries abroad there is need for extraordinary tact and understanding on our part, arising from the very fact of our preponderant wealth and power. The possession of wealth and power does not in itself confer a title to leadership. It is much more becoming for us to accord sincere appreciation to Belgium for its stupendous achievements in developing the Congo than to suggest ways in which we might have done it differently. It is not certain that we should have done it better. If now and in the future we are in a position to offer substantial help in this task, it should be done in a way which will confirm the friendship of the peoples of the Congo, of Belgium, and of America and not in a way which would engender suspicion or enmity among us.

It is particularly important for Americans to realize the fear which the size and power of the United States can engender in a smaller nation like Belgium. America could conceivably be plotting to take over the Congo completely. Some Belgians find it hard to believe we have no intention or desire to do so. Rumors as to American designs on the Congo find ready acceptance both in Belgium and among the Belgians in the Congo. American projects to aid the people of the Congo which might otherwise be useful and effective may be unwelcome to the government or unable to secure needed local collaboration if they seem to portend an increase of American involvement there.

# BELGIAN CONGO AND THE UNITED STATES

THE UNITED STATES GOVERNMENT

Intergovernmental relations are handled through Belgium as the power administering the Congo. The United States government interest in the Congo relates especially to security, defense, and vital materials. Apart from the production of such materials there is the matter of assuring adequate transport facilities, especially roads and railways. These in turn involve questions of labor recruitment and training, the provision and use of mechanical equipment, and other factors which ramify into the whole economy of the colony. Thus the strategic needs of the United States are linked indirectly with the whole question of African welfare and human development which has been sketched above. In the light of this discussion, and of past experience, it would seem to be incumbent upon the United States government to proceed with due concern for the total welfare and development of the colony. The following suggestions may be noted in particular.

1. Sharp fluctuations in demand for strategic materials and sudden changes of policy should be avoided. A relatively small change in the United States military spending, for instance, may cause a disastrous fluctuation in the much smaller total economy of a colony like the Belgian Congo.

2. United States purchases and other spending in relation to the Congo should be so planned as to assure the largest possible coincidental present and future benefit to the people of the Congo. Their economic and social implications should be recognized.

3. United States government aid to the Congo has been confined chiefly to funds and equipment for such objectives as road-building, in which strategic considerations are paramount. If an understanding could be reached which would allay Belgian fears of United States domination, there are other major projects, such, for instance, as the utilization of the Congo River for electric power, in which intergovernmental co-operation would be highly productive.

4. There are also certain types of activity in the field of technical assistance which might be as valuable in the Congo as they

have been in other areas. In view of the excellent research and development work already being done, or projected, under Belgian auspices, and of the advantage of prior acquaintance with local conditions, it may be that the most fruitful form of collaboration would be the temporary attachment of Belgian specialists and trained Congolese to existing operations in other areas as observers. Reciprocally, certain methods and projects of the Congo government might usefully be adapted to other situations.

5. The United States government might also promote better understanding by facilitating the interchange of personnel between the Congo and the United States, as is being done in other areas. Visitors from the Congo would necessarily be chiefly persons of European origin for the present, but, as higher education progresses, there should also be an increasing exchange of African and American students especially at the graduate level. Meanwhile there will be occasion for visits to the Congo of a certain number of specially qualified people in various fields.

THE UNITED NATIONS

Belgium is responsible to the Trusteeship Council for the administration of Ruanda-Urundi, a small but densely populated area closely related to the Congo for administrative purposes. The Trusteeship Council examines the annual reports of administering powers in considerable detail, makes suggestions, and occasionally sends missions of inquiry into the various trust territories. Inhabitants of the territories are also permitted to send petitions to the United Nations in case of real or fancied grievances.

In respect to the Congo, Belgium is required by the Charter of the United Nations to report on matters of social and economic development and education. These reports are referred to the Committee on Information from Non-self-governing Territories, which is not empowered to make recommendations in relation to any specific territory. It does, however, study the reports and prepare working papers on various colonial questions.

The United Nations therefore has no direct oversight over the

Belgian Congo. It has no power to criticize Belgian administration or to propose changes. However, the supervision exercised by the Trusteeship Council over Ruanda-Urundi is in fact a potent means of bringing to the attention of the government of the Belgian Congo suggestions which might advantageously be applied there as well as in the trust territory. For example, the concern expressed in the Trusteeship Council for the provision of higher education in Ruanda-Urundi is finding response first of all in the development of a university in the Belgian Congo. Ruanda-Urundi may thus serve at times as a kind of pilot operation in relation to the Congo.

It would be highly unwise for the United States representatives in the Trusteeship Council to presume upon this relationship. Their concern is rightly limited strictly to developments in Ruanda-Urundi and the other trust territories. It is the prerogative of the government of the Belgian Congo to decide for itself how far such suggestions may wisely be extended to that colony.

The United Nations Organization is committed to work toward the political independence or autonomy of the trust territories as rapidly as possible. It wisely recognizes that other factors, including economic development, education, and a certain degree of political experience, are necessary prerequisites. It is beset on the one side by the impatience of the anticolonial powers and on the other by the recognition of the real tasks confronting the powers administering trust territories. Americans would do well to understand the complexity, the difficulty, and the importance of its task.

The delegates of Belgium in the United Nations have repeatedly pointed out that nonself-governing ethnic groups exist within the territories of many nations, including the United States, Russia, and India, which tend to be critical of the so-called "colonial powers." These retarded groups are not always administered with as much concern for their welfare and advancement as colonial peoples receive. It appears that in our currently accepted nomenclature the geographical accident of noncontiguity to the homeland of the ruling power must combine with nonself-government to make a territory qualify as a colony. Belgium argues that instead of nonself-governing *territories* the United Nations might well concern itself with nonself-governing *peoples* wherever they are found. In that way the experience of colonial administrators could be put to the widest use, and the criticism of anticolonialists might be turned into collaboration in facing this larger task. It is improbable that this view will prevail in the policies and structure of the United Nations, but it would seem appropriate for the United States to express its interest in the advancement of backward peoples irrespective of where they are.

### BUSINESS INTERESTS

In the past the Congo has not been very hospitable to non-Belgian business interests or investment capital. Corporations were in general required to have Belgian head officers and at least 51 per cent Belgian capital. In highly productive and profitable fields of activity sharp competition from firms related to one or more of the major syndicates was a certainty. It may be that the evident need for rapidly increasing private capital investment will result in more favorable conditions, especially in relation to new types of enterprise. As a result of the war many firms moved their corporate headquarters from Belgium to the Congo, and local incorporation in the Congo is now common. The constructive fiscal policies both of Belgium and of the Congo have made the Congo franc practically as strong as the dollar. It would seem therefore that American businessmen concerned for the development of backward countries might well study the possibility of developing in the Congo activities which would be socially useful there as well as affording a profitable return. If such developments tend to promote skills and craftsmanship among their employees, and if direction and ownership can gradually be transferred to local hands—especially to Africans—so much the better.

### PRIVATE PHILANTHROPIC AGENCIES (MISSIONS AND FOUNDATIONS)

Much of the most-needed help to the Congo must be provided by private agencies, which alone are in a position to establish the most effective person-to-person relationships between Africans and those who want to help them. Christian missions are such an agency, and the one through which American concern for the Congo has been most abundantly and effectively expressed hitherto. This help expresses itself in many ways. It has developed African churches to which more than a tenth of the population of the Belgian Congo are related and which provide a highly important focus of reintegration in the changing pattern of African life. It has provided schools attended by hundreds of thousands of the children of the Congo—schools the more important because it is the policy of the government to intrust all education to Christian missions rather than to encourage the rise of secularism among the people.

In this connection, however, Americans who cherish religious freedom may well ask whether this policy will not produce certain negative results in the long run. Granting that Christian character and high moral standards are qualities greatly to be prized in tomorrow's citizens and leaders, will they most abound where anyone who wants an education must attend a Christian school to get it, or where there is free choice between religious and secular schools? Will not the former promote merely superficial conformity on the part of many pupils and thus nullify to a large extent the religious life of the school? Will it be possible to approach the goal of compulsory education for all without either doing violence to the religious convictions of many or providing secular schools for those who want them? Will the mission-conducted schools renounce the right of selection among applicants they now enjoy and accept all comers? Yet, when there are no secular schools, is not that right of selection itself a form of coercion which violates the principle of religious freedom? These are vital questions which some of the missions are beginning seriously to ponder.[2]

The missions have also developed a widespread medical service which gives millions of treatments to the people of the Congo every year. They have reduced to writing many of the lan-

2. Since these paragraphs were written the government has instituted a new educational policy which undertakes to provide nonconfessional schools in the larger cities at least.

guages of the Congo, compiled dictionaries, translated the Scriptures and other books, developed rapid methods of adult literacy, and so laid the foundations of mass education. In their rural stations and outposts they have established model villages and taught improved techniques of housebuilding, sanitation, hygiene, child welfare, nutrition, and farming.

All this needs to be augmented and expanded. There are still far too few such demonstration projects of community betterment; this in particular is a field which American philanthropy would do well to cultivate intensively.

The cities of Africa, and especially of the Congo, present a challenge to social reconstruction great enough to enlist the combined efforts of the local government and every private agency that can be mobilized to help.

Higher education is a field in which international collaboration can be of particularly great value. Universities in the Congo will have a primary relation to those of Belgium, but they should also be related to those in other parts of Africa where common problems will be studied; and international linkages and support, opening to them the whole resources of the academic world, would be extremely valuable. This is particularly true because of the need for greatly increased and better co-ordinated research in many fields related to Africa. There is reason to suppose that American interest and aid in this field would be welcome.

Through all these agencies, and perhaps others, it is to be hoped that America will collaborate fully and effectively in helping the peoples of the Congo rise to their full stature in the family of nations. Our concern is genuine and deep; the problem is to find means of expressing it within the realities of the total situation—political, social, economic, and strategic—which necessarily govern American policy.

# MOZAMBIQUE

### Eduardo Mondlane*

I SHALL depend mainly on my own observations in Mozambique, since I was born and bred there. Mozambique has an area of 297,654 square miles and a coastal line of some 1,700 miles. Most of this coastal line is sandy and swampy; however, two of the most important ports in Africa are located there: Lourenço Marques and Beira. The northern and southern provinces are flat and tropical in climate, whereas the central provinces have high mountains and small plateaus. Mozambique is rich in water resources. Two of the five most important rivers in Africa have their mouths in Mozambique; one of these, the Zambezi, has a large estuary.

The northern part of Mozambique falls within the Tropic of Capricorn, and the southernmost point is on the twenty-ninth parallel. The summers are hotter and wetter and the winters are drier and warmer than most of South Africa. The warm Mozambique current has a great deal to do with these climatic conditions.

The population of Mozambique consists of 48,213 Europeans, 1,613 Goans, 12,630 Indians, 25,149 persons of mixed ancestry, and 5,640,000 Africans, of whom 4,349 were in the category *assimilado*, according to the most recent data. Population density is 7.5 per square kilometer. Most of the European population is Portuguese, who live in the southern province, where the capital, Lourenço Marques, is found. The European population is growing rapidly due mainly to a government scheme of colonization intensified soon after the second World War.

The African population is composed of two major groups: the Swahili-speaking northern group, mainly Mohammedan in reli-

* [Mr. Mondlane is a citizen of the Republic of Portugal, studying in the United States preparatory to a professional career among his countrymen in Mozambique. Born a member of the Shangaan people, he achieved the status of *assimilado* and attended schools of higher learning in the Union of South Africa and the United States, most recently at Northwestern University. This is, then, an African's report on his land, which is governed by a European power.—EDITOR.]

gion, and the Bantu-speaking central and southern groups, who worship their ancestors. Within these groups there are vast differences in language and culture. Among the Bantu-speaking peoples there are now over 100,000 Christians, both Roman Catholic and Protestant.

Most of the East Indian population are engaged in business, especially barter trade with the Africans. They import different kinds of cloth, which they exchange for agricultural products such as peanuts, cashew nuts, and African beans.

Culturally the Africans of Mozambique, like those of any other African political territory, do not form a single unit. They are part of the cultural groups belonging to the adjoining territories. For example, the Tsongas of southern Mozambique make up about half of the whole Tsonga people, who extend over into both the Union of South Africa and Southern Rhodesia. This is also true of the Ndjau people of the central provinces of Mozambique, who extend into the eastern section of Southern Rhodesia.

Portuguese is becoming little by little the lingua franca of the peoples of Mozambique. This is quite obvious to anyone who visits the coastal ports, where most contacts between the different cultural groups take place. It is possible to foresee a future time in which the Portuguese language will be the main means of communication among the peoples of Mozambique, just as English is in West Africa.

Politically, Mozambique is part and parcel of the Portuguese empire, which includes, besides continental Portugal, the Azores and Madeira, the West African provinces of Angola, Guinea, the Cape Verde Islands, São Tomé, and the Fort of San João Baptista de Ajuda, in East Africa the province of Mozambique, in Asia the State of India (not to be confused with the Republic of India), and Macao. In Oceania there is the territory of Timor.

Before the constitutional amendment of 1950, the whole of the empire outside the mother-country and India was known as the "Portuguese Colonial Empire." Since the amendment the designation of "Colonial Empire" became "Overseas Provinces." This move to change the legal status of the overseas territories from colonies into provinces took place at its appropriate histor-ical time. As everyone knows, the problems that colonial powers face today in relation to their colonies are not to be minimized. Portugal, like all other colonial powers, desires to maintain its sovereignty over these territories without having to answer questions raised by such organizations as the United Nations. By this I do not mean that, when the new amendment of the constitution was made, its authors deliberately wanted to avoid embarrassing questions. It is rather that the point is pertinent when viewed against the perspective of world politics. After all, the French Union or the overseas territories of the United States are conceived in more or less the same spirit.

In a way this new designation gives a new and somewhat bet-ter status to the average Portuguese citizen inhabiting an over-seas territory. For the natives of the territories that are classi-fied legally as civilized in culture, such as Cape Verde Islands and India, the designation of province does give a social status which approaches that of metropolitan Portuguese. But for the native of Mozambique and Angola (for reasons that I am going to explain presently) this is something still to be attained.

According to the constitution already mentioned, the people of Mozambique and Angola are divided into two main groups. On one hand, there are those people who, either by birth or adoption, have acquired sufficient Portuguese culture to be con-sidered full citizens. They must at least be able to speak, read, and write the Portuguese language. Other qualifications, such as having only one wife and an arbitrary standard of living held necessary for a minimum enjoyment of basic European culture, are important but not essential requirements. Recently, in both Angola and Mozambique, the mere passage of a certain grade in high school confers citizenship. On the other hand, there are the so-called African natives who have not yet acquired the basic elements of European civilization and who as a conse-quence must still be guided and tutored to full citizenship.

Not long ago there used to be a system of recruitment of full-fledged citizens from the native population known as *assimila-dos*, similar to what is known among French-speaking peoples as the *évolués;* but with the new constitution this is no longer necessary. Anyone who is born and educated in a Portuguese territory is, at least legally, a Portuguese citizen.

This legal separation of the Mozambican Portuguese and the native suggests a number of questions. One of these would be: "What are the political consequences of this system?" The aim of the Portuguese government is to have Portugal one and indivisible, united in culture, language, and spirit. In order to achieve this general aim, the Portuguese government has recruited the contribution of two important institutions within the nation; namely, the Roman Catholic church, with its missionary organization and machinery, and the Nationalist party, with its devotion to the glories of the Portuguese past and the revolution that has been going on for the last twenty-five years, at the head of which is Dr. Salazar, the present prime minister. The Roman Catholic church's function is to educate the natives. As the constitution says, "The Overseas Portuguese Catholic missions . . . shall be protected and aided by the State, as institutions of education and of assistance and instruments of civilization according to the provisions of the concordat and other agreements entered into with the Holy See." This means that the Roman Catholic church is intrusted with the task not only of converting the natives and making them good law-abiding citizens but also of instilling in them the national spirit. This the Roman Catholic church has accepted.

So far the majority of the Africans have not been converted and thoroughly civilized according to the required standards. They are allowed to continue to maintain their social and political organizations under the supervision of the proper authorities.

The whole province is divided into districts and circuits, and each circuit into *regedorias*. Heading each district is a district administrator, and at the head of each circuit lesser administrators with authority over a number of chiefs. At the capital of each circuit there is a judicial council, composed of the administrator, his secretary, and a number of chiefs, which deals with all criminal and civil cases from all over the circuit. The chiefs take care of all minor cases in their regions of influence as well as all taxation, which is set by the higher authorities.

Next to the governor-general is the director of native affairs, who is appointed because of his knowledge of native life and problems. He is usually one who has previously been an administrator. It is through this authority that the right of appeal to the governor-general is obtained. In case of disagreement with the justice of the local chiefs, the individual native can appeal directly to the circuit administrator with or without the permission of his chief.

Labor contracts, which are regulated by law based on the constitution of Portugal, are negotiated with the co-operation of the chief and the administrator. With reference to the recruitment of labor the position of the government is as follows: "The labour of natives in the service of the State or in that of the administrative bodies shall be remunerated." This also applies to "all systems under which the State undertakes to furnish native labourers to any enterprises working for their own profit; and all systems under which the natives in any territorial area are compelled to work for such enterprises no matter under what heading."

A reservation to this principle is implied in Article XX, which states: "The State may only compel natives to work on public schemes of general benefit to the community in occupations the proceeds of which belong to them in execution of judicial decisions of a penal nature or of the fulfillment of fiscal obligations."

Article XXI, however, states: "The system of labour contracts with natives shall be based on individual liberty and on the right to a fair wage and assistance, the public authorities intervening only for purposes of supervision."

The difficulty of interpreting these sections of the law has given cause to certain abuses which could have been avoided if the law had been more explicit.

A large proportion of the African labor in the southern part of the province of Mozambique is recruited by the Witwatersrand Native Labour Association to provide the Union of South African gold and coal mines with their work force. According to a contract made between the Portuguese government and the Union, the province of Mozambique furnishes 86,000 ablebodied men annually as mine workers. Although this is the official number, it is common knowledge that a similar number of men cross the frontier without official permission to work in the homes of South African whites as servants as well as on the farms and in the sugar plantations of Natal and in the growing secondary industries in the cities. While this is a great gain for the Union of South Africa, it is a source of economic and social as well as spiritual impoverishment for Mozambique. But, unless our economic resources are properly developed, there is no way of stopping this. We will have to put up with it until such time as our many and rich natural resources are developed.

Of late the government has been interested in developing co-operative farming for both Africans and whites. How successful these co-operative schemes will be only time can tell. So far no usable statistics have been published concerning the progress of the co-operative agricultural schemes. Technologically, African agriculture, in the main, utilizes the hoe, though more and more Africans are coming to use plows. The government has given special encouragement to Africans who engage in agriculture. Africans produce rice, cotton, peanuts, and vegetables, though no statistics of their production are available. The production of cotton in Mozambique has grown tremendously ever since 1930. According to the latest statistics, in 1931 Portugal imported 14,000,000 kilos of cotton, of which only 3,000,000 were from Portuguese territories. Between 1941 and 1945 continental Portugal imported 24,000,000 kilos, of which 5,000,000 were from Angola and 14,000,000 from Mozambique. Between 1946 and 1951, 40,000,000 kilos were imported, of which 16,000,000 were from Angola and 24,000,000 from Mozambique.

Viewing this from the figures above, one would say that there has been a great gain for Mozambique, especially taking into consideration the fact that it was mainly the result of African labor. Yet, in an analysis of the methods used by the private corporations to induce the natives to produce the cotton, one would see a number of problems. One of these problems is related to the traditional African agricultural activities. Most Africans in Mozambique are accustomed to subsistence agriculture. They cultivate those crops that are primarily used for direct consumption. From this, one can have an idea of how difficult it would be to induce Africans to produce cotton for commercial purposes. Where there was reluctance on the side of the Africans to co-operate with the cotton corporations, the government often had to step in and aid the corporations, using methods which were not quite popular with the Africans.

The same applies to the production of rice for commercial purposes. Most Africans would be willing to produce rice, but they do not like to submit themselves to the prices fixed by the government or to sell the quantity of rice which they would want to use for their family consumption. But since most of their farm implements, and even seed, have been donated by the rice-distributing companies through the government, they are often required to sell all their produce. This has been a source of discouragement for many African farmers. Many of them have given up farming and have gone to the Union to work either in the mines or in the factories.

In the southern province the government is spending thousands of dollars to irrigate the land which lies along the basins of the Limpopo and Incomati rivers. This region produces maize, potatoes, beans, rice, and tropical fruits. A number of private corporations are developing fruit plantations to supply the city of Lourenço Marques and the South African cities of Johannesburg and Pretoria as well.

Certain regions along the river basins have been set aside for European colonization. In almost all these areas Africans who belong to the class of *assimilados* are allowed to settle on the same basis as Europeans. It is the policy of Portugal to encourage Portuguese individuals and families to come to Mozambique and settle in special areas set aside for them. For this the government spends thousands of dollars. However, this settlement scheme does not seem to be a success. First of all, it seems as though the kind of white families who are encouraged to go and settle in the overseas provinces are those who do not have sufficient education to make a success of it. They leave Portugal with the idea that they are going to be rich within a very short period, and, when they discover that they are not even allowed to hire native labor unless they pay the right wages, they get discouraged to the point of returning to Portugal or migrate to the Union of South Africa without the proper documents. In 1949 about five hundred of these persons were rounded up by the South African police and ordered to leave the Union of South Africa. Those who remain in Mozambique tend to become government charges, for they cannot compete successfully with the African farmer unless the government aids them.

One of the most acute problems in Mozambique is the development of slum conditions in the cities, owing to overcrowding caused by the migration of young people from the rural areas. This phenomenon, of course, is found all over Africa. The government has tried to stop or, better, to regulate this movement. In the city of Lourenço Marques the government has started a housing scheme which thus far mainly accommodates the municipal employees. Since the city of Lourenço Marques has over 60,000 Africans, and municipal employees comprise less than 10 per cent of this population, one can imagine the housing problems that the rest of the Africans must be facing. Of late a whole section of the African population which for generations has been inhabiting the beach section of the city has been removed to enable commercial bathing developments to take place. But, since no housing projects for these people had been developed, most of them are plunged into areas where slum conditions were making headway. Compared with the Union of South Africa, one can say that there are no slums in Mozambique, but slum conditions are a function of the speed with which industrial development takes place.

The economic development of Mozambique is closely related to that of the adjoining countries: the Union of South Africa and the Rhodesias. The ports of Lourenço Marques and Beira are the natural outlets of the industrial areas of the Union and Rhodesia, respectively, and provide work for both Africans and European workers.

Before closing I would like to point out three of the most important problems that Mozambique is facing. One concerns the education of Africans. It is known that the educational standards in the schools for native Africans in Mozambique are far below those of neighboring countries. The reasons are many, but the most important is a material one: not enough money.

## MOZAMBIQUE

There are two systems of education in Mozambique. The state takes care of the education of white children and children of the families who fall in the class of *assimilados*, as well as of Asians. The justification for this separation, as explained before, is based on a difference in culture and, even more importantly, in language. In the past it was necessary for a child to present his birth certificate or the certificate of assimilation of his parents in order to be enrolled in a white school. Under the new constitution perhaps this will not be necessary. In Lourenço Marques practically all the white primary schools have some African children as well as a large number of Asian children.

In the high schools (lyceums) the number of African children is negligible due to the age limit which is imposed upon all children. Thirteen is the oldest age at which one may enter a government high school. This, however, is too low for the few Africans who manage to finish their elementary education. There are a number of private high schools, however, which accept children of all ages as long as they can pay. Since most African parents cannot afford the tuition, this really is no help at all.

There are technical schools in the cities of Lourenço Marques, Beira, and Nampula, and these are open to all citizens of the nation. Though there is no age limit, the comparatively small fee that must be paid is, in effect, prohibitive. Yet, despite this, there are more African students in technical schools than in high schools.

The government runs a school of arts and crafts for Africans in each district. These schools were the pioneers in preparing African craftsmen in Mozambique for the production of European goods, and this has been a great economic asset to the nation. Yet, of late, a new problem has appeared; namely, the new assembly-line production of the same goods that the professional craftsmen are producing. As manufacturing industries grew in number, they came to produce all the goods that were produced by the school-trained artisans. Since these factories do not necessarily need to be manned by trained workers (except a very few), the craftsman is put out of trade. And, when he employs himself in the factories, he is forced to accept the same wages as the unskilled wage-earner. I am sure most people know the consequences of this phenomenon, and I shall not elaborate on it. The question, however, could be asked, "Are the trained craftsmen going to fit into the new set-up or are they going to compete successfully, and how successfully?"

Before the concordat with the Vatican which intrusted to the Roman Catholic church the education of all native children in African Portuguese territories, there was a government-supported teachers' training school located in the southern province. During the war this school was closed down and the campus used for military purposes. After the war the school was reopened under Roman Catholic leadership. This means that now it cannot train people who do not share the same faith with the Roman Catholic church. Since there are no other teachers' training centers, those who are not of the Faith cannot be trained as teachers in Mozambique. This applies only to the people classified as "natives." This state of affairs, viewed in the light of the whole political policy of the nation, is easy to understand.

The second problem is that of health. The Portuguese government has done everything within its power to eliminate disease in Mozambique. The health department of our government in Mozambique is one of the most forward-looking and most successful in Africa. These last ten years have seen a tremendous expansion of the health services to reach most parts of Mozambique. There are nurses' training centers in all the important cities in Mozambique. Scattered over the territory are dispensaries and maternities staffed with well-trained nurses. The Portuguese doctor is one of the best friends one would like to have by one's bedside during sickness. The government has made it easy for a number of privately owned hospitals to take care of the natives, mainly in those areas the government has not been able to reach. Practically all these hospitals are maintained by missionary bodies, both Roman Catholic and Protestant. Nurses trained in state hospitals are allowed to practice in private hospitals.

The third problem is that of the migration of labor especially to the Union of South Africa. Besides the fact that our young men provide the cheapest labor force that the Union can get in the whole of South Africa, it creates a number of other problems of a social and emotional kind. It is easy for anyone who has an inkling of the social organization of any nonindustrial people to see that the migration of men from their homes to other regions for more than two years at a time causes all kinds of family and social maladjustments. The moral consequences of separation from one's family are known to all of us here. One needs only to read Alan Paton's *Cry, the Beloved Country* to get a feeling of it. Unfortunately, though social scientists are thoroughly aware of the problems, not enough people with responsibility are interested in doing anything about it; this is true of most of South Africa. Directly connected with this is the problem of old age. In the Union of South Africa all people who are sixty years old and over are eligible for social security benefits, although, compared with the whites, Africans receive very little (ten shillings per month in the rural areas, thirty shillings in the cities, and twenty-five shillings in the small towns, while white people receive twelve pounds in the rural areas, twenty pounds in the cities, and fifteen pounds in the small towns). Still it is something helpful compared with the Mozambican African, who does not receive any old age security benefits at all. Yet the Mozambican African provides one of the most important sources of wealth for the Union of South Africa. It is the opinion of many Africans in Mozambique that the Portuguese government should negotiate with the Union to provide social security for all the men who have given a large part of their most productive years to the Union gold- and coal-mining industries.

In the city of Lourenço Marques the government maintains an old age home for Africans. This is run by the Catholic church with government assistance. Here again the problem of religion is very important. Old age is the time when a person's religion is well established. This system restricts the inmates' opportunities to avail themselves of their native religion at just the time when they need it most.

In conclusion I would like to mention that, while Mozambique, as a Portuguese territory, presents problems that are unique, it is necessary to keep in mind that the problems of Africa as a whole, and especially those of South Africa as a region, have a great deal in common. It is a well-known fact that, when two or more cultures come into contact with each other, a great many changes take place. South Africa is experiencing cultural, economic, and social change as the result of the impact of the Europeans. Many of these gains and losses cannot be assessed in terms of material goods.

After having lived in Europe for over a year, as it has been my fortune to do, I have come out with the impression that one of the most lamentable losses that Europeans living in Africa have suffered is respect for people, regardless of their racial and cultural group. In Europe I found no color line. But in Africa the average white man has acquired what is known as a "colonial mentality." In some degree this is true even of recent immigrants from Europe. Although the Portuguese government is against discrimination on grounds of race and religion, one often finds it in hotels, restaurants, theaters, and boarding houses in Mozambique. This phenomenon is aggravated by contact with the Union of South Africa and the Rhodesias, where discrimination is even legalized.

We come, then, to a statement of fundamental questions confronting us in Portuguese Africa: Will the Portuguese be able to resist the influences of the Rhodesias and the Union of South Africa in forming their attitude toward Africans, in view of the close economic relationship with these territories? Will pressures in this direction increase as more Portuguese settlers are brought to the country as it develops economically, as occurred elsewhere in Africa?

Will Portuguese Africans who work in the Union of South Africa—in a segregated society which tends to breed hatred against white people—be able to identify themselves with the Portuguese as co-citizens of the same country?

Will Africans throughout the continent tomorrow have an attitude of appreciation for what Portugal is doing, and may do in the future, for development of opportunities for Africans? Will these Africans feel resentful toward Portugal?

The answers to all these questions will depend upon how the high ideals of the Portuguese government are implemented by the European Portuguese working in harmony with the indigenous peoples in such a way that Africans will feel that their cultural values are appreciated and that nothing stands in the way of the advancement of the African peoples.

# THE CHANGING ECONOMIC STRUCTURE
# OF THE UNION OF SOUTH AFRICA

### Leonard H. Samuels
*University of the Witwatersrand*

#### INTRODUCTION

LESS than a century ago the Union of South Africa was a remote, isolated area at the tip of the African continent. Trading connections with the outside world were tenuous; the interior was difficult of access; and, except for parts of the Cape, the wants of its scattered population were restricted and largely satisfied by a primitive form of subsistence farming. Today the economy is in most part highly organized, with a striking capacity for growth.

The Union's economic expansion has significant lessons for all underdeveloped areas, though it has also been affected by the presence of people of different cultures and skin colors. From the outset the white society, which took root at the Cape during the second half of the seventeenth century, was profoundly influenced by its relations with the aboriginal peoples. First, there were the Bushmen and Hottentots, whose numbers were increased by slaves imported to labor for the white colonists. As the whites expanded the frontiers of their settlement northward, they also came into contact with African tribes advancing southward. Contact between these white and black immigrant communities inevitably resulted in a series of clashes, in part since both were essentially pastoralists, with the same requirements for grazing and water. Each clash between these two vigorous groups perpetuated the colonists' dependence on the labor of the conquered people, because it left large numbers of black laborers at the beck and call of the farmers.

Running throughout the Union of South Africa's economic history is this conflict: the growing dependence on the black man's labor, however great the distaste for his person or the fear of his competition for land or for jobs. Despite repeated attempts by the various administrations to keep whites and nonwhites apart by military frontiers or, after the middle of the nineteenth century, by a policy of geographic separation through the creation of reserves for blacks, economic contact between the different groups intensified. Indeed, the process by which the whites acquired the bulk of the land increased the interdependence between the conquerors and the dispossessed.

Today in the Union of South Africa, which covers an area of almost 473,000 square miles, there are about 13,000,000 people, including some 2,700,000 whites and 8,800,000 Africans. There are over 1,100,000 Colored people, descended from the Bushmen, Hottentots, slaves, Africans, and whites. There are, in addition, about 400,000 Indians, first brought to South Africa in 1860 as indentured workers, who constitute the fourth element in this complex multiracial society.

Though outnumbered nearly five to one, the whites constitute the elite group in this deep south of the African continent. Their higher economic standards reflect, in part, differences in skill and productivity, but these standards are also due to the whites' strong bargaining position and to such factors as tradition and color prejudice. The dominant position of the white group within the political and social structure flows from its control of political and military power, its superior education, and its Western heritage.

The story of the Union of South Africa has often been told in terms of this formidable structure to defend a "white South Africa." Yet perhaps the most significant aspect of the Union's economic development has been the gradual breakdown of all those barriers which have impeded the interdependence of its inhabitants. Increased co-operation has resulted in higher standards of living for all sections of the population; all sections have been drawn into the modern economy. Insofar as these higher standards have depended upon increased co-operation and interdependence, the different groups are destined to become even more closely integrated if the economy maintains its present rate of expansion.

One of the most potent forces making for these changes has been the high economic and cultural aspirations of the small white settled population. The whites have been able to satisfy their desire for greater material welfare through their skill, initiative, and growing command over the means of production. In the process they have attracted the less-developed African and Colored peoples into the ambit of an exchange economy and have constructed with their aid a modern state closely linked to, and dependent on, the world economy.

### STRUCTURAL CHANGES IN THE UNION

The diamond and gold discoveries of the sixties, seventies, and eighties of the last century wrought an economic revolution in a society still largely feudal. They provided wealth on a spectacular scale, produced an immediate expansion of the market, quickened the tempo of commercial life, drove up land values, and led to a rapid creation of capital gains. Moreover, the mineral discoveries led to a substantial influx of capital and immigrants from abroad to the largely inaccessible interior. Here, indeed, were the surplus wealth and the technical skills necessary to develop the country's resources and span it with a network of communications.

It is not possible to review more than briefly the economic changes initiated by the mineral discoveries which were destined to destroy the largely static, rural society. The sudden establishment of new, large-scale activities threw a heavy strain on a farming system with its small surplus production. The expanded demand for meat and other foodstuffs, together with the pressure of rising land values, required a more settled agriculture with intensive stock-raising as an alternative. Farmers, driven onto poorer and smaller areas of land, acquired mainly through the process of subdivided inheritance, became increasingly incapable of adjusting themselves to the economic development taking place in the rest of the economy. They were bound to fail, since the farming techniques with which they were familiar were suited only to the primitive methods of exploitation used by large landowners, who depended upon an abundant supply of "cheap" labor. Thus there emerged a growing class of rural poor, who tended to join the ranks of those landless whites, the bywoners. They were called "bywoners" because they lived on the land of relatives or friends for whom they worked in one capacity or another but without any real economic status. These landless whites became at last what they were called, "poor whites."

Each shock to the agricultural economy disturbed the loose hold of some of these agriculturists on the land and sent a fresh wave of them into the towns. Agriculture in the Union has had many shocks, apart from the droughts, pests, and other natural disabilities which afflict it. In this century the most serious shocks have been the Anglo-Boer War of 1899–1902 and the collapse of agricultural prices after the boom following World War I and during the great depression. Despite the general growth of agriculture, therefore, farming as a whole has become progressively less able to support either a working or a dependent population. Today, less than one-fifth of the white working population is engaged in agriculture. About half the Union's working force is officially estimated to be employed in farming, while its "share" in the national income amounts to less than one-seventh of the total.

The declining importance of agriculture as a source of livelihood was doubly important because of the very large part it had always played in South African economic and political life. Thus, it was not strange that the exodus of population from the countryside and the growth of a poor white class should have dominated economic policy until the thirties. This problem of rural depopulation and white impoverishment was not, of course, peculiar to the Union, though it had a number of singular features.

In a homogeneous society individuals tend to rise or fall according to their capacities and to find occupations suited thereto. In a society stratified along color lines, however, this vertical diffusion between classes is interrupted. The members of the dominant group who would ordinarily occupy the lowest stratum of society are inhibited by the national sentiment from undertaking menial tasks, quite apart from the difficulty of competing for such jobs at the low wages acceptable to their colored competitors. There were, moreover, limited outlets for such white workers in the more remunerative occupations.

From the outset, mining and ancillary activities have been

organized on the basis of a small, highly paid white labor force and a large supply of African labor performing manual work at much lower rates of pay. This pattern of wages and employment arose because of the original scarcity of the artisan, trading, and professional classes. It has been perpetuated by legal and social conventions in the interests of the white group. Thus, it was not easy to fit the unskilled white workers into this peculiar economic organization. Many became destitute, and this created a special and embarrassing problem of poverty that would not have existed in a country with a homogeneous population.

Today, unemployment is insignificant among the white community, largely because of the remarkable expansion of the field of employment, particularly in the manufacturing and service industries. Between 1918–19 and 1938–39 the net output of manufacturing expanded more than threefold and has more than trebled again since the outbreak of World War II. Since the end of World War I, the number of white workers in factory production has increased more than sixfold.

The growth of the manufacturing industry is the product of deep-seated changes in the Union's economy. As real incomes have grown, an increasing proportion of disposable income has been diverted from food and other necessities to the purchase of services and manufactured products. These changes in consumption patterns created the conditions for an expansion of the industrial structure. There can be little doubt, however, that this process of industrialization was greatly accelerated by the authorities' growing preoccupation with measures to mitigate the serious problem of urban white unemployment. These measures took the form of a "civilized labor" policy, which deliberately encouraged the use of white rather than nonwhite unskilled labor in certain occupations and aimed at enlarging the field of white employment in the growing manufacturing industries.

Since the twenties the scale of manufacturing activity has been expanded by a policy of tariff protection, by the establishment by the government of undertakings such as power, iron, and steel production and engineering works, and by close connections with important firms in the United Kingdom and elsewhere. In recent years the government has actively encouraged a variety of projects, either through the state-controlled Industrial Development Corporation or through the establishment of state enterprises such as Sasol (South African Coal, Oil, and Gas Corporation).

The important role played by the state in encouraging manufacturing is indisputable. Nevertheless, the spectacular growth in manufacturing during the past decade in particular could hardly have taken place without the impetus provided by the war and postwar conditions. The dislocation and destruction at the end of the war and the excessive demands which have existed since the early forties in relation to the existing flow of goods and services have made practically any production profitable. In this situation the existing price and marketing controls affecting agricultural products, as well as the operation of import restrictions, have increased the profitability of manufacturing as compared with activities such as farming and mining.

Today, manufacturing activities employ almost twice the number of workers engaged in gold-mining; they account for some 24 per cent of the country's national income, compared with about 7 per cent before the war of 1914–18. During the same period the "contribution" of gold-mining and other mining activities to the national income has declined from 28 per cent to about 13 per cent at the present time. The conclusion drawn by some is that gold-mining is now of much less importance compared with its role during previous periods of the Union's economic history. These changes in the South African economy, however, require careful interpretation.

The "net product" of a given industry, or the size of its labor force, is not a true index of its role in generating income, nor is it an index of the relative importance of any industry to the economy. The extent to which a single industry, say, mining, acts as a prime generator of income cannot be assessed on its net product alone. Thus, the mining industry's activity influences the size of the figures of the other component classes of the national income, such as agriculture, wholesale and retail trade, transport, and manufacturing. The net products of the engineering, metals, and power industries, for example, are largely dependent on the demands of the gold-mining industry.

The interdependence of income-creating industries should thus not be overlooked, while it is important to recognize the still great dependence of manufacturing industry on gold-mining both as a customer and as a source of foreign exchange. Though the contribution of manufacturing to the Union's export trade has expanded substantially, its ability to finance its requirements of imported raw materials and other supplies out of its own exchange earnings is still limited. The value of manufactured exports, including semiprocessed gold, only amounts to about 18 per cent of the Union's total exports. Thus, manufacturing has still to reach the stage where it can rely on its own exchange earnings to finance its activities and their expansion.

There is reason to believe that the very rapid growth in manufacturing since the outbreak of the war has been, in part, at the expense of the Union's export production, with a consequent slowing-down in the rate of its economic growth. A complementary expansion in manufacturing activity as export incomes increase is an inevitable development. It is, however, a different matter when attempts are made to force the pace of industrialization as a means of relieving unemployment and poverty.

This is a lesson which is sometimes overlooked when industrialization is suggested as a policy to improve standards of living in the underdeveloped regions of the world. An attempt to expand incomes by diverting labor and other resources from the export industries to activities producing for the home market can have quite the contrary result. Economic development in the Union demonstrates the importance of maintaining exports either in the form of additional manufactured products or in the form of raw materials. A reduction in the scale of activities in which a country enjoys a comparative advantage will result in a fall of real income, unless this loss of income can be made good by using resources otherwise unemployed.

### GROWTH OF THE NATIONAL INCOME

It is an extraordinarily difficult matter to express statistically the immense expansion which has taken place in the Union's economy since the mineral discoveries. National income statistics, available only since 1911, have a number of defects and are of limited utility when they relate to long periods of time. Nevertheless, they provide some indications of the trend and magnitude of economic activity.

The market value of all goods and services increased annually by about 8.5 per cent during the period from 1911–12 to 1919–20, while the average rate of growth amounted to 4.4 per cent per annum in the twenties and to 8.7 per cent in the thirties. Since the outbreak of war in 1939, the net national income produced expanded at an annual rate of almost 11 per cent. These figures make no allowance for the rise in prices or for the growth in population. Allowance for these factors reveals that the rate of expansion in the thirties was more than double the corresponding rate of increase in the twenties, while the rate of growth in the twenties, in turn, appeared to be almost double the rate attained during the period from 1911–12 to 1918–19.[1] This is an astonishing achievement, though this rate of growth has not been maintained, despite the immense expansion during the past decade.

In spite of this rapid economic advance during the last forty years, average incomes of the bulk of the population are still extremely low. A rough computation suggests that average real incomes per person in the Union are about one-third or less of real incomes per head in Australia, the United Kingdom, and Canada and about one-fifth of real incomes in the United States. Such international comparisons have, of course, only a limited validity, but they reveal that the Union of South Africa is still a poor country when judged by the standards of its total population.

Current statistics of income, however, tend to obscure the real significance of those changes which have swept the bulk of the population into the modern economy. There has been a persistent and significant improvement in average incomes per head since the turn of the century. In the case of the white population the improvement has been remarkable. Allowing rough-

1. The estimates are those of Professor Frankel. The twenties relate to the period from 1922–23 to 1928–29; the thirties refer to the period from 1932–33 to 1938–39. Though not strictly comparable, each of the periods chosen commences a year after a depression or recession reached its lowest point, and each period ends with the peak year of the subsequent boom (see S. H. Frankel, assisted by H. Herzfeld, "An Analysis of the Growth of the National Income of the Union in the Period of Prosperity before the War," *South African Journal of Economics*, XII [June, 1944], 147–49).

ly for the share of nonwhite incomes and for various measures of prosperity, such as passenger motorcars and university students in relation to the white population, the money and real incomes of the whites are, after the United States and Canada, among the highest in the world.

Incomes of the nonwhite inhabitants are very much lower than the incomes of the white population. Yet the significant comparison is between the relatively high living standards of the African workers drawn into the orbit of the exchange economy and the low standards of those still lodged in their primitive subsistence economy. Incomes, both in cash and in kind, derived from the tribal economy are extremely low. According to a fairly recent investigation, incomes from agriculture and other activities appear to have averaged about $70 a year per family of six in the Keiskammahoek district in the Ciskei Reserve. Earlier investigations placed the average reserve money income at about $40 a year for a family of five in the Ciskei.[2] In the Keiskammahoek area *family* incomes in cash and kind, including remittances from those working outside the district in urban areas and elsewhere, averaged approximately $140 a year.[3] In contrast, average earnings of nonwhite workers in manufacturing activities are about two-and-one-half times as high at the present time.

### URBANIZATION

Rural poverty and the growing disparity between incomes received from urban and farming activities have been chiefly responsible for the steady depopulation of the countryside. A half-century ago the exodus of the white rural population was a trickle. Since the twenties, it has gained in momentum as a result of the immense expansion in mining, industrial, and other activities. During the last forty years the proportion of whites in rural areas has declined from 52 to about 25 per cent of the total white population. This migration of the white inhabitants

2. See *Report of the Witwatersrand Mine Natives' Wages Commission* (Union Government Reports, No. 21 [Pretoria, 1944]), p. 12.

3. See D. Hobart Houghton and D. Philcox, "Family Income and Expenditure in a Ciskei Native Reserve," *South African Journal of Economics*, XVIII (December, 1950), 423.

has been paralleled by the movement of the African, Colored, and Indian peoples into the urban areas, though this process only became significant at the end of World War I. In 1921 one-eighth of the African population lived in the cities and towns; the percentage is now one-quarter.[4] Today, the total population in the urban areas is about 60 per cent greater than before the war.

At the present time the white inhabitants account for about 40 per cent of the population in the cities and towns, the Africans for about 41 per cent, the Coloreds for 13 per cent, and the Asiatics (Indians) for some 6 per cent. Thus, the towns are now, in reality, mixed areas, with the different elements of the population closely interwoven in economic life. In manufacturing activities, which are mostly located in the urban areas, African and other Colored workers account for about two-thirds of the labor force. In mining, Africans constitute about 89 per cent of the workers employed. This dependence of urban activities on nonwhite labor is also a characteristic feature of the rural economy. The rural African population outside the native reserves is about four times as great as the whites in the rural areas and provides over 90 per cent of the workers in farming.

About two-fifths of the African population still live in the native reserves and constitute the only compact bloc of one racial group in the Union. The separation of this group from the rest of the South African economy, however, is more apparent than real, since the reserves are closely integrated with the labor market. At any time, as many as one-third to one-half of the able-bodied population may be at work outside the reserves. Competent investigators[5] have repeatedly stressed the disastrous consequences for tribal economies and family life of this

4. The figures relating to the African population in the urban areas are not a true indication of the extent of permanent urbanization. Many of the Africans enumerated in towns are not permanent residents but are migrants who leave their families behind in the reserves in order to supplement their income by working in the mines or in other urban activities. Pressure on the land in the congested native reserves as well as the Africans' expanding range of wants are leading to a more settled urban African population. This is borne out by the decrease in masculinity rates, which are now 185 males per 100 females in all urban areas. According to several sample surveys, some 40 per cent of the African population in the towns appears to be permanently urbanized.

5. *Report of the Native Laws Commission, 1946–48* (Union Government Reports, No. 28 [Pretoria, 1948]), p. 17.

continuous exodus of adult males from the reserves. This migrant labor system is a product of complex factors. It reflects, in part, the insecure position of the African in cities and towns, the lack of accommodation for his family, as well as the limited opportunities for his cultural and social advancement. For many Africans a plot of ground in the reserves is a safeguard against loss of employment and, therefore, their right to remain in the urban areas.

Large-scale migration and urbanization always give rise to difficult social and economic problems. There is the need to provide housing, food, and the other requirements of a rapidly expanding urban population as well as the creation of conditions to ease the transition to urban life. In the Union of South Africa these problems have been aggravated by color and cultural differences and by the reluctance of the central government and of local authorities to accept the facts of the social processes taking place. Thus African men and women who have been detached from their old pattern of social relationships have largely been left to their own devices to make complicated adjustments in an unfamiliar urban society, in which their opportunities to become productive members are restricted. In these circumstances their requirements for adequate housing and other needs remain unsatisfied and, indeed, appear to be beyond the existing capacity of the economy. Solution of these problems requires an immense expansion in national production through more effective use of the Union's working population as well as greatly increased contributions by the nonwhite peoples to their own economic and social betterment.

## OBSTACLES TO EXPANSION

The growing incorporation of all sections of the population into the economy has been accompanied by a steady improvement in economic position. On the basis of these trends, it is tempting to forecast that average incomes per head will expand continuously—except for temporary setbacks—owing to improvements in techniques as the developing industrial society acquires more knowledge and enjoys the economies of more effective methods of co-operation. Yet there is nothing automatic about the growth of a country's national income. It depends on the natural resources available; the literacy, skill, and well-being of the population; the effectiveness with which the society uses its factor endowment; and its ability to adapt itself to the changing circumstances which improved co-operation implies.

In the Union the expansionary process is taking place within a framework of custom and legislation which seeks to confine the use made of African and other Colored labor. Since the early years of this century the organization of labor on the gold mines has been dominated by a legal color bar,[6] while restrictions also operate in such "sheltered" trades as printing and building and in the engineering and other industries. The industrial color bar operates largely through trade-union pressures, and it has prevented nonwhites, particularly Africans, from being apprenticed and gaining access to the skilled trades.

The opposition of skilled artisans to the entry of competitors into their occupations is not confined to South Africa. In the Union, however, the fear of lowered standards because of the competition of cheap labor is intensified by color distinctions. The result of this stratification of the labor force along color lines has been to create an economic society composed of noncompeting groups. In this society of privilege and caste the great bulk of African workers is largely confined to unskilled tasks, with limited opportunities to promote themselves along the rungs of the economic ladder. As a result, wide disparities exist between the incomes of the different color groups. In mining, where the pattern took root because of the original scarcity of technical and other skills, this disparity is most marked. Nonwhite workers, who outnumber the white workers by about eight to one, receive about half the income of the white miners.

This peculiar economic organization must not be regarded as entirely rigid. The speeding-up of industrialization and the

6. In terms of the Mines and Works Act, the government is authorized to make regulations to provide for the issue of certificates of competence in mining, or works where electrical power is used, and to limit the issue of certificates to white or Colored persons. The only other legal color bar operates through the Native Building Workers' Act, which was enacted in 1951. This legislation makes provision for the training and employment of Africans in the building of houses for Africans and for the proclamation of areas in which Africans may not be employed in the erection and maintenance of buildings for the use of non-Africans.

scarcity of workers during the war and postwar years have made considerable breaches in the system. Indeed, the very growth of manufacturing activities has tended to dissolve the complex of the color bar by opening up an expanding range of work for semiskilled operatives. Today work which is classed as "semiskilled" appears to be distributed in more or less equal proportions among whites, Africans, and other Colored workers. According to investigations of the Wage Board, 35 per cent of semiskilled workers are Africans, 33 per cent whites, and Asiatics and Coloreds combined represent 32 per cent.[7] On the other hand, about 84 per cent of the skilled workers in the same trades and industries were whites.

The penetration of nonwhite workers into the more skilled occupations has been greatly affected by historical circumstances. In older trades, governed by craft traditions, and on the mines, trade-union pressure reinforced by law has retarded the advance of nonwhite workers. Despite these barriers, there has been a substantial modification of the racial composition of the labor force. In the metal and engineering industries, employing over one-quarter of those engaged in private manufacturing industry, more than 20 per cent of the labor force consists of semiskilled, nonwhite operatives. In the newer industries, such as clothing, furniture, leather, and light steel manufacturing, the employment of African and Colored workers has proceeded apace in an increasing range of occupations. In the clothing industry, for example, the proportion of white workers (mainly females) has declined from 61 per cent to 29 per cent of the total labor force during the last fifteen years.

Given the continued growth of manufacturing activities, it is inevitable that nonwhite workers will increasingly undertake not only the semiskilled work but also a growing proportion of the skilled tasks. The future rate of growth of the different sections of the population, as well as the growing tendency for

7. These statistics are based on investigations between 1937 and 1950 of sections of the manufacturing industry, although other important groups, such as the distributive, catering trades, and motor industry, were also included (see *Report of the Industrial Legislation Commission* [Union Government Reports, No. 62 (Pretoria, 1951)], pp. 22–28).

white workers to move into the distributive and commercial trades, is likely to hasten these developments.

The movement of Asiatics, Coloreds, and to an increasing extent African workers to the more skilled occupations is bringing about significant reductions in the disparity between the wages of workers exercising different classes of skill. The wage of the unskilled laborer (mainly nonwhite) on the railways, for example, now constitutes about 18 per cent of the wage paid to the skilled worker, compared with about 7 per cent before the war. In the clothing industry, where the gap between skilled and unskilled wage rates has always been smaller, the proportion has grown from 33 to 39 per cent during the same period. Indeed, there is reason to believe that during the past decade the gap between the real earnings of white and nonwhite workers has narrowed even more than the gap between their cash wages. In general, remuneration in kind constitutes a greater proportion of the total earnings of nonwhites than of whites; this factor weighs heavily in favor of nonwhite workers during periods of rapidly rising prices.

There can be little doubt of the constructive and liberalizing influence of the expanding manufacturing and service industries on the Union's economic life. Yet, the capacity of these industries for generating change within the existing institutional framework is limited. Throughout the war and postwar years the dependence of the growing manufacturing industry on the exchange earnings of the export industries has been masked, in particular, by the immense inflow of funds from abroad, while the war and the postwar inflation have provided exceptional opportunities of expansion.

These conditions are now changing. In the process they are bringing into sharp focus the basic contradictions between economic expansion and the survival of those legal and conventional restrictions which prevent the full utilization of the efforts of the working force. Despite the great economic advance which has taken place, the national output relative to the total population remains distressingly low. The low volume of production, in turn, restricts the growth of the market and prevents changes in the industrial structure from propagating themselves in a cumulative fashion. Thus, the Union is denying itself the full benefits of those forces of growth which are the real dynamic factors in an advancing economy. It is significant that the manufacturing industry after more than a quarter of a century of protection is still unable to compete effectively in world markets.

There have been substantial modifications of the peculiar labor structure which restrains the growth of manufacturing and prevents progress taking place in a co-ordinated fashion throughout the economy. Nevertheless, far too many barriers still circumscribe the productive powers of the bulk of the workers and stunt ambition. Thus, their opportunities of acquiring and exercising skill remain limited and, consequently, impede the development of those faculties, habits of industry, and discipline required in an urban society. In addition, a complex structure of controls restricts the freedom of movement of African workers into the urban areas and their right to acquire property in these areas. Underlying this policy is the assumption that the African is a temporary dweller in the towns and that his permanent home is in the native reserves.

As a result of restricted social and economic opportunities, the African worker has little incentive to improve his efficiency or to remain in a job. Thus productivity remains low, and labor turnover is high.[8] High labor turnover combined with the inefficient system of migrant labor on which are still based the mines and the Natal sugar plantations, as well as certain farming areas, prevents the development of skills and specialized abilities. The existence of a large, undifferentiated mass of unskilled and illiterate workers leads to their substitution for less efficient methods, and this severely restricts the scope for mechanization. Thus is perpetuated a vicious circle of low efficiency, low earning, and high labor turnover.

An economy condemned to operate in this manner below optimum capacity cannot easily maintain an uninterrupted rate of economic growth. Indeed, there are unmistakable signs of a

8. A detailed analysis of the employment histories of 251 firms showed that one-half of the jobs taken by Africans lasted less than six months, three-quarters less than one year, and 90 per cent less than two years (see Department of Commerce, Witwatersrand University, *Native Urban Employment, 1936–44* [Johannesburg]).

slowing-down in the pace of economic expansion, despite the immense constructional, mining, manufacturing, and transportation activities during the postwar years. During the period 1947–51 the average annual increase in "real" income (i.e., at 1938 prices) per head of population amounted to about 5 per cent, which represents an extremely rapid rate of growth. Nevertheless, the annual rate of growth of the economy during this period was less than the rate of expansion achieved during the thirties.

Conclusions drawn from simple comparisons of rates of growth during periods which are not strictly comparable require careful interpretation. During the period 1933–39 the Union's economy expanded at a phenomenal rate, largely owing to the rise in the price of gold in terms of sterling and dollars, with a consequent improvement in the real value of South Africa's exports (including gold) in terms of imports. On the other hand, a complex set of factors helped to restrain the expansion in output during the period 1947–51. There can be no doubt, for example, that the insignificant increase or even decline during this period in the output of gold, wool, and hides and skins, which still account for about half the Union's export income, has been a vital factor in the declining rate of economic growth in the Union. This decline in export production reflects the diversion of labor and other resources to those activities, notably manufacturing, which have benefited most from the inflationary growth of money incomes and prices. At the same time the real value of South African exports in terms of imports has shown a steady tendency to decline, largely because of the diminishing quantity of goods obtained for each ounce of gold.[9]

Whatever the precise explanation, the signs of strain in the Union's economy are evident in significant aspects of its economic life. Though the value of farming production is now more than three times as great as in 1938–39, the output of agricul-

9. In 1949 a unit of exports (including gold) bought only 85 per cent of the imports it bought before the war. To some extent this position was adjusted by the devaluation of currencies in September, 1949, and by the sharp rise in commodity prices until the early part of 1951 (see Economic Co-operation Administration [Special Mission to the United Kingdom], *The Sterling Area* [London, 1951], pp. 247 ff.).

tural and pastoral products is little more than one-third higher than before the war. The failure of farming output to respond to rising incomes and prices has produced a precarious balance between existing supplies and inflated money demands. As a result, there have been repeated shortages of wheat, dairy produce, and other products during the postwar years. The incapacity of such key industries as transportation, power, and coal to cope with growing demands has undermined the efficient operation of the economy. In mining, the strain is apparent in the steady rise in gold-mining costs, which is fundamentally due to the fairly rigid racial composition of its working force. This has weakened the industry's ability to retain its complement of workers in competition with the manufacturing and tertiary activities. Today, the mining industry has to draw more than 60 per cent of its workers from outside the Union's borders.

The inability of the Union's major branches of activity to expand output sufficiently has severely strained the economy's capacity to provide housing, food, education, and other amenities of a rapidly growing urban population. Its flagging ability to undertake these economic tasks is evident in the rapid growth of money incomes and prices unaccompanied by a commensurate expansion in output. Since the outbreak of war, aggregate money incomes have expanded rapidly; but the real value of production has only grown at about half the rate. The result has been unsatisfied demands, economic waste of resources, and social distress, which has been accentuated by the prevailing distribution of incomes.

### WHAT OF THE FUTURE?

In less than three-quarters of a century the white inhabitants of the Union have fashioned with the co-operant efforts of the African and Colored peoples the most modern economy in Africa south of the Sahara. In the process, average incomes of the white group have risen to levels found in advanced economies, while the living standards of the nonwhite groups drawn into the orbit of the modern exchange economy are much above the standards of those still engaged in subsistence production. The drive behind these immense economic advances has come from the economically and culturally more highly developed white inhabitants of the country.

The problem of the future is to hasten the pace of development and to bring about an all-round improvement in living standards, while reducing gross disparities in wealth and income. Without a substantial increase in the volume of production, it will be difficult to raise significantly the consumption standards of the mass of the population. This will require an economy in which full opportunities exist for developing the skills and capacities of its members. Failure to develop new social and economic structures to replace the disintegrating tribal societies will leave the indigenous people uprooted and incapable of integrating themselves into meaningful social and economic relations in the new industrial society. The social and political dangers of precipitating men and women into unfamiliar economic societies in which they are not fully received have become increasingly obvious. This is not a task which can be accomplished by the wave of a magic wand. It requires patient experimentation with new forms of economic and social organization and the creation of devices for smoothing the transition of those ill adapted to cope with economic change.

Throughout the Union's modern history the need to make those fundamental changes required by an expanding economy has been obscured by a series of economic windfalls in the past. Today, there is again the danger that the immense increase in incomes in prospect from the new gold-mining developments in the Orange Free State, the Far West Rand, and the Klerksdorp areas, as well as the exploitation of the Union's uranium resources, will once more reduce the urgency of these adjustments. Yet, these very developments are demonstrating in a vivid fashion the economy's increasing inability to cope with its growing economic tasks. Indeed, the present acute shortage of labor in gold-mining at current wage rates is not merely curtailing the lives of many of the existing gold producers but slowing down the rate of development in the new gold fields. Thus, the beneficial flow of additional gold and uranium exports, on which such great store is being placed to buoy up the economy in the immediate future, is likely to be delayed.

The white community is evidently facing a choice of alternative policies: the progressive relaxation of restrictions inhibiting the growth of labor productivity or the perpetuation of existing legal and institutional barriers to development, with their depressing effects on consumption standards as well as on the relationship between the different racial groups. It will not be an easy decision for the whites to forego their monopolistic position in the South African society and to expose themselves to the continuous effort and the incessant vigilance necessary in the interests of efficiency and social justice.

The white inhabitants are in this respect not very different from people everywhere who attempt to maintain their income standards through restrictive practices. They are, besides, filled with apprehensions and doubts, a product partly of their frontier history and partly of their human frailty. However ill founded, their fears are facts of deep psychological and historical importance. The white man is uneasy as he observes the Africans' educational progress, their rise in economic and social standards, their attempt to strengthen their bargaining position, and the growth of African nationalism. He fears the growth of native political rights and the possibility that some day numbers will predominate in the government of South Africa. Chiefly, he fears that present development will ultimately lead to social mixtures, to race mixtures, to the destruction of "white South Africa."

Fear has a cramping influence on men's minds. Yet, economic experience is a hard taskmaster, and its lessons cannot be easily ignored. Continued resistance to full co-operation with the African and Colored people will inevitably lower the Western standards of life achieved in the Union: the African population, after all, constitutes a most important part of the resources on the utilization of which depends the economic prosperity of the whole society. If through the application of restrictions economic growth is brought to a halt, nonwhite competition will almost certainly grow progressively keener, and restrictions will become at the same time more necessary and more difficult to impose.

A surer basis for dealing with the Union's complex social and economic problems is through a policy of expansion. If economic development can be pushed on more rapidly, the demand for white, African, and Colored labor will increase, and the field of competition will be narrowed. It is, in any case, in an advancing and expanding phase of industrial activity that those qualities which distinguish the white inhabitants will be in greatest demand. Thus a policy of justice and wisdom can be made to coincide with economic interest.

*PART III*

CONCLUSIONS

# SOME CONTEMPORARY DEVELOPMENTS IN SUB-SAHARAN AFRICA[1]

MELVILLE J. HERSKOVITS

*Northwestern University*

## I

THE subcontinent of Africa south of the Sahara, when considered as a unit, shows certain widespread patterns of response to situations which derive from the play of similar historical and psychological forces. To recognize these patterns is not, of course, in any way to deny either the reality or the importance of the regional and local differences which mark off geographical provinces, culture areas, and political entities from one another. These differences have very properly come to provide points of focus for the attention of research scholars and men of practical affairs.

For reasons we need not elaborate here, there has developed a reluctance to speak and think of Africa as a whole, until today the danger exists that, in overstressing this, we may fail to recognize the existence, to say nothing of the significance, of the unities on which such differences impinge. We need not be misled by the many works which, though dealing with restricted parts of the continent, employ the word "Africa" in their titles, or the all-too-prevalent tendency to stereotype the entire sub-Saharan continent in terms of a particular part of it. The broad view and the more restricted approach has each its place. It is not a question of the cameo versus the mural. We derive only profit when we project detailed information against over-all patterns and assess widespread similarities in the light of the different forms they take in different situations.

1. The field investigation on which this paper is based was conducted during the period December, 1952—September, 1953, under grants from the United States Educational Commission in Great Britain (Fulbright Fund), the Graduate School and Program of African Studies of Northwestern University, the Penrose Fund of the American Philosophical Society, the Social Science Research Council, and Special Aid Funds, Inc., to all of which grateful acknowledgment is given.

As a point of departure, we may hence first of all ask what the historical and psychological forces are which must be kept in mind as we consider certain manifestations of the dynamics of the African scene.

On the historical level the fact that in all the area of Africa with which we are concerned the African, despite his enormous preponderance in numbers, is rarely a free agent is basic. This is perhaps what is meant when, in most discussions of sub-Saharan Africa, it is pointed out that this is a colonial area, where all sources of power lodge outside the region where it is exercised. Though this is akin to the point just made, it is not the same. For to the conventional statement the reservation is at once expressed that Liberia and the Union of South Africa—and Ethiopia, when it is included in the area under discussion, as it is not here—are self-governing and are therefore exceptions. In terms of our formulation, however, this political distinction has no relevance. For the African in the Union in no way determines his own destiny, and even in Liberia it is only recently that President Tubman's policy of "unification" has begun to bring members of the tribal majority, the peoples of the interior, into the government.

Conquest, then, is the historic fact that has dominated the last half to three-quarters of a century of recent African experience. It is the force in the psychology of all those who are involved in its present-day working-out, setting up drives which shape the thought and mold the behavior of the inhabitants of Africa, whoever they may be and wherever they live. Professor Frankel has put the proposition in this way: "If I were asked what have been the two poles about which the human forces in Africa have played with the greatest tension, I would say land and status; both for African and non-African these and little else have in the past spelled the security which they sought and still seek."[2]

Yet in these terms we must recognize that the complex problems of the allocation and use of land are the direct result of the dislocations and readjustments that have flowed from the so-

2. S. H. Frankel, *Economic Impact on Underdeveloped Societies* (Oxford, 1953), p. 169.

cial, economic, political, and religious impulses set in motion when Africa came under foreign control and the rules that governed the lives of indigenous peoples began to be made by outsiders. Nor is it only indigenous peoples whose responses have been involved. It is widely recognized that one of the great political realities in the Union of South Africa today is the Boer War; certainly the present tensions between English- and Afrikaans-speaking South Africans cannot be comprehended without taking this historic fact into full account.

The question of status is of a similar order. It is another manifestation of the working-out of the same historical principle, its essential expression psychological, as shown in the attitudes and characteristic reactions of all those who participate in the African scene—European, African, or Asian, ruler or ruled. It is too often forgotten that living in any society where differences in status are continuously in the foreground of experience, in every sphere of life, symbolic as well as tangible, leaves its mark on all those who are a part of it. The European official who confesses, "Try as I may, I cannot overcome the distaste I feel when an African comes into my office wearing shoes and speaking my language properly," is exhibiting one kind of response to living in this situation. His reaction differs only in form from that of the trained African teacher who, commenting on salary differentials, says, "And, in spite of this, I am reproached for not maintaining the standard of living set by my European colleagues, which I am constantly told is expected of me."

Out of these broad historical and psychological patterns come the nationalist movements, the separatist churches, and all those other types of reaction to the frustrations which so many Africans feel when they assess their present position. And it is these same factors that are at the base of the soul-searching, the aggressions, the endless debates among Europeans as to ways and means of resolving situations that are as frustrating for the privileged minority as for the underprivileged majority.

No approach to the African scene is realistic unless it takes all those concerned into account. The great bulk of African population, by its very size, exerts much more influence on the course of events than is ordinarily recognized. One need only talk with those who are charged with implementing policy to realize this fact—to those who direct relocation or community development or housing schemes, determine educational policy, or institute new agricultural or grazing practices. The European settler, industrialist, and trader, no less than the Asian in South and East Africa, are likewise imponderables in the scene. The wisest statesmanship in Africa has discovered that the success of unilateral action can by no means be taken for granted, whether it be a decree to control fishing by Africans or to revise the constitution of a Central African dependency.

When we turn to some of the developments that are responses to the play of the dynamic forces in African life, we may name four that are far-reaching in their implications for the future. The first is the drive on the part of the African for European education. The second, which follows on the attainment in significant measure of the first, is the re-examination and selective re-establishment by the African of the values in his indigenous social institutions and modes of cultural behavior. The third is the problem posed by the European or Asian settler in African territories. Finally, we must consider a development that lies on the ideological level and hence assumes peculiar importance as a cultural rationale for racism.

## II

"If we establish a technical school with a capacity for two hundred students," said a high official of the Belgian Congo, "five hundred candidates present themselves on the opening day." He was speaking in the idiom of European Africa, since the term "technical school" is applied to what elsewhere is called a "trade school," where pupils are trained to become masons, carpenters, shoemakers, tailors, mechanics, and other craftsmen. But the significance of his comment is the reflection in it of the pressure from Africans, everywhere, on administrations to permit them to have access to the resources of the peoples who, through their superior technology, were able to conquer them in the first instance and, living among them in maintaining their rule, opened vistas of standards of living, of health, and of other material benefits available only to those who have the educational key that will unlock the door to this treasure-trove.

The widest manifestation of this drive is the demand for literacy. In the psychology of the African it has been the ability to read and write that has given the European his controls over man and nature. It is this, therefore, that he seeks for himself and, above all, for his children, so that they will have more adequate control of this power and, to an extent not vouchsafed him, will be enabled to apply it in solving their own problems. A letter from an African teacher in Nigeria shows how, on the local scene, this desire for literacy dominates the thinking of the villagers who live near the boarding school in which he teaches:

> I am giving my spare time in helping in the Adult classes in the village. Our big disease is the wrong conception of "education" which to our people is the ability only to read and write. People in this area as in most of Africa are underfed, diseased (hook-worms), [live under] unsanitary conditions, etc. We have organized a small team of students . . . to help in showing the villagers to dig cess-pits so that they can stop going to the bushes, to stop erosion by planting trees and grasses, and [give] simple hygiene lessons . . . ; but strangely enough their one big desire is to read and write.

This drive for literacy is shown in the official statistics, which tell their tale of a steady increase in number of schools, number of teachers, number of pupils, or the amount of funds allocated to education from year to year. We take at random the figures for primary-school pupils in various parts of sub-Saharan Africa. In Nigeria these increased in number from 933,333 in 1949 to 970,768 in 1953; in the Belgian Congo from 913,100 in 1946 to 962,812 in 1950; in French West Africa from 105,607 in 1947 to 170,378 in 1951; in Northern Rhodesia, on a longer-term basis, from 30,023 in 1937 and 93,505 in 1943 to 146,909 in 1951. In addition, we have also witnessed a steady increase in secondary education and, beyond this, the continuing force of the same impulse creating a demand for study on the more advanced levels. This has resulted in the establishment of the various university colleges in British West and East Africa, the Institute of Higher Studies at Dakar, the proposed Lovanium center near Leopoldville, and the projected Rhodesian University at Salisbury, in addition to motivating African student migration, in substantial numbers, to universities in England,

France, the United States, and now Germany, Italy, and Middle Eastern European countries.

The statistics, however, and the institutionalized representations of this drive that can be named as its tangible results, afford those who seek to understand the patterns of present-day life only a framework for the realities of attitude, behavior, and achievement. These realities one senses as one attends the graduation ceremony of a remote Mass Education center in the Northern Territories of the Gold Coast, visits classroom exercises in a modern *lycée* in Brazzaville, watches a primary class being drilled in simple sums at a thatched single-room school in a village deep in the swamps of the Upper Congo, or sees boys and girls on a Rhodesian native reserve learning their letters by tracing them with their forefingers in the dust of the school compound.

One comes even closer to this reality when a worn taxi-driver in Southern Rhodesia, summoned to meet an early plane, confesses that he has worked until three o'clock that morning; that his long hours are of his own choosing, because he is paying for the schooling of two younger brothers, one at Fort Hare, the other at Adams College, both in the Union of South Africa. There is pride in his voice as he tells of the good record both are making and as he expresses his hope that the elder, when he has finished work for his B.A. degree, may go to England or the United States for further study and then return to be a teacher. "It's what we need more than anything else." Nor can we fail to be struck by the power that this drive for literacy, all unwittingly, places in the hands of those who can provide it, as when an executive of a missionary society states that one way of enforcing Christian discipline is to withdraw the teacher from the school of a village where drums have been played and African dances danced.

The very intensity of the feelings of Africans about what literacy can do for them, however, has implications that must be explored with care. Literacy, at first blush, is regarded as the means for the satisfaction of all hopes and aspirations; and the discovery that this is but the first step in a long process can open the way to disillusionment and bitterness. Experience corrects this misconception; but more serious, because it is more fundamental in terms of our knowledge of cultural processes, has been the tendency to regard "education" as something peculiar to the literate societies, which they alone possess and which they alone can therefore make available to those of other ways of life. Historically, the earliest educators in Africa took for granted that to educate Africans meant just this. An educational philosophy which held that there might be values in African social life and customs on which a curriculum for Africans could be built did not exist in the intellectual currents of their day. Yet Africans, for all the centuries that their societies have existed, have educated their children, training them in indigenous patterns of morals as well as in the techniques of getting a living, in proper modes of conduct in interpersonal relations, in the creative expression of their culture—graphic arts, dance, oral verse and narrative—and in maintaining an equable balance with the rest of the universe.

What the European brought, and has in larger measure continued to bring, to the African was schooling, which is but a portion of the total process of social and cultural learning that comprehends the education of the individual. The schooling they brought was European schooling, drawn from the background of the metropole, something which accorded with the prior experiences of the European child but which, transplanted *in toto* to Africa, constituted for the African child a most serious discontinuity between the school and the rest of his environment. In this situation, unlike that of the school whose curriculum derives from the cultural setting in which it is found, teaching could take nothing in the way of experience or sanction for granted; or, more frequently, it took these for granted to the bewilderment of the learner—a bewilderment that often went unexpressed because of the play of African patterns of polite behavior.

The result has tended to be stress on form and memory. It is not so long ago that the French textbook in which African children learned that "the palm tree is a plant which does not grow in our climate" was replaced by one which, to the African child, is somewhat more realistic. It is relatively recently that the re-

[[ 273 ]]

peated charge made by Africans trained in the schools of British territories that at the end of their secondary schooling they knew the geography of Britain far better than that of their own country brought about changes in the school curriculums. Everywhere in sub-Saharan Africa, even in bush schools, one finds insistence on African pupils conforming to the schedule of the metropole, regardless of relevance to the African scene. The word, early and late, was that the African child required discipline; but that the African child, like any other, had the discipline of his culture, which might be built on in giving meaning to what in too many cases became rote learning and meaningless memorization, was not taken into account.

This wholesale transplanting of educational systems has reached into the highest levels of African training. The curriculums of the African institutions of higher learning, the contents of the subjects taught, and the examinations based on them are, without significant exception, those of the universities of the metropole. It is understandable that the curriculums of schools of medicine or engineering necessitate little recognition of the fact of cultural variation; a bridge to be built, a patient to be cured, represent problems that, under the rubric of scientific method, are similarly approached wherever they may be. But in the humanistic disciplines or the social sciences—the latter the most cognizant of the factor of cultural differentials—African values and institutions would seem to have considerable relevance for the teaching of Africans. Nonetheless, one finds professors of philosophy continuing to teach Plato, Aristotle, Nietzsche, and Bergson to the exclusion, even by so much as formal recognition, of the philosophical systems that function to regulate life and thought just off the campus or, more than they know, on it, insofar as their students are concerned. One finds professors of comparative literature who, in teaching the European classics, remain oblivious to the values in the oral narrative and verse forms of the societies to which the very men and women to whom they lecture belong. ·

One hears, again and again, that what the African gets from his schooling is the form but not the meaning of what he is taught; that his objective is the passing of the examination, the winning of the degree, not the pursuit of knowledge. That this charge is by no means justified need scarcely be noted. The manner in which Africans, wherever opportunity offers, and to the degree they are permitted, function effectively in the phases of African life most responsive to European influence demonstrates its untruth. It is, indeed, a tribute to the determination of the Africans to whom European education has been made available that this is so, in view of the psychological and educational handicaps imposed on them as the result of their having been compelled from earliest school years to adjust to acquiring a type of knowledge and modes of behavior that, because they have no meaning in terms of the real life of the student, require such application to penetrate and master.

This fact of the relevance of schooling to the life of the pupil, then, presents the basic problem to be faced in meeting the demand of the African for schooling; nor are signs lacking that educators, African and European alike, are increasingly becoming sensitive to it. "We need education," as the Asantehene, the ruler of the Ashanti, put it, "but we must have education that will not give disrespect to the Ashanti way of life." The recognition and the changes in curriculum and method of teaching that will result will undoubtedly bring in turn a more satisfactory resolution of the difficulties faced everywhere by educational administrators in furnishing the facilities and, above all, the teachers so desperately needed to supply the ever increasing pressure of African demand for more schools, better training, and longer schooling.

Even the question of the use of the "vernacular," the somewhat invidious term employed for the unwritten languages of Africa, may in this spirit be solved—whether it be the nationalistic clamor in some parts for more teaching in the language of the people or, on the contrary, the protests heard from Africans in such regions as the Union of South Africa that the enforced teaching in the native language for the first years of schooling handicaps them in the use of English. Or it may bring about a realization of the arbitrary nature of the ruling, as in Portuguese African territory, that prohibits teaching in any school, at any grade, of any subject except the catechism in any tongue but that of the metropole; and interposing for Africans three years of "rudimentary" education before the elementary stage, which makes it all but impossible to attain the educational qualification for admission to the secondary school, the *liceu*, until after the age limit for admission has been passed.

The African, in his desire for literacy and for schooling, has discerningly followed the leads of his recent history. The danger is that the presence of ethnocentric rigidity in the European administration of educational programs may make for a reaction to schooling that can have serious repercussions for all concerned in the African scene, Africans no less than others. Discussions like the one in *The Cockerel*, the student magazine of the University College of the Gold Coast, debating the relative value of Twi and English as languages, have little point, since all languages are valid instruments of communication. Yet, in indicating that each language has its qualities, the author quite correctly goes on to say, "It is clear that no one has the right to expect English to do the work which Twi does," adding that "no living language has yet been found which lacks the means of expressing new ideas which the speech community has acquired." Arguing that translation into Twi of works of all kinds thus presents no difficulty, he continues: "People talk of raising educational standards as if it was a matter of pressing a button. How can you raise educational standards if you have first to teach your pupils for ten years the language with which you are going to educate them, and that poorly? You really get nothing done accurately until the upper forms of secondary schools or in the University where all the work is concentrated. The English name for this is cramming, not education." And, observing that "English is . . . not part of our life, it is external to it," he ends his article with the assertion: "No society can depend on a language the making of which it has no hand in. It is the vernaculars which have any real hope, not English."

This passage is cited not because it solves the most difficult problem of which it treats but because of the attitude it reveals. And this attitude, intimately connected with the question of schooling, as it clearly shows, is at the heart of the question raised by the second development to be treated here, to which we now turn.

## III

The pattern of African reaction to European culture seems, on broad lines, to be reasonably well established. It appears to fall into three well-defined stages, marking a path which, in its full length, has been followed as yet only in a few parts of the continent.

In the first stage, after peaceful assumption of control, or the imposition of rule by force, the European is accepted as a remote being, endowed with superior power, and therefore to be heard with respect and emulated insofar as comprehension of his strange ways and ability to tap his awesome resources permit. Where he is accepted with reservations, these are well concealed, because of fear of the powers of all kinds he controls. This is the day of the isolated district officer, the remote mission station. The strangers are councilors, judges, and, where friendship can cross the deep gulf of status, friends; it is they who can deal with the forces of the new world that has come to the African—forces against which he is powerless.

With continued contact, cracks in the armor begin to appear. Europeans become more familiar; they are found to have the frailties of other human beings. They war with each other; where they come to preach a new belief, their doctrines are not always in harmony, and they contest for the allegiances of the Africans living near them. More is learned about the machines that aid them in conquering time and distance; Africans as well as Europeans can operate and repair them. The knowledge of how to read and write is acquired, and Africans experience at first hand this outside world and learn that what has happened to them is not unique. Questions arise as to their present position and their hopes for the future. They begin to see that the values of their own cultures, often denigrated by themselves in the first flush of their acquisition of the cultures of Europe, are not of the inferior quality they had come to believe they were.

At this point the path bifurcates. Here reaction to the teachings, the things, that have come from the outside can take the line of appraisal and selection, as is clearly occurring in the Gold Coast, in Nigeria, in French West Africa, and elsewhere. Or continued frustration can lead to rejection and the preachment of return to the traditional ways, with the demand for the ejection of the European, the carrier of this way of life now held undesirable, by violence if need be, as in Kenya.

It may be well asked, "What of the third possibility, in which the African wholly accepts European culture—civilization, as it is called by those who envisage this—gradually becoming the equal of the European and ultimately raising himself, as the terminology goes, to the same social, moral, economic, and technological level?" This is an alternative that must be considered, for many in Africa hold the inevitability of its achievement an article of faith, and it is a stated objective of official policy in Belgian and Portuguese Africa and, to a substantial degree, in French Africa as well.

To this, as to the question whether the aims of the Africans who would return to the old way of life can be realized, the answer is the same. Culture, being learnable, not only can be learned by any people who have access to the knowledge, the techniques, of any other people but in some measure always is learned; so that peoples never come into contact without experiencing some alteration in their ways of life. Every people, that is, has its culture, and there are thus no fresh cultural slates on which a foreign way of life can be newly inscribed. What is taken over is projected against pre-existing patterns, and the result is never identical with the model. By the same token, cultures are never exported in their totality. Hence it is as much, but no more, fantasy on the part of Africans to believe that they can recapture the ways of life that existed before European contact as it is for Europeans to anticipate that Africans will become identical in their thoughts and acts with those who would act as their model.

In essence, this means that African culture change will be selective and that the variation in result, represented in the greater or lesser numbers of European elements in an African setting, will reflect the historic situation in which the African cultures of the future will individually develop. Here the experience of the African and his descendants in the New World throws significant light on what can be anticipated in Africa itself. For in the Americas and in the Caribbean, where these peoples have been in contact with Europeans and their cultures far longer than has occurred in any but the smallest fraction of their ancestral continent, we find that elements of the earlier African cultures have persisted, in instances to an unsuspected degree of purity, but more frequently in changed but analyzable form. This at once clarifies the issue. For how, in their own home, can the cultures of Africa be expected to undergo more far-reaching change than could be achieved through the attack on these cultures that occurred during the regime of New World slavery?

It so happens that most of the reports of changing Africa are the work of non-Africans or, where they are made by Africans, are in most instances by those fascinated by the machine cultures of Europe and America and the possibility for changed standards of living these offer. Such accounts, in the nature of the case, tend to stress change, which in these terms means the substitution of European for African ways. In addition to this, the fact must not be forgotten that change in the behavior of a people is not only easier to discern and assess than stability but, in the prevailing climate of interest, becomes the obvious aspects of any situation under consideration. All this goes to explain why the dynamics of changing Africa are so rarely presented in balance and why the present scene is so seldom considered in its totality. With retention of the old considered as unimportant, a rounded account becomes impossible.

Yet, when we turn to the cultures of Africa with the object of discerning totality, we find that, in the life of a people as actually lived, the old may assume great functional as well as symbolic importance. Thus, for example, over the leading story in the *Accra Daily Graphic* for October 12, 1953, is the headline: CEREMONY ENDS GA DISPUTE. The appended photograph is that of Kwame Nkrumah, the prime minister, in European clothes, shaded by an umbrella of state, surrounded by chiefs and people in African dress, reading from a manuscript into a microphone. From the text we learn that a four-year-old dispute between two important chiefs of the capital city had been settled by a commission appointed by the prime minister. On this occasion he had presented a bullock, which was slaughtered to mark the reconciliation, at the ancient place of sacrifice, as is required by customary law, and the proper officials had dipped their staves of office in the blood as a symbol of unity in the Ga state. The prime minister also gave the bottles of gin from which the essential libations were poured; after one of the disputants had paid homage to the Ga Manche, the head of the state, his opponent, a vote of thanks was moved on behalf of the divisional chiefs, who reaffirmed their allegiance to their leader.

No European was concerned in this ceremony, which illustrates the statement made before that the selective process in cultural change, as evidenced in a recognition of the values in both old and new ways, has gone farthest in the Gold Coast. It takes no special insight to discern how both African and European elements meet in this event, so important in the political life of the capital of the country. The microphone, the dress of the prime minister, the vote of thanks—these are clearly European; the offering of the bullock, the dipping of the staves in its blood, the libations, the state umbrella as a symbol of rank, and the formal reaffirmation of allegiance are as clearly African. One might stress the former aspects, as one might the latter; to do either would be to throw the resulting account out of focus.

In actuality this kind of situation can be found almost anywhere in Africa, even where for the most part the earlier stages of reaction to contact with European culture still prevail. Thus, for example, in northern Tanganyika, where people such as the Masai are scarcely touched in their mode of life by cultural contact, one may witness among the Arusha, culturally similar to them, a traditional dance honoring a literate chief, dressed in European clothing, who has his office in the substantial near-by building and has been elected by a democratic vote of the people. The VaMwila, a cattle-keeping people in southern Angola, originally nonpecuniary, who have manifested little interest in the aspects of European culture urged on them by missionaries and administrators, have fully accepted the value of Portuguese money and show no reluctance at all to pose for photographers when they realize that they will profit from this.

# SOME DEVELOPMENTS IN SUB-SAHARAN AFRICA

Once we understand the fact that change in Africa is selective and take account that culture has many facets, no two of which change at the same rate; that some aspects may not change at all, while others may be completely altered, instances of all these come to hand. A native ruler in Central Africa complains that his people have lost their old customs; that nothing is as it was. Yet a simple question as to whether the old family structure and the clan have disappeared at first startles him and then restores the balance. Yes, he agrees, these have remained, and diet, and much of clothing, and the value of the cattle, and many more things. What he meant is that he no longer gets the revenue he did or has as much free labor, that some of the court rituals are no longer possible, that new crops are being grown, and that money is being used.

In almost any urban center one finds that town living, work for wages, and the steady application to labor required by industrialization has by no means erased the allegiances of the Africans to their villages and to many of the patterns of their nonindustrial society. Thus, for example, in Leopoldville one hears the doctor in charge of a maternity clinic tell of the difficulty of computing vital statistics, since many pregnant women return to their villages before parturition and may lose their infants there and never return to the clinic; or of how a woman who brings her sick child to him will take it away if medical care does not yield prompt results, so that a native practitioner can treat it. Or he may tell how an assistant, trained in nursing, in need of an operation would not consent to its being performed until she obtained permission from her maternal uncle, living in a distant village; and, this being refused, she would not permit it. Another instance of this selective adjustment to urban living may be taken from Johannesburg, where old family forms cannot function as on the reserves, and realignments have been necessitated. In one case, when an elderly man died there, and his oldest son could not come to officiate at the funeral, as Zulu custom demands, all the clansmen of the dead man gathered to perform the modified type of traditional ritual of death now becoming customary in South African cities.

That it is essential to probe deeply the nature of the changes in African culture now taking place, especially as concerns the fact that the selectivity of these changes is the result of a positive affirmation of values in traditional ways, need not again be underscored. The political or educational officer who complains of "atavism" when a clerk or teacher asks leave to attend the rites for his ancestors or the European headmaster in the mission school who is hurt by the fact that students, conscientiously taught, turn to native, unsanctioned music and dance for recreation—to cite only two examples out of the endless number anyone familiar with the African scene can recall—is reacting unrealistically to the situation of which he is a part. In doing this, he is helping to create a climate of emotional tension, the consequences of which can be disastrous for adjustment, individual or social. As the European values his own culture, so the African; and he weighs what in his contact with Europe he finds good. It is not without significance that, as one moves about the continent, one finds the greatest relaxation, the best co-operation between races, where this fundamental fact in modern African life is best understood.

## IV

We now turn to the next development we shall consider, the problem of the white settler class or, as it may be termed, of a population of European Africans. It is linked to the fourth topic we shall take up, standing somewhat in the same relationship to it as we saw the development of schooling to stand with regard to the changing attitudes of Africans to their own body of custom. The final two, however, differ from the others in one respect; they exhibit greater variation, in some instances being entirely absent from large areas of sub-Saharan Africa.

On the sound principle of scientific method that it is profitable to give attention to those instances where a phenomenon does not exist, it will be worth while to turn briefly to British West Africa, where the settler problem is not present. Comparing the territories here with other parts of the continent, we see that certain aspects of the total situation emerge as unique to them. Thus, in British West Africa there are no native reserves in the country or locations in the urban centers, while such large-scale operations as mining or mechanized agricultural projects hold their land on leases which bring rent and sometimes royalties to the African owners. There is no official color bar or what Lord Hailey has aptly called the "culture bar"; services such as those of transport, hotel accommodations, and restaurants are available to any who can pay their cost. The Africanization of government services, of the managerial ranks of trading companies, and of the staffs of educational institutions is a matter of policy and is in process everywhere. The problem of race relations is by African standards minimal, this fact deriving from economic as well as political causes. The ideal of equal pay and perquisites for those who do the same work is much further toward realization than elsewhere, especially in government or in institutions of higher learning. Furthermore, on the level of personal relations, especially in professional circles, a give and take between members of the two groups on the basis of individual preference is possible to a degree found nowhere else on the continent.

The uniqueness of their position does not escape those West Africans who compare it to situations found elsewhere. An article in the *Lagos Daily Times* early in April, 1953, entitled "The Mosquito in Politics," written by an African member of the faculty of University College, Ibadan, begins: "Let us imagine for a moment that in the process of biological evolution nature omitted to put in that tiny little item, the mosquito. . . . What sort of Nigeria would you and I be living in today?" After answering his question, and considering what the situation in other parts of Nigeria would be, he makes the point that the mosquito, the carrier of malaria, fatal to Europeans but not to Africans, has been the prime cause of the absence of European settlement. "While Negroes in mosquito-free parts of Africa are deprived of the elementary right of voting, we, over here, hold ministerial portfolios." The article ends with this encomium: "Let us give thanks therefore to that little insect, the mosquito, which has saved the land of our fathers for us. We cannot ring its praises too often. The least we can do now is to engrave its picture on our National Flag."

We recognize, of course, that no simplistic approach to the

complexities of a changing social situation, such as presents itself everywhere in Africa, yields more than a partial explanation. In the present case the article is essentially valuable as an analysis of attitude, since it leaves out numerous other causes which have resulted in the present ordering of affairs, to say nothing of the fact that medical discoveries of the past decade have quite removed most of the fears Europeans may have earlier held of the carrier of malaria. Nonetheless, the fact remains that, where one variable in contrasting social configurations remains as constant as does the factor of European settlement in the African scene, it must be regarded as a contributing cause of some magnitude in making for the observed differences. This, in essence, is the reason why it must be placed in the first rank of those developments in Africa which merit consideration.

Thus, in terms of tensions between racial groupings, it is obvious that these have mounted highest in the Union of South Africa, where permanent settlement of Europeans has the longest history and where Europeans are more numerous than anywhere else. Other areas of tension—the Ivory Coast, the "White Highlands" of East Africa, British Central Africa—are similarly, but to a lesser degree, ones where permanent settlement by Europeans is an accomplished fact. Uganda offers a test of our proposition worth considering, for it is the informed consensus that the tensions between Africans and Europeans in Uganda are much less strong than in the neighboring territories of East Africa. We find that, in 1948, of a population of 4,958,520, Europeans numbered but 3,448. But we also find that there were 33,767 Indians, 1,448 Goans, and 1,475 Arabs; and one is not long in Uganda before he finds that racial tensions, arising from attitudes of Africans toward Asians, do exist. This would seem to indicate that the fact of the presence of permanent foreign residents in positions of power, political or economic, is the significant element and not the fact of European settlement per se. Nothing is more certain, however, than that the uneasiness of the African inhabitants of Uganda at the possibility of an East African Union arises out of their fears that they will be then in a situation where both political and economic power will lodge in the hands of the same minority group of permanent residents who have come from outside the continent.

Granting, then, that permanent settlement of Europeans in African territory creates special problems, it is worth considering the approaches toward this question taken by various governments and something of the manner in which they envisage the results of the positions they have assumed. The Belgian Congo, where colonization in the sense of permanent settlement is being urged, is a good case in point. One can quote the discourse of M. Maleingreau, president of the Federation of Colonists (Fédacol), at the opening session of the Commission du Colonat in Brussels, in June, 1953, as to the aims of colonization. His remarks, as reported in the *Essor du Congo* (June 6, 1953), were addressed to the Minister of Colonies of the government of Belgium:

> To base the conservation of the principles of our civilization and the respect for economic rights acquired by the Belgians on the expectation of recognition of them by primitive peoples is a psychological enormity. Gratitude is not a sentiment of the mass. On the other hand, if the black man is not affected by that which he does not perceive or which does not strike his imagination, he is extremely capable of liking what he does see and his attachment to the person who protects and guides him is proverbial. At the present time our duty is clearly outlined: to people the Congo with inhabitants of the white race so as to realise its potentialities and raise the level of its populations and, to preserve the peace inside the country, to place those who govern under the eyes of the blacks and in direct personal contact with them.

The point of view expressed here is not essentially different from what one can hear in British East and Central Africa or in Portuguese territory. In the latter case, it has been clearly enunciated by General Norton de Matos, a functionary of long service as governor-general of Angola, in his book, published in 1953, entitled *Africa nossa*, with the subtitle, "O que queremos e o que não queremos nas nossas terras de Africa" ("What we want and what we do not want in our African lands"). "We want," he says at the outset of his work, "to assimilate to us, completely, the black inhabitants of Angola, Mozambique, and Guinea; we wish to people, intensively and rapidly, these African provinces of Portugal with Portuguese families of the white race; we wish the nation to comprise a single people, composed of descendants of our race and the races we have assimilated to us; we wish a civilization which permits men of various races to live a full life, in peace and harmony, in the same region; we wish One Nation, the result of complete and perfect National Unity." On the other hand, "we do not want our African lands to be solely for the Africans; we do not want these lands only for Portuguese of the white race; we do not want separation by race or color in Portuguese lands, wherever they may be; we do not wish the least social, political, or administrative discrimination to exist among the Portuguese people."

It is instructive to follow General de Matos somewhat further in his argument. He tells how the policy of Portugal, from its first contact with peoples other than the Portuguese, has been in accordance with Christian morality, and how "from Christian equality we pass readily to economic equality" (p. 15). He continues: "In Africa, to convert the blacks, to lift them from the moral and material misery in which they are found, to teach them, to clothe them, to give them human dwellings, to make them rural proprietors or transform them into artisans having their own shops, this was what we had in mind." But, he adds, "we are not thinking of giving them political equality at once, to make them politically equal to us." This, General de Matos feels, is inadvisable, and he cites as his example the English, who, in East and West Africa, have "too rapidly passed from Christian equality to political equality." Portugal, he says (on p. 50), must move as rapidly as possible to develop its lands economically, peopling them with white families, teaching all in its own language, aiding all with social assistance of every sort. "But we must have the greatest care as concerns the rest, with mentality quite unknown to us, as in Kenya and elsewhere, care above all not to allow a press published in native languages, or fetichism and its rites."

The extent to which immigration of permanent settlers to various parts of the continent is taking place is not easy to determine. Returning to Portuguese policy, it is said that one aim is to settle 100,000 Portuguese annually in Angola. In 1952, 24 farming families, numbering 134 persons, arrived to initiate a settlement project at Cela, in the province of Benguela; and it was expected that 250 families would soon thereafter depart from the metropole for this colony, which, it was hoped, would have 1,500 inhabitants within the year—an estimate regarded by some officials as optimistic. One unusual point in this project is worthy of mention; under terms of the contracts made with the immigrants, they may not employ African labor because of its scarcity in the colony.

In the Belgian Congo the European population is rising by about 10,000 annually. On January 1, 1953, the Minister of Colonies gave the figure of about 80,000 whites; the census of a year earlier had enumerated 69,000 of them. How permanent this population is, it cannot be said; unlike in East and Central Africa, or in the Angola highlands, Europeans in the main work in the towns or in the mines, and only the minority live off the land, which, in the Congo, is mostly cultivated by Belgian companies which operate large plantations. As in French territory, the inflation of recent years has greatly increased the cost of bringing and maintaining white workers. A Leopoldville employer has estimated that to employ a European automobile mechanic costs the equivalent of about $1,000 a month. In large part, this is because, as one economist has put it, the system of employee benefits for Europeans is one of the most remarkable of its kind in the world. Employers are required to furnish European employees and their families free housing, furniture, and medical care in all its aspects, plus vacations of six months in Europe, with salary and travel expenses, once every three years. Most firms, in addition to these minimums, pay for the domestic servants of their European employees and provide daily transportation to and from work. Family allowances are made to those with children, and there are adequate pension, insurance, sickness, and disability plans.

The minimum salary per month for Belgians is 10,000 francs ($200); for Europeans recruited locally, 8,100 francs ($162). It should be noted that employers of African labor also furnish homes in the *centres extra-coutumières,* or native locations, or provide allowances in lieu of housing and other benefits. The absolute minimum wage for Africans, as set by law, is about 26 francs (53 cents) a day in Leopoldville, excluding allowances;

but shortage of labor causes most firms to offer more. Clerks, typists, and others in positions requiring special skill receive higher pay; the case of one such African drawing 7,000 francs ($140) a month, including allowances, may be noted.

The pattern of colonization in French territory is somewhat different from elsewhere. Here, again, though the person who comes from the metropole to make his residence and career is encountered, these are in the minority. The most striking divergence from Belgian, English, and South African practices, where the financial responsibility of Europeans proposing to emigrate is more carefully scrutinized before the necessary permits are issued, seems to lie in the fact that so much of French immigration derives in large measure from the lower economic levels of French society. In the cities one finds that shopgirls, taxi-drivers, clerks, and others in positions below those ordinarily held by whites elsewhere may as likely be Europeans as Africans, and in post offices, banks, and other establishments persons of both races will be seen working side by side. With the customary wage differentials, this makes for tensions that result from the competition for jobs.

A situation seems to be developing in this regard that may with time come to parallel the South African "poor white" problem of a decade ago—something that in the Union is being prevented from spreading by the measures just indicated. A similar situation, on a smaller scale, obtains in Mozambique and Angola, though here it is hoped that the interposition of the system of rudimentary education will provide an obstacle to Africans competing with whites; in the words of a Portuguese description of this new system, through it and special vocational courses, it is intended "to avoid the development of an urban proletariat, de-tribalized individuals not being abandoned, but led in the direction of assimilation in such a way as to avoid competition between Europeans and Africans."

This development in the African scene could be pursued much further with profit, since it is apparent that it constitutes one whose implications for the future are of the utmost significance. This is particularly true where, in British East, Central, and South Africa, and increasingly in Belgian, French, and Portuguese territories, appreciable numbers of European men and women, and, in the former, Asians, born in Africa, have come to regard it as their home. Studies of possible differences in their psychology and those of newly arrived or temporary residents —in motivation, attitude, and value systems—should throw much insight on the situation of which they are a part and materially aid in predicting the future course of events where they are concerned. As a permanent feature of the African scene, they must be taken into full account in any approaches to the contemporary problems of Africa, whether concerned with analysis as such or with the determination of policy.

## V

From the earliest days of contact with the African, Europeans have speculated on the reasons why his modes of life, no less than his physical type, differed from theirs. The tale is a long one; it will be enough for our purposes to note that these explanations have changed with the changing currents of thought of the times, so that now one, now another, reason came to prevail. During the first four decades of this century, cultural differences were most often explained in terms of differences in innate abilities, reflected in the physical characteristics of the types concerned.

This came to be called "racism," and in racist terms the African was held to have failed to achieve the standard of civilization of other races because his biological equipment did not permit him to do so. Various forms of this explanation were to be encountered; reference was made to differences in brain weight or complexity of convolution, or a thicker skull which knit at an earlier age than in persons of other races, or an inherent tendency to rapid development in infancy and in early childhood, followed by failure to continue this progress into adulthood. Long before the Nazi debacle, with the consequent discredit cast on the racist hypothesis that provided one of the important elements of its ideological base, human biologists and anthropologists had destroyed each theory by patient investigation. The downfall of its principal proponents now impressed the validity of the scientific findings on a large segment of public opinion.

# AFRICA IN THE MODERN WORLD

One of the most striking current developments in Africa has been the change in the explanations as to why the African, pressing for educational, economic, and political opportunities, cannot be given what he asks. For, relatively speaking, one rarely encounters a racist explanation of this or seldom hears the expression of an opinion that the African is a second-class human being, incapable, by the very nature of his endowment, of scaling the heights of civilization the European achieved long ago. Not only are the abilities of the African admitted but, more often than would be expected, their recognition is urged. The argument now lies on the level of learned, that is, culturally and historically acquired aptitudes, rather than biologically determined innate abilities and has thus shifted from a racial to a cultural basis. Because it rests on intellectual foundations that scientifically are no more valid than were the reasons based on innate differences—whatever the social, political, and economic considerations involved in the solution of the difficult problems of adjustment in Africa today—it must be thought of as the cultural equivalent of the earlier doctrine of racism. The African, that is, is held to act like a child because his cultures have lagged behind the civilizations of Europe, not because he is destined by his nature to remain one.

This is, of course, not always clearly expressed, for earlier habits of racist thinking do not slough off easily. Yet a letter entitled "Responsibilities in Africa," which appeared in the *East African Standard* of Nairobi on August 13, 1953, will show the prevalent point of view well enough. "The human race is a family of nations," the writer states after discussing the responsibilities of parents and children within a family; "some mature in political and social affairs while others are just emerging from the nursery of elementary human experience." He points out that, "whatever may be the opinion of certain aspects of western civilization, it has at least the background and heritage of some centuries of struggle, endeavour and achievement that gives it the right to claim a position of leadership." The indigenous peoples of East Africa, prior to about 1890, had not appreciably "advanced along the long road of civilized development"; and this prompts the question, "Are we wrong in regarding Africans as among the youngest members of the human family, and therefore not yet morally or intellectually equipped to share fully in the complicated mode of living that the west has suddenly introduced into their midst?"

It is not necessary here to follow the development of this argument further, since these excerpts adequately interpret the position of the writer, the very figure of the African as the child in the family of nations making the point. Nor need other instances be cited; they are abundant. One finds a protest in a Belgian Congo newspaper against certain acts of the Trusteeship Council of the United Nations couched in terms of the argument that tutelage implies control and direction of a culturally younger people by one more experienced. The same philosophy pervades a definition of "partnership" proposed for the new Federal party in the Rhodesian Federation: "The realization that the European is the senior and the African is the junior partner; that the latter requires to be guided by the former and that each should be rewarded according to his contribution to the welfare of the community." Yet it is to be noted that here, as elsewhere, the ability of the African to develop is not denied, the next proposal urging "the extension of political rights and privileges to those who conform to civilized standards of behaviour and conduct." Perhaps on the level of unconscious reaction, this point of view is implicit in the consistent use, by French, Belgians, Portuguese, and Afrikaans-speaking South Africans, of the second-person singular—the form used ambivalently for children, inferiors, intimates, and animals—when speaking to Africans, even when their degree of adequacy to handle European culture is considerable.

Certain points mark the affirmations of the person who takes this culturist position. Most often heard is the statement that, since it took Europe five hundred years—the time varies, now being a thousand, now two hundred—one cannot expect the African, hardly more than fifty years from the bush, to grasp its intricacies. The element of truth in this statement gives it its sanction; that it runs counter to scientific knowledge concerning cultural learning—that this is a function of opportunity, not generations—is not recognized. It is quite true that the

African, living his aboriginal way of life, is not culturally equipped to live in terms of European patterns; but so, for that matter, is the reverse, as Europeans who attempt to hunt lions with spears have learned to their cost. As was customary when racist misconceptions were faced with the scientific findings, so with the precepts of culturism. The African professional man is regarded as the exception; the success of the Gold Coast in moving toward self-government is held to be the result of three hundred years' contact with Europeans—the implications of the fact that the conquest of Kumasi occurred at about the same time as the occupation of the "White Highlands" being quite passed over.

There is no question of the earnestness or honesty with which this position is held; rather the fact is important that, in assuming it, the lessons taught by the scientific study of culture are ignored, with results that cannot but be far-reaching in the future. And just as racism had its presumed scientific justification, so the beginnings of a presumed scientific base for culturism is appearing.

Early in 1953 there was published, under the auspices of the World Health Organization, a monograph by a psychiatrist, Dr. J. C. Carothers, under the title *The African Mind in Health and Disease: A Study in Ethnopsychiatry*. The author, rejecting the racist explanation of African behavior, says: "It is a main theme of this monograph that African culture has developed on such lines as to reduce the exigencies of living to a minimum, and that the integration which the rural African apparently achieves, is founded on the continuing support afforded by his culture and has but little independent existence in himself." This is not the place to discuss the validity of the ethnographic materials which are marshaled to support this thesis; suffice it to say that Dr. Carothers is obviously not a competent ethnographer. Few of the studies of African life written out of a sophisticated field technique are cited by him, and the degree of generalization in his work blots out the variations in African cultures and, with this, the African as he actually lives. In reality, he has had recourse to an outworn concept of so-called "primitive" life which, based on inadequate methodology, saw only the patterned modes of conduct and ignored the variations that since have been found everywhere, even in the "simplest" societies, to play about them. Such peoples, in the view of this theory, long since rejected by students of culture, but here advanced anew, lived in a kind of cultural strait jacket, all individuality suppressed, the individual a social automaton.

From this point Dr. Carothers proceeds to apply the findings of psychiatry. "In general," we are told, "it seems that the rather clear distinction that exists in Europeans between the 'conscious' and the 'unconscious' elements of mind does not exist in rural Africans. The 'censor's' place is taken by the sorcerer, and 'splits' are vertical, not horizontal. Emotion easily dominates the entire mind; and when it does, the latter's frank confusion takes the place of misinterpretation." Psychiatrists, the discussion goes on, are not in accord as to the neurophysiological causes of this difference, but, whatever the position, the author says, they seem to agree that " 'frontal idleness' accounts, at least in part, for the divergencies observed in Africa, and that a 'fragility of higher psychic functions which contributes to a liberation of automatic psychomotor centers' includes this part."

From the cultural point of view, the relevance of all this for Dr. Carothers derives from the argument that "for full development of both aspects of intelligence," that is, the impersonal and social aspects, "both early infantile and later childhood experiences must follow certain lines and that neither of these lines is followed, early or late." In other words, we now have an explanation of African failure to function in the European setting in terms of the influence of cultural experience on individual development. And this, in turn, is given a neurological explanation: "The main function of the frontal lobes seems to be the integration of stimuli arriving from other parts of the brain [thalamus and cortex]. . . . When integration is lacking, the frontal lobes would be relatively idle since they alone subserve no other function. The African, with his lack of total synthesis, must therefore use his frontal lobes but little, and all the peculiarities of African psychiatry can be envisaged in terms of this frontal idleness."

It must not be assumed that the cultural equivalent of racism is restricted to the African scene, any more than its latency in earlier years is belied by the fact that it has today moved to the forefront. Its importance for Africa is that of the importance of any ideology, everywhere, and at all times. Ideologies derive their force from the fact that their logic and the facts employed to bolster them fit in with the preconceptions of an age, an area. They are thus in themselves data of the highest order in analyzing the situations in which they are found; as socialized rationalizations they illuminate the underlying psychosocial drives that give rise to them. In observing the play between the developing facets of African life—the desire for education and the reassertion of the values in African native cultural patterns, on the one hand, and the growing number of non-Africans permanently domiciled in Africa, with their newly developing ideology, on the other—we can look down vistas of the years to come with realism and weigh the more surely the possible resolutions of differences and tensions these developments portend.

# THE RISE OF AFRICA IN WORLD POLITICS

Vernon McKay

*School of Advanced International Studies*
*The Johns Hopkins University*

T HE rise of African issues in the controversies of world politics during this turbulent postwar decade has forced many governments to give serious attention to Africa for the first time. In the diplomatic crises precipitated by the scramble to partition Africa in the late nineteenth century, only the governments of Europe were primarily involved. Today, as its long isolation rapidly comes to an end, Africa attracts not only governments but peoples and not only Europe but all the continents. Viewed in the long time span of history, this will perhaps appear as the natural culmination of a four-hundred-year process of Western expansion. At the moment, however, the underlying cause of the rise of African issues in world politics appears to be the profound revolution in power relationships among the nations of the world. The centers of world power have shifted away from western Europe to the United States and the Soviet Union, and the West finds itself at the same time confronted by the awakening Africans of a strategic continent, by the newly independent Arab-Asian states, which strongly support African aspirations, and by the threat of Soviet imperialism. The wide scope and the significance of the resulting African problems are perhaps best mirrored in the United Nations, where the sixty members of the General Assembly annually discuss a growing number of more or less explosive issues ranging over the whole continent. This notable development, in addition to its repercussions in Africa, is embittering international relations. It may therefore be useful to look behind these international controversies over African issues in order to analyze the general factors responsible for the emergence of Africa and to highlight some of their effects on the foreign policies of the many powers concerned.

I have found it convenient to select arbitrarily seven factors, or combinations of factors, that seem relevant. Their relative importance varies from time to time and place to place. These factors are:

1. *The strategic factor.*—This includes Africa's military bases, critical raw materials, military manpower, and its potentialities as an industrial and military supply center.

2. *The rapid development of nationalism.*—This development, using the term in its broadest sense, covers the many types of political aspirations.

3. *The revolt against economic hardship.*—Even were colonialism and racialism wiped off the face of the earth, conflict would continue between peoples who are industrial and well to do and peoples who are poor and predominantly agricultural.

4. *The international concern over the colonial question.*—Along with this concern there is the consequent growth of the principle of international accountability for colonial administration.

5. *The threat of communism.*—Communism has thus far made relatively little headway. Party membership is limited, for the most part, to the areas in which industry has developed and to which Europeans have come in large numbers: French North Africa and the Union of South Africa. How many members the party has is unknown, but I would guess not more than 25,000, of whom perhaps 15,000 are concentrated in Algeria. In the vast expanse of tropical Africa there are no Communist parties and only scattered individual Communists. These thus far have had little influence, save in French West Africa, where a new postwar political party called the Rassemblement Démocratique Africain was for several years under Communist control.

The threat is there and cannot be ignored. At least some of the preconditions for Communist expansion are present, and, if European controls suddenly collapsed, the situation might become very dangerous. Although Africa may be last on the Kremlin's timetable, the Soviets have found in the United Nations a ready-made forum for wooing African nationalists and for subverting the friendship of the Western allies. This fact alone makes communism a significant factor in our problem. Numerous African leaders know that it is the Soviet delegates who say the things they like to hear and that it is the Western representatives who do not say these things. Moreover, many nationalists are impressed by what they hear about Soviet achievements in the quick economic development of a backward area. As for the East-West conflict, many African leaders have neutralist inclinations. Some of them may sympathize with the view of those Indians who oppose both communism and colonialism but, of the two, would rather see communism operated anywhere in Asia by Asians than colonialism operated anywhere in Asia by non-Asians.[1] For all these reasons it would be highly desirable for the West to build up some kind of counterattraction to Soviet propaganda, a task that is exceedingly difficult, because the irresponsibility of the Russian position makes it impossible for the West to outbid Soviet appeals to colonial peoples.

6. *The present effort by colonial powers to counteract the Soviet appeal.*—As the annual reports on many territories reveal, there has been since the end of World War II a steady increase in the number of Africans holding responsible posts in the government, a considerable increase in production and trade, a remarkable rise in the number of Africans in school at every level of education, and a steady growth in the number of doctors, hospitals, co-operatives, and other assets. The irony in this situation is that, instead of satisfying the nationalists, these gains only foster more and stronger demands for self-government sooner.

7. *The contribution to European recovery.*—There has developed a widespread belief in Europe after 1945 that Africa can make a significant contribution to European recovery. It is a fact that the Gold Coast, Nigeria, and Northern Rhodesia have earned hundreds of millions of dollars for the sterling area, and the Belgian and Portuguese territories have earned dollars on a smaller scale. The French territories, on the other hand, have been a liability in this respect.[2]

These seven factors have all been stimulated powerfully by

1. Ronald Stead, *Christian Science Monitor*, April 28, 1953; quoted in Eugene Staley, *The Future of Underdeveloped Countries* (New York, 1954), p. 130.

2. Philip W. Bell, "Colonialism as a Problem in American Foreign Policy," *World Politics*, V (October, 1952), 86–109.

World War II. If they are underlying causes which in their origins antedate the war, history may nonetheless record that it was the war which served as the catalyst for the emergence of Africa.

I

The growing bitterness of international controversy over African issues is having a significant influence on the foreign relations and foreign policies of many governments. In addition to the small number of states with the most direct interests in Africa, more than fifty other states are today forced to focus attention on many African problems because of their membership in the United Nations. The system of bloc politics which has developed in the United Nations provides a convenient basis for a few general observations concerning their views, bearing in mind that there are many divergent interests and variations in the voting positions of individual delegations within each bloc.

On African issues the most aggressive group is the Arab-Asian bloc. This may be considered to contain sixteen members: six Arab, eight Asian, and two African states (Afghanistan, Burma, Egypt, Ethiopia, India, Indonesia, Iraq, Iran, Lebanon, Liberia, Pakistan, the Philippines, Thailand, Saudi-Arabia, Syria, and Yemen). Developing in December, 1950, during the Korean crisis, the bloc met often thereafter to discuss specific issues. Thirteen of its members (excluding Ethiopia, Liberia, and Thailand) joined in a successful endeavor to get the Moroccan question, the Tunisian question, and the item on race conflict in South Africa on the agenda of the General Assembly. In addition to their hostility to colonialism, these states share a common and related interest in fighting racial discrimination against people of color and in seeking ways and means for the economic development of their underdeveloped countries. Through bloc politics they gain additional strength and influence and are able to win membership for a larger number of their members in various United Nations organs and offices. Three presidents of the General Assembly have come from the Arab-Asian states. It is these facts which hold the bloc together despite the differences and rivalries of its members.[3]

On the main peace and security resolutions emanating from the General Assembly, the Arab-Asian bloc has generally supported the Western powers, although there has been a high percentage of abstentions on the part of India. On African issues, however, the last several sessions of the General Assembly have revealed the depth of the antagonism between the East and the West. Previously, the conflict between the East and the West was predominantly the cold war between Russia and the Western powers, but today there is a second East-West conflict between the West and the non-European world. As one observer has written, the United Nations has become "one of the principal mechanisms by which race relations are transformed into international relations. . . . If the two East-West conflicts did become amalgamated, it might well turn the over-all balance of power against the West, and the UN is one of the means through which such a merger is being sought."[4] This, of course, is a big "if." Nonetheless, the West cannot afford to overlook the possibility that it may have greater difficulty in keeping the two East-West struggles apart if bitterness over African issues in the United Nations continues to grow.

The Latin-American bloc has also achieved a good deal for its members despite differences of view which are sometimes sharp and acrimonious. Because of their large number of votes in the United Nations, they often hold the balance on heated colonial issues. Since they are (1) former colonies, (2) racially mixed, and (3) relatively underdeveloped, they are in general on the anticolonial side of the Assembly. Only three or four of them, however, consistently vote with the extreme left on African problems in the General Assembly. The remainder take varying positions between the left and the center. Although they dislike French colonial policy, the voting positions of some Latin delegations have been moderated by their traditional affection for France and French culture. A similar attitude of cer-

3. Harry N. Howard, "The Arab-Asian States in the United Nations," *Middle East Journal*, VII (Summer, 1953), 279–92.

4. Cora Bell, "The United Nations and the West," *International Affairs*, XXIX (October, 1953), 466.

tain Latin countries toward Italy affected their voting on the Assembly's disposition of the former Italian colonies.

The systematic exploitation of African issues in the propaganda of the five members of the Soviet bloc will be referred to later. A few words should be said, however, about the voting positions of the administering authorities, the western European countries, and the white Dominions of the British Commonwealth. With the United States, these are generally considered to constitute a bloc. Although the group may not always be identifiable as a single bloc, it has tended to draw together on African issues as the attacks from the extreme anticolonial group have mounted in intensity. However, the voting position of the United States and the Scandinavian countries, and occasionally Canada and New Zealand, continues to be more affirmative than that of other members of the group.

To conclude this brief survey of bloc politics, it should be re-emphasized that the existence of the United Nations has forced all sixty of its members, whether or not they have direct interests in Africa, to focus more or less regular attention on a wide variety of political, economic, social, and educational problems ranging over the whole African continent. This is a fact of major significance for both Africa and the United Nations. It not only reflects the rise of Africa in world politics but is in itself a powerful though often intangible force contributing to further change in that continent.

Bitter controversy over African issues could also have a grave effect on the United Nations itself, which depends for its strength on the co-operation of its members in accepting recommendations which the United Nations does not normally have the power to enforce. In England and France it is occasionally said that, if events force a choice between the Commonwealth and the United Nations, or between the French Union and the United Nations, British and French interests would require the end of the United Nations connection. And, in India, Prime Minister Nehru told the House of the People on June 12, 1952: "If the whole of Asia and Africa combined cannot get a subject discussed [Tunisia] because two or three great Powers object, then the time may come when the Asian and African countries will feel that they are happier in their own countries and not in the UN." One may hope that the larger interests of these countries will be strong enough to overcome their discontents over the colonial question, but it might be unwise to disregard such a statement entirely. Already the French and South African delegations have temporarily walked out of, or refused to participate in, certain General Assembly discussions affecting them; the Belgians have withdrawn from the important Committee on Information from Non-self-governing Territories, and the United Kingdom and Australia have indicated that they will no longer co-operate if the Assembly takes certain decisions in the colonial field which they consider objectionable.

## II

Let us now examine the effect of international controversy over African issues on the powers with the most direct interests in Africa, beginning with Britain and France. It is not easy for British representatives in the United Nations to sit and listen as they are publicly berated by fellow-members of their own Commonwealth of Nations, as happened in November, 1952, for example, when the representative of Pakistan accused all the European colonial powers of having "a beautiful front and a very large and stinking back yard" extending over the whole continent of Africa. Yet the British are now engaged in a notable effort to transform the Commonwealth of Nations from a white into a multiracial organization. Three new Asian members, India, Pakistan, and Ceylon, have already joined the "club," and a number of emerging African states will soon be ready. The flexible relationship between Britain and the older dominions has its unity in their common ideas and ideals, traditions, feelings, interests, and symbols. But the Asian and potential African members of the new commonwealth have a very different cultural heritage. Can the experiment suceed, or is it doomed to failure by these cultural differences? Its success is vital to Britain, which would drop from the ranks of the world powers if it lost the economic and strategic assets and the prestige which go with the commonwealth. To the West as a whole, moreover, a successful multiracial commonwealth would provide a valuable link with Asia and Africa.

The task of building the multiracial commonwealth would be difficult enough even if the only problem were to surmount the tensions and disagreements resulting from cultural differences. But the existence of the United Nations has injected a new factor into the problem, namely, that these tensions and disagreements are now aired before the eyes and ears of the world under the glare of merciless publicity. The new commonwealth's chances of success might be much greater if these conflicts could be discussed in private over the conference table by Prime Ministers Eden, Nehru, Mohammed Ali, Strijdom, Nkrumah, and others. But in the General Assembly of the United Nations, where orators speak to a world audience, including their own supporters at home, the temptation to go beyond the bounds of diplomatic propriety is often too great.

As H. Duncan Hall has recently written, the old British Commonwealth of states with a common cultural background carried on its business in private and with certain rules, even if mostly unwritten. Members kept each other informed; they did not negotiate with foreign governments without considering the interests of other Commonwealth members; they did not involve each other in active obligations without first obtaining the assent of all concerned; and they aided each other against military aggression.[5] Will Asian and African members obey such rules? Can the rules be modified to make allowance for such bitter controversies as the annual attacks of India and Pakistan in the United Nations on the Union of South Africa over its treatment of peoples of Indian origin in the Union; or the action of Gold Coast Prime Minister Nkrumah, even if only in his unofficial capacity as head of the Convention People's party, in sending a petition to the United Nations Ad Hoc Committee on South West Africa attacking the administration of Prime Minister Malan?

Controversy over African issues not only endangers the prospects of the multiracial commonwealth but is playing into the

5. "The British Commonwealth of Nations," *American Political Science Review*, XLVII (December, 1953), 997–1015.

hands of those South Africans who have wanted for some time to take the Union out of the old Commonwealth. Leo Marquard has estimated that possibly one-fourth of the Nationalist party supporters "want a republic soon and outside of the Commonwealth."[6] Prime Minister Malan declared in February, 1951, that Britain and the United Nations between them were killing the Commonwealth. In his opinion the British experiment in the Gold Coast was bound to fail, for it was an example of the good principle of democracy wrongly applied and making itself ridiculous. Moreover, he contended that Britain had recently admitted India, Pakistan, and Ceylon to the Commonwealth without consultation or approval of other Commonwealth members, who were linked by a homogeneity and feeling of solidarity that did not include the Asian members.[7]

The Nationalist government's attitude toward continued membership in the Commonwealth was set forth in an interesting way during a debate in the South African House of Assembly on July 7–8, 1953, when the leader of the opposition, Mr. Strauss, introduced a motion that the House, *inter alia*, "should express its conviction that continued membership of the Commonwealth by the Union under its present constitution was in the best interests of the Union and would promote national unity and the material welfare of the country." Prime Minister Malan attacked the proposal as an "anti-republican motion" in which Mr. Strauss sought "to bind us permanently to the Commonwealth and . . . to kingship." He then proposed an important amendment to the motion, which was adopted by a vote of 84 to 56. In this amendment, after indorsing co-operation with the Commonwealth in principle,

the House further takes cognizance of the republican policy of the Government and the assurances given therein, viz., (i). That such a constitutional change to a republican form of state, though it offers a great contribution to true national unity and is best adapted to the traditions, circumstances and aspirations of the South African nation, can be brought about only on the broad basis of the national will, and with the faithful observance of equal rights in all respects of the two sections of the European population, and as

6. *The Peoples and Policies of South Africa* (London: Oxford University Press, 1952), p. 163.

7. As cited in *East Africa and Rhodesia*, March 1, 1951, p. 696.

the result of a special and definite mandate from the European electorate, and not merely by a parliamentary majority obtained as the result of an ordinary election. . . .

In addition, the amendment made it clear that "the proclamation of a republic and withdrawal from the Commonwealth have become two separate questions which need not be answered simultaneously."[8]

The rapid changes now under way in Africa are also affecting another aspect of the Union's foreign policy: its attitude toward the rest of Africa. One indication of present policy came from the prime minister in March, 1952, when he spoke against a proposal in Parliament to call on the government to negotiate with Southern and Northern Rhodesia "with a view to their joining the Union in the formation of a greater union of southern states in Africa." He recalled that, when South Africa had taken the initiative in proposing the incorporation of Southern Rhodesia into the Union some years ago, Rhodesia had rejected it. Any fresh negotiations, he said, should be started by Rhodesia. It was of the utmost importance, however, that the Rhodesias and the Union should co-operate in maintaining Western European Christian civilization in Africa. A united Rhodesia could become an important bulwark between the Union and the pressures from the north, but it might also become a bridge, with all the dangers to South Africa that would follow. The prime minister went on to say that he was prepared to throw in his weight to get a Charter of Africa such as that between North and South America. As long as the open-door policy toward Asiatic immigration existed, the future of white civilization was not safe, still less that of the natives. It was therefore necessary, he felt, to reach an agreement with the various European powers with interests in Africa.[9]

An issue that further endangers friendly relations between South Africa and the United Kingdom is South Africa's desire to incorporate the three British High Commission Territories of Basutoland, Bechuanaland, and Swaziland. This is an old ques-

8. *Journal of the Parliaments of the Commonwealth*, XXXIV (October, 1953), 792–803.

9. *East Africa and Rhodesia*, March 13, 1952, p. 822.

tion which has been raised on numerous occasions since the passage of the South Africa Act by the British Parliament in 1909. Herein the government pledged that Parliament would have the opportunity to discuss and, if it wished, to disapprove the transfer of the territories to the Union and also that the wishes of the inhabitants of the territories would be ascertained and considered before any transfer took place.[10] The Nationalist government has revived the issue, and, if it is aired publicly, it could arouse a great deal of emotion in Britain, South Africa, the three territories, and the United Nations. The inhabitants concerned, despite their close geographical and economic relationship with the Union, would no doubt strongly oppose the proposed transfer. The situation is further complicated by the fact that Southern Rhodesia, on several occasions since it attained self-governing status in 1923, has approached the United Kingdom government with a claim to at least a part of the northern Bechuanaland Protectorate. It is possible that the new Federation of Rhodesia and Nyasaland might press this claim more vigorously.

The attitude of the Union and of Europeans in British East and Central Africa toward Asians is one of the important influences on the foreign policy of India and Pakistan. These two governments have many internal problems to solve, and their long-range policy toward Africa is difficult to foresee. There are a half-million Indians in Africa today, however, and the protection of their interests is a matter of immediate concern. In the United Nations, India has become a leader of the anticolonial states which are fighting for self-determination and against racial discrimination. Scholarships have begun to be offered for Africans to study in Indian universities, and in recent years there has been a growing tendency for African and Indian political organizations to work more closely together in Africa. These various developments have aroused considerable alarm among numerous Europeans and have resulted in the spread of various emotional rumors, including an alleged plan to establish an Indian state in Tanganyika supported by the United

10. *Basutoland, the Bechuanaland Protectorate and Swaziland: History of Discussions with the Union of South Africa, 1909–1939* (Cmd. 8707 [London: H.M. Stationery Office, 1952]), p. 6.

States! The official policy of India, however, was stated as follows by Prime Minister Nehru in a foreign policy debate in the House of the People on September 17, 1953:

> We have been accused of interfering in the affairs of other countries, in Africa. We have also been accused of some kind of imperialist tendency which wants to spread out in Africa and take possession of those delectable lands which now the European settlers occupy. As a matter of fact, this House knows very well that all along, for these many years, we have been laying the greatest stress on something which is rather unique . . . we have rather gone out of our way to tell our own people in Africa . . . that they can expect no help from us, no protection from us, if they seek any special rights in Africa which are not in the interests of Africa . . . we have told them: "We shall help you naturally, we are interested in protecting you, your dignity or interests, but not if you go at all against the people of Africa, because you are their guests, and if they do not want you, out you will have to go, bag and baggage. . . ."[11]

The Commonwealth of Nations thus has many problems to work out before it can evolve into a successful multiracial community. It is sometimes argued that the existence of the United Nations is a safety valve which permits Commonwealth members with divergent views to let off steam which might otherwise explode. Possibly this view contains an element of truth, but it is a risky asset which may be more than offset by the additional tensions created by intemperate and widely publicized denunciations. In any event, it is to be hoped that the political inventiveness of the peoples concerned will be equal to the task, for the evolution of the British Empire into a successful multiracial Commonwealth of Nations would be a notable achievement.

## III

The rise of African issues in world politics is having a significant impact on the foreign policy of France and on the evolution of the French Union. The severity of international criticism of French colonial policy, particularly in the United Nations, has often tended to rigidify the French attitude and to undermine French prestige. At the same time, the lessons of the loss of Syria, Lebanon, and Indochina, and critical uprisings in Madagascar and French North Africa, have shaken the confidence of many Frenchmen in the validity of the concept of the

11. *Journal of the Parliaments of the Commonwealth*, XXIX (October, 1953), 813–14.

French Union. Confronted by all kinds of pressures from the nationalists, from French liberals, from the Kremlin, from the United Nations, and from the policies of Britain and the United States, a growing number of Frenchmen are advocating a colonial arrangement with a more flexible spirit. They believe that in French West and Equatorial Africa, they have an opportunity to develop a new type of relationship that will avoid what they regard as the dead ends of nationalism and communism as well as the outmoded concept of assimilation. The results of the 1951 elections indicated to this group the growth of aspirations in tropical Africa for autonomy within the French Union, as opposed to the present constitutional status of the overseas territories as an integral part of the French Republic.

Developments in the two United Nations trust territories under French administration, Cameroons and Togoland, may also influence the evolution of the French Union. Constitutionally these are Associated Territories, with an international status different from that of other parts of the French Union. Under pressure of the United Nations, which has encouraged the demands of the local inhabitants, the French are accelerating the rate of political progress in these territories. It is also an interesting fact that the French delegation in the United Nations Trusteeship Council, under close questioning by Council members, has on several occasions committed France to the principle that, if the two trust territories at the appropriate time want to achieve their independence outside rather than inside the French Union, they can do so. This recognition of the right of secession is unique for French Africa.

The French political observer, "Pertinax," has suggested that Africa may also provide the basis for another significant development in world politics, namely, the revival of the Anglo-French Entente Cordiale. He bases this belief on the grounds of the convergence of French and British interests in Africa, as indicated by the fact that Britain and France not only have joined to defend these interests against attacks in the United Nations but also have held many technical and some political conferences since 1948 to work out a policy for common African interests.[12] In this view, however, "Pertinax" seems to have underestimated the differing political methods and objectives of the two governments in West Africa, which are so deeply rooted that co-operation can hardly go far beyond the technical field in the immediate future.

## IV

The scope of this article permits only brief mention of the effect of Africa's emergence on the foreign relations of the remaining powers with African territory: the four metropolitan governments of Belgium, Portugal, Spain, and Italy and the four independent states of Ethiopia, Liberia, Libya, and Egypt.

The continuance of Belgium's relative prosperity and status among Europe's powers depends to an important extent on the maintenance of the profits and prestige which come from the Congo. Though strongly democratic in the Western tradition, Belgium has followed a colonial policy markedly different from that of its British and French allies. While the latter have fostered higher education and participation in government for Africans, the Belgians have concentrated on African economic and social development and primary education. Before the rise of Africa in world politics, the Belgians were able to move calmly along in this direction without concern or unusual criticism. Today, however, Belgium is also under severe attack in the United Nations, and its initial reaction has been to stiffen its resistance and even to walk out of the Committee on Information from Non-self-governing Territories. When the United Nations began its career, certain liberal-minded Belgians were interested in the possibility that United Nations influence might help them break down the "old colonial spirit" which retarded Congo progress. Today, however, most Belgians seem to feel that United Nations excesses have destroyed whatever value it might have had in this regard. In an effort to counteract what they regard as unfair criticism, Belgian delegations in United Nations organs now publicize Congo progress in contrast to conditions in certain independent countries and have recent-

12. André Geraud, "Rise and Fall of the Anglo-French Entente," *Foreign Affairs*, XXXII (April, 1954), 374–87.

ly launched an interesting but ineffective effort to induce such countries, primarily in Asia and Latin America, to report to the United Nations on their own tribal peoples whom the Belgians contend are just as nonself-governing as the Congolese. Whatever the validity of such an attitude, it may increasingly complicate Belgium's international relations.

Portugal still manages to keep its African territories outside the main stream of world politics. Like Spain, Portugal is not a member of the United Nations and is spared the attacks undergone therein by the other colonial powers. Portuguese admission to the United Nations would change this situation. Portugal would presumably contend that its territories, having the constitutional status of integral parts of the metropole, had attained self-government. Hence, Portugal might refuse to report on these territories under Article 73(e) of the Charter. But this would not prevent the General Assembly from making annual efforts to induce Portugal to make its colonial administration accountable to the international community. The present Portuguese controversy with India over the status of Goa, however, may foreshadow further international difficulties for Portugal over the colonial question.

Spain has only slight holdings in Africa, but it has found in France's difficulties with the Arab world an opportunity to strengthen Spanish prestige among the Arabs of North Africa. Since the end of World War II the Spanish have taken steps to cater to the Arabs and, as a consequence, have created international difficulties between Paris and Madrid. Spain and Portugal, it should be recalled, were not directly involved in World War II; this is another fact which has kept the pace of change slower in their African territories.

The effect of Africa on Italy's international position is illustrated by its fight to retain the former Italian colonies after World War II. Despite the fact that these impoverished territories were a heavy annual drain on the Italian treasury, Italy fought hard to retain them. This illustrates the great importance of the prestige factor as a motive for empire. Although it succeeded only in regaining Somaliland under a ten-year trusteeship, Italy is doing effective work in trying to build an economic, social, and educational basis for the political independence scheduled for Somaliland in 1960. Although the U.S.S.R. has vetoed Italian membership in the United Nations, the Italians have been granted the right to participate without vote in matters affecting Italian Somaliland. Italy is also seeking to protect and develop the remaining Italian interests in Libya and Eritrea. It is interesting to note that among the advocates of the new concept of Eurafrica are theorists from Italy, Germany, and the Netherlands— three powers which have lost all or most of their empires. Another development worthy of study is the current effort of these three countries to expand their African markets.

The official visits to the United States in 1954 by the emperor of Ethiopia and by the president of Liberia symbolize the growing desire of these two states to expand and strengthen their foreign policies as Africa assumes new importance in world politics. Perhaps the best measure of Ethiopia's wish to play a larger role was its sending of troops to join the United Nations forces in Korea. Another Ethiopian achievement has been the United Nations decision to federate Eritrea with Ethiopia. The emperor has also had considerable success in obtaining economic aid and technical assistance from the United States and the United Nations. On May 22, 1953, Ethiopia and the United States signed an agreement providing military base rights for the United States. Ethiopia has recently begun the exchange of diplomatic representation with a number of new countries, including Yugoslavia, which the emperor also visited in 1954. Finally, it should not be overlooked that the only Soviet diplomatic post in tropical Africa between the Sahara and the Union is in Addis Ababa, where the U.S.S.R. maintains also a hospital and a permanent Soviet exhibition.

Under the leadership of President W. V. S. Tubman, Liberia has made notable progress in the last decade in both internal and external affairs. Liberian consulates have been opened in the Gold Coast, Sierra Leone, and Nigeria. A widely publicized visit to Liberia was made in 1953 by Gold Coast Prime Minister Nkrumah. In the United Nations Liberia and Ethiopia have joined the Arab-Asian bloc as a means of increasing the effec-

tiveness of their views on foreign affairs. Like Ethiopia, Liberia
is one of the chief African beneficiaries of the Expanded Technical Assistance Program of the United Nations. Monrovia has
become the site of the only United Nations Information Center
in Africa south of the Sahara. In another interesting development, the Liberian United Nations Association in April, 1953,
organized a West African seminar on teaching about the United
Nations and its specialized agencies. Sponsored by UNESCO
and the World Federation of United Nations Associations, the
seminar was attended by five delegates from Sierra Leone, five
from the Gold Coast, one from Nigeria, one from British
Cameroons, two from "Western" (British) Togoland, one from
"Eastern" (French) Togoland, and forty-five from Liberia.

Libya, the newest of Africa's independent states, has a foreign
policy still in a formative stage. Its creation by the United Nations has established an important precedent, and its evolution
is under close scrutiny in many quarters. Libya has joined the
Arab League, but it has such important financial and military
ties with Britain and the United States that some of its leaders
speak of Libya as a bridge between the West and the Arab
world.

Although Egypt is normally considered a part of the Middle
East rather than Africa, a number of signs of the times indicate
that the makers of Egyptian foreign policy may have a different
idea. Among these are the expansion of Egyptian influence in
the Sudan at the expense of Britain, the attention Egypt is devoting to Libya and Italian Somaliland, and the African conference held in Cairo recently. One may also wonder what will
ultimately be the political effect of the spread of Islam in Africa
south of the Sahara.

## V

Finally, what effect has the emergence of Africa and the consequent rise of African issues in world politics had on the foreign policies of the two great powers? For the foreign policy of
the Soviet Union, the problem is relatively simple. In sharp
contrast to the United States, which would lose much from the
weakening of western Europe, the Russians have much to gain.
Because it thrives on disorder and instability outside its own

borders, Moscow can be completely irresponsible in its efforts to make the evolution of Africa toward self-government as disorderly as possible. Moreover, the dynamics of the situation play into the Kremlin's hands, for the powerful levers of nationalism and race are themselves doing its work of disrupting Western control of Africa.

In the United Nations the U.S.S.R. has found its best forum for its stock denunciations of all the varying colonial relationships of the Western powers as imperialist exploitation. Since the end of World War II the theme of this political weapon has been expanded to attack the United States as the leader of an imperialist bloc seeking to transform Africa into a base of military operations for the aggressive wars which it is preparing against the U.S.S.R.

Although the Kremlin has doubtless had too many irons in the fire to concentrate much of its attention on Africa in the past, a Communist party was established in the Union of South Africa as long ago as 1921, and today the new strategic importance of Africa poses additional problems for the makers of Soviet foreign policy. Although communism has had relatively little success thus far, a number of new channels for Soviet influence have opened up since the war. One of these is the French Communist party, the postwar strength of which enabled it to make considerable inroads in the French territories either directly or indirectly for several years. Another is the vastly increased number of African students in European universities who are systematically cultivated by French and British Communists and, in a few cases, are granted scholarships for study behind the Iron Curtain. A third is the trade-unions, which have undergone a remarkable growth in British and French West Africa, where they now number several hundred, as well as in the more industrialized areas of South Africa and French North Africa. A fourth is the press and radio through which the Communist line reaches a considerable number of Africans in certain towns, although during recent years local governments have taken more vigorous steps to prohibit the dissemination of Communist propaganda. And, finally, the dissemination of the official records of the United Nations in Africa, particularly in the seven middle-African trust territories, provides the Soviets with a valuable opportunity to drive the Soviet line home by constant and deliberate repetition. This could become of considerable importance in the case of growing numbers of petitioners to whom the United Nations sends direct a voluminous collection of records in which the petitioners find that Soviet spokesmen appear to have been their chief friends and advocates.[13]

No one can foresee what the final results of this Soviet effort will be. Many African leaders whose thinking is dominated by their hostility to Western colonialism seem to be unimpressed by the threat of Soviet imperialism. Even though they may be aware of the hypocrisy of Soviet aims, and may dislike Russian political methods, some of them admire what they regard as outstanding Soviet achievements in the social and economic field. Even if the Russians fail to convert Africans to communism, they could still achieve a considerable victory if emerging Africa decides to wish "a plague on both your houses."

If international controversy over African issues has presented the Soviet Union an opportunity, it has confronted the United States with a dilemma, as Professor Morgenthau has pointed out in his analysis of United States policy toward Africa.[14] In face of this dilemma, the United States government has reviewed its attitude toward Africa and has attempted the formulation of a policy adapted to the changed conditions of the mid-twentieth century. The result has been the issuance of two major policy statements, one by the Assistant Secretary of State in charge of African affairs under the Democratic administration on May 8, 1950, and the other by his successor on October 30, 1953, under the Republican administration. Both statements reaffirm the traditional American faith in the principle of self-determination, which has been enunciated by many Presidents and Secretaries of State. In both, however, is found a new emphasis on the idea that the transition to self-govern-

13. I have discussed communism in Africa in more detail in my article, "Communist Exploitation of Anti-colonialism and Nationalism in Africa," in C. Grove Haines (ed.), *The Threat of Soviet Imperialism* (Baltimore: Johns Hopkins Press, 1954), pp. 258–74.

14. See below, pp. 317–25.

ment should be orderly if it is to succeed. This is particularly true of the later statement, a major portion of which is devoted to the amplification of the theme: "We believe in eventual self-determination for all peoples, and we believe that evolutionary development to this end should move forward with minimum delay."

Thus the words "orderly," "eventual," and "evolutionary" have entered the American vocabulary of self-determination. There are perhaps two main reasons for this new emphasis. One of them stems from the fact that the United States has assumed the leadership of a Western coalition against the threat of Soviet imperialism. To quote the 1953 policy statement again: "It will be one of the great tragedies of our time if the peoples of Asia and Africa, just as they are emerging from generations of dependence, should be deluded by the fatal lure of the new imperialism and return thereby to an age of slavery infinitely more miserable than they have ever known before." At the same time the United States itself would be in grave jeopardy if the rest of the world were overrun by communism. It is this Soviet threat that complicates our Africa policy. Because of it we need military bases and strategic materials in Africa, as well as the co-operation of the colonial powers in building the Western defense arrangements. The United States cannot have these things without the friendship of Europeans. At the same time, we need the friendship of Africans, whose leaders are often so intense in their aspirations that they may turn against the West if self-government is long delayed. This is the dilemma.

A second reason for the new emphasis in American policy is that a growing number of those who have studied Africa's problems are impressed by the fact that, generally speaking, the old colonialism is dead or dying and that progress toward self-government, in certain territories at least, is steady and relatively rapid. Moreover, this progress is priming its own pump and will inevitably accelerate. Meanwhile, the continued economic and technical assistance of the metropolitan powers is building the economic, social, and educational pillars necessary for responsible self-government and the full enjoyment of political freedom. The two policy statements imply that the Department of

State hopes to find in this fact at least a partial solution of its dilemma. If Africans can achieve self-government through orderly transition, perhaps a mutuality rather than a conflict of interests can be developed, to the benefit of all concerned.

Unfortunately, the success of this policy of moderation is jeopardized by the fact that we live in an age of ferment which seems to place a premium on extremism. Whether or not it is fair or helpful to do so, the leaders of a majority of the world's peoples understandably believe with deep emotion that the world has a moral obligation to give independence to all colonial peoples. In view of these deep emotions and of our conflicting interests, some observers have felt that the United States should keep silent on controversial African issues and work quietly behind the scenes toward its objective of orderly evolution toward self-determination. But the existence of the United Nations makes silence impossible. As a loyal member of that organization, in the success of which we also have a vital interest, the United States must take a stand on every controversial African issue that is forced to a vote, and normally the United States has to explain its position, thereby exposing itself to public criticism. It is not an enviable role.

Meanwhile, if I may conclude on a note of optimism, it may at least be said that people are learning much from this international controversy over the future of Africa. The colonial powers are acquiring a better understanding of the depths of emotion aroused by the idea of colonialism and are learning that they must take it into account if they are to deal successfully with anticolonial nations on other issues. The anticolonial group is learning more and more about the progress Africa is making under new colonial policies and is finding that it can push the administering authorities only so far without undermining the machinery of international supervision. Africans, meanwhile, are learning some valuable lessons in international politics, including the fact that the United Nations is constitutionally incapable of doing for Africa what they had hoped. And in the United States, the location of the United Nations in New York has been one of the important factors stimulating American interest in Africa. In the last five years various American committees to aid Africa, including African petitioners who come to the United Nations, have been organized, and a movement to learn more about Africa has spread from coast to coast through groups of scholars, students, businessmen, churchmen, and civic organizations. Only five years ago it was possible for the small number of specialists in the African field to keep in relatively close touch with African studies, interests, and organizations in this country. Today it is no longer possible, the field has grown so rapidly. The new public awareness and knowledge of Africa, moreover, is enabling the government to employ more and better-trained personnel to formulate and implement United States policy.

If this analysis of the causes of Africa's emergence in world politics and its effects on international relations is tentative and incomplete, it may nonetheless serve a useful purpose by suggesting profitable lines of study to others, who can undertake detailed analyses of subjects which are only highlighted here. In the perspective of history it is possible that current international disputes over African issues may appear less significant than they do today in the heat of battle. For Africa is not a passive land of military bases and strategic materials but a continent of men who are even today shaping their own destiny.

# UNITED STATES POLICY TOWARD AFRICA

Hans J. Morgenthau

*Center for the Study of American Foreign Policy*
*University of Chicago*

THE topic of this paper requires answers to four questions: (1) What are the interests of the United States in Africa? (2) What are the problems the United States is facing in the pursuit of these interests? (3) What policies does the United States actually pursue? (4) What policies ought the United States to pursue?

I

The United States has in Africa no specific political or military interests. As in other parts of the world, American interests in Africa are a by-product, as it were, of the East-West struggle. In other words, the American policy of containing the Soviet Union on a world-wide scale requires the United States to pursue in Africa certain interests which serve the over-all objective of containment.

The policy of containment proceeds everywhere on two levels: the military and the ideological. The United States attempts to prevent the military forces of the Soviet Union from stepping over the line of military demarcation which was established at the end of the second World War, and it tries to prevent Communist ideology, being at the service of Russian imperialism, from making inroads on this side of the Iron Curtain. Applied to Africa, the American interest consists in the denial of the African continent to military and ideological conquest by the Soviet Union.

This general interest is translated by the specific conditions under which it presents itself to American policy into certain specific interests which American policy must protect. They are of a military, economic, and political nature.

The military importance of Africa for the United States is twofold. The westernmost part of Africa forms the closest jumping-off place for a military attack upon the Western Hemisphere. Viewed in terms of traditional strategy, the route from Dakar to Brazil's Natal constitutes the shortest route for the invasion of the Western Hemisphere. Hence, in hostile hands West Africa would constitute the most direct physical threat to the integrity of the Western Hemisphere. Furthermore, the safety of the shipping lanes around the coasts of Africa, connecting Europe and Asia, must be a vital concern of the Western world, especially if the Mediterranean should become impassable. Hostile control of part of the African coastline might sever seaborne communications between Europe and Asia.

Modern technology has made Africa an important supplier of rare and vital raw materials, such as uranium, cobalt, manganese, rubber, and industrial diamonds. The United States is not only interested in retaining free access to these raw materials; it has also perhaps an even greater interest in denying access to these raw materials to the Soviet bloc. Furthermore, in view of its interest in the economic stability of its Western allies, it must also be interested in their continuing ability to make full use of the economic potentialities of Africa.

The over-all American interest in the containment of communism requires political stability in Africa. Yet political stability, as applied to Africa, is an ambiguous concept, for political stability may mean the maintenance of the status quo at any price. Conceived in such terms, political stability is indeed maintained by the present government of the Union of South Africa. Political stability may also mean the establishment of viable relations between the white minority and the black majority, and, then, political stability requires the satisfaction of the native aspirations for self-government and social justice compatible with such a viable relationship. In other words, the United States is interested in the maintenance of a viable social and political order in Africa—an order which in present circumstances can mean only an uneasy and precarious compromise between the maintenance of white rule and the satisfaction of native aspirations.

## II

The policies which the United States has pursued in support of these interests have been beset by three dilemmas.

First, with the exception of Ethiopia, Liberia, and the Union of South Africa, the United States has no direct access to the problems of Africa but can approach them only through the intermediary of the metropolitan governments which control the main bulk of the territory and population of Africa. In other words, the United States can pursue its policies with regard to Africa only insofar as the metropolitan governments are willing to execute them or will allow the American government to do so. The metropolitan governments stand between American interests and the satisfaction of those interests, and that satisfaction is dependent not only upon the wisdom of American policies but also, and primarily, upon the wisdom of the metropolitan governments.

Second, the interests of the metropolitan governments are not necessarily identical with the interests of the United States. For instance, the United States has no stake in the maintenance of colonial rule as such but is interested in its maintenance only insofar as it serves the interests discussed under Section I. The metropolitan governments, on the other hand, are interested in the maintenance of colonial rule per se, an interest which, while changing in intensity from territory to territory, is always sufficient unto itself and exists independently of any transcendent considerations of the policy of containment. This basic difference in the orientation of policy makes it inevitable that the objectives of American policy will at times be at variance with those of the metropolitan nations, that at times they will coincide by accident rather than in view of their intrinsic identity, and that more frequently they will be identical in appearances and short-run objectives rather than in their ultimate goals.

Finally, and perhaps most importantly, American policy with regard to Africa is beset by two types of inner contradictions. A policy required by American interests in Africa taken in isolation is bound to have all kinds of repercussions upon the metropolitan nations. It may impair metropolitan control and run counter to metropolitan economic interests and thereby weaken the over-all power of the metropolitan nations. It may also create resentment against the United States within the metropolitan nations which may hold the United States responsible for their decline in national power and economic returns. In view of its over-all political and military interests, the United States cannot afford to neglect these repercussions of its African policies. For instance, if France is weakened by the policies which the United States pursues in Africa, the loss which the containment policy of the United States thus suffers must be weighed against the gain which accrues to it. More particularly, the gain from the success of a particular African policy may be more than offset by the resentment of France which will at the same time strengthen the Communist opposition to the Western orientation of French policy and decrease the domestic influence of a French government which has proved itself unable to prevent this decline in French power. In one word, the United States cannot pursue its policies with regard to Africa without regard to its general policies within the Western alliance, and it cannot afford to pursue policies in Africa, justified in terms of its interests in that region, which might jeopardize the position of, and its relations with, its allies in western Europe.

The other type of contradiction operates between the different policies pursued by the United States itself. American policy, inspired by the objective of military containment of the Soviet Union and by ideological opposition to communism, may well fail completely to gain the support of the native population or may gain it only accidentally and temporarily if this policy does not actually and patently meet native aspirations. The interests of the native population are not necessarily identical with those of the United States. Quite naturally, the native population thinks in terms of freedom from colonial rule and of social improvement and is indifferent to the issue of containment as such. Nor does it take sides in the struggle between East and West in view of the respective merits of competing ideologies. Whichever side can persuade it of its willingness and ability to satisfy its aspirations will gain its allegiance.

For instance, American interest in the smooth supply of uranium from South Africa may well be incompatible with a policy friendly to the native aspirations for independence and social justice, which may result in short-term disturbances. Similarly, American long-range policy of technical assistance for the sake of the economic and social betterment of the natives may be incompatible with the short-range interest in a maximum supply of strategically important raw materials. Confronted with such an incompatibility, the United States must either make a choice between its short-range economic and military interests and a long-range policy favoring political and social stability in the relations between whites and natives. Or else it must reconcile its own objectives with native aspirations and must present its objectives in terms immediately recognizable to the natives as meeting their aspirations.

Or, to give an example of a different—ideological—order, the domestic policies which the United States pursues toward the American Negroes cannot help bearing a direct influence upon the effectiveness of the ideological policies which it pursues toward the native population of Africa. To a lesser degree, American policies toward colored races elsewhere, especially in Asia, reflect upon the reception of its policies in Africa.

## III

It stands to reason that no policy which must steer its course between the multiple Scyllas and Charybdises of these dilemmas can live up to an ideal standard of perfection. It is bound to leave much to be desired and to be criticized for any number of different reasons. Granted the immense difficulties which beset such a policy, one can, however, ask the question as to what the actual character of this policy has been and whether it has been able to maximize its opportunities and to minimize its liabilities.

If one considers the over-all record of American policy with regard to Africa, two salient facts stand out. The United States has tended to opt in virtually all respects for the policies of the metropolitan powers, however modified and qualified in detail, and it has subordinated its long-range interest in the autonomous development of the native population to short-range considerations of strategy and expediency.

When confronted with the dilemma between its own interests in Africa and the inaccessibility of Africa save through the intermediary of metropolitan governments, the United States has, by and large, channeled the promotion of its interests through the policies of the metropolitan powers. The effect has been disadvantageous to the interests of the United States on two counts. First of all, the United States has been identified by the native population with the metropolitan powers, and its interests and policies have been considered, however mistakenly, as being a mere continuation and implementation of the interests and policies of the metropolitan powers. Furthermore, the very policies pursued by the metropolitan powers with the financial and technical support of the United States have frequently provided experimental proof for that assumption; for, inevitably, a government receiving financial and technical assistance without effective strings attached will use that assistance for its own purposes rather than those of the assisting nation.

It follows from this observation that the United States has generally solved the dilemma between its own interests in Africa and those of the metropolitan powers in favor of the latter. It has generally voted in the United Nations in favor of the position taken by the metropolitan nations, however halfhearted, hesitant, and qualified the support might have been at times. It is important to note, in view of the American long-term interest in winning the contest with communism for the allegiance of the native population, that the United States has hardly ever appeared as the champion of the interests of the native population against their white masters. At best, it has pursued a hands-off policy, while paying lip service to the ideals of independence and social justice, or has tried to mitigate the policies of the metropolitan nations. Of this attitude, the following statement by Charles A. Sprague, made in November, 1952, in the Ad Hoc Political Committee on the occasion of the Arab-Asian complaint against South Africa, is a characteristic sample:

We would leave enforcement to the lively conscience of the citizens of each country and to the power of the public opinion of the world. This course may not satisfy those eager to crack down on a member whom they regard as a delinquent. It will not satisfy those who, not recognizing the limitations of this organization, want the United Nations to do something about distressing situations. But in the long run, this course may accomplish far more than abrupt and direct action. Let us not impute evil purpose or lack of intelligence to the people of South Africa. Rather our attitude should be one of neighborly helpfulness in working out just solutions to the difficult problems they face in the field of race relations in their country.[1]

Finally, confronted by the dilemma between its own policies, the United States has invariably sacrificed its long-term interests either for short-term advantages or a position requiring a minimum of change and immediate risk. As elsewhere, it has subordinated the long-range objectives of technical assistance to short-term military advantages. Ports, airfields, and railroads are built primarily in view of immediate military contingencies rather than for the long-term improvement of the living conditions of the native population. The United States remains overtly indifferent to the policies of the Union of South Africa with regard to the native population, because for the production of fissionable material in required quantities the smooth flow of South African uranium is indispensable. Likewise, the United States has refrained from making any drastic changes in its policies vis-à-vis the American Negroes, changes which would appeal to the imagination of the native population of Africa, because the exigencies of domestic politics have made a less dramatic and more gradual policy appear to be more expedient.

## IV

Even if one keeps constantly in mind the handicaps under which American policy labors with regard to Africa, there can be little doubt that it could be greatly improved. We are here concerned not with improvements in detail or in technical efficiency, but with two fundamental changes in the attitude with which the United States has approached the problems of Africa. One concerns American policy toward its allies; the other, the realization of its leadership of the free world.

The fact that the United States is able by and large to influence developments in Africa only through the intermediary of the metropolitan governments poses a general problem of American foreign policy. For the dilemmas which face the United States here are only specific instances of a general dilemma which confronts the United States in its dealings with its allies.

1. *Department of State Bulletin*, December 1, 1952, p. 870.

This dilemma is the inevitable result of the inequality of power within a coalition of which the United States is the predominant member. Thus it is upon the United States that the responsibility rests to see to it that measures be taken best calculated to protect and promote its interests, which in their fundamental aspects happen also to be the interests of its allies. For that purpose and for that purpose alone, the United States extends political, military, and economic support to its allies. It is committed by the very logic of these relations of interest and power to make certain that its aid is used by the recipient countries with maximum efficiency for the furtherance of common ends.

However, we have not been able to fashion policies which would meet these requirements of interest and power. Instead, following the time-honored, yet obsolescent principle of nonintervention, we have pursued a policy of "no strings attached," interrupted from time to time by sudden and quickly subsiding bursts of interference. Yet this policy can be effective in promoting our interests in Africa only insofar as our notion of the policies to be pursued coincides with that of the metropolitan powers. In case of conflict the preferences of the metropolitan powers will prevail.

This policy, however favorable it has been to the metropolitan powers, has not gained us their support. They tend to resent our policy as meddling in their own affairs, if not as an attempt to undermine their position in the colonies, and it is the very vacillation and ineffectiveness of our policy which discredits it in the eyes of the metropolitan powers. Those very qualities, together with the emphasis on short-term military and economic policies, have discredited it also in the eyes of the native populations, who see in it primarily an attempt to bolster or take over colonial rule.

It is hard to see how our policy with regard to Africa can avoid these liabilities, which are inherent in the very situation with which we have to deal, without transcending that situation itself. These liabilities result from one great power attempting to pursue policies within a sphere which is controlled by other great powers and where great-power policy is discredited per se. The solution to this problem seems to lie in a concerted, large-scale effort to internationalize our policies with regard to

Africa. An international agency, within or outside the framework of the United Nations, ought to take responsibility for the policies which the United States and the metropolitan powers have been pursuing separately. Such an international organization would be composed not only of representatives of the United States and the metropolitan powers but also of representatives of non-European nations and of the native populations concerned. Only such an organization would seem to be capable of removing from American policy the stigma of great-power intervention which has in the past impaired its effectiveness via-à-vis the metropolitan powers and the native populations alike.

However, by thus merging its own policies toward Africa in the policies of an international organization, the United States risks losing its position as champion of freedom and social improvement in the ideological struggle with communism. This position is already seriously impaired by the policies of vacillation and expediency to which we have referred before. Hence, a reaffirmation of that leadership is needed in view of the traditional policies pursued by the United States as well as of the new ones recommended here.

Such reaffirmation must consist in deeds rather than in verbal declarations, and the deeds must be of a spectacular nature, carrying a symbolic significance. There has been a tendency on the part of the United States government to hush up incidents in which colored visitors to the United States have been subjected to discrimination; instead, the United States government ought to make the incident into a *cause célèbre*, demonstrating toward the world its own convictions and policies. The importance of such symbolic acts has been greatly underestimated by all Western governments, which, however enlightened some of their substantive policies have been, have not realized the depth of the longing for "freedom from contempt" by which all colored races are possessed, of the resentment at its continuation, and of the suspicion of the white man's intentions. The psychological ineffectiveness of otherwise beneficial policies which the United States has pursued in Africa and Asia results in no small measure from the neglect of these intangibles, which may well weigh decisively in the future world balance of power.

APPENDIX

# LIST OF PARTICIPANTS OF THE TWENTY-NINTH INSTITUTE OF THE NORMAN WAIT HARRIS MEMORIAL FOUNDATION

MARTIN J. ALIKER, Department of Anthropology, Northwestern University

DAVID E. APTER, Center for International Studies, Princeton University

ROBERT ARMSTRONG, 2820 Jessup Road, Cincinnati, Ohio

ARNE BARKHUUS, M.D., Department of Trusteeship and Information from Non-self-governing Territories, United Nations

WILLIAM BASCOM, Department of Anthropology, Northwestern University

ROBERT D. BAUM, American University

WILLIAM O. BROWN, Program of African Studies, Boston University

GEORGE W. CARPENTER, Africa Committee, Division of Foreign Missions, National Council of Churches

JAMES B. CHRISTENSEN, Department of Sociology and Anthropology, Wayne University

ROBERT I. CRANE, Department of History, University of Chicago

PIERRE DEVISÉ, Consulate-General of Belgium, Chicago

ST. CLAIR DRAKE, Roosevelt University, Chicago

ELLSWORTH FARIS, Department of Sociology, University of Chicago

CORA FELD, Washington, D.C.

NICHOLAS FELD, United States Department of State

HERMAN FINER, Department of Political Science, University of Chicago

E. FRANKLIN FRAZIER, Department of Sociology, Howard University

ROBERT GRAY, M.D., Marshall, Minnesota

RIGHT HONORABLE LORD HAILEY, Royal Institute of International Affairs, London

MELVILLE J. HERSKOVITS, Department of Anthropology, Northwestern University

ELIZABETH HOYT, Department of Economics, Iowa State College

RICHARD HUGHES, Robins Ridge Farm, West Hill Road, New Hartford, Connecticut

W. SENTEZA KAJUBI, Department of Geography, University of Chicago

FRANK LAMACCHIA, United States Department of State

GASTON LEDUC, University of Paris

CARLOS MEYERS, Department of Trusteeship and Information from Non-self-governing Territories, United Nations

JOHN MITCHELL, Committee on International Relations, University of Chicago

EDUARDO MONDLANE, Department of Sociology, Northwestern University

HANS J. MORGENTHAU, Center for the Study of American Foreign Policy, University of Chicago

G. M. MORRIS, Public Administration Service

ERNEST P. MOSES, Department of Sociology, University of Chicago

AFRICA IN THE MODERN WORLD

Edwin S. Munger, Institute for Current World Affairs
John A. Noon, United States Information Service
Pius Okigbo, Department of Economics, Northwestern University
Sebastian Opon, Department of Political Science, University of Chicago
Leslie Paffrath, Carnegie Endowment for International Peace
Alan Pifer, Carnegie Corporation of New York
Darrell Randall, Committee on Planning, University of Chicago
Fred W. Riggs, Public Administration Clearing House
J. Fred Rippy, Department of History, University of Chicago
Kenneth Robinson, Nuffield College, Oxford University
Virginia Robinson, United States Foreign Operations Administration
Emory Ross, Phelps-Stokes Fund
Simon Rottenberg, Department of Economics, University of Chicago
Harry R. Rudin, Department of History, Yale University
Leonard H. Samuels, University of the Witwatersrand
William B. Schwab, Haverford College
W. Lloyd Shirer, Tamale, Gold Coast
Ruth C. Sloan, United States Information Service
Burton Stein, Department of History, University of Chicago
Calvin W. Stillman, The College, University of Chicago
Frank Untermyer, Roosevelt University, Chicago
Kimani Waiyiki, Roosevelt University, Chicago
Derwent Whittlesey, Department of Geography, Harvard University
R. Richard Wohl, The College and the Division of the Social Sciences, University of Chicago
Robert J. Wolfson, Committee on Economic Development and Cultural Change, University of Chicago
Quincy Wright, Department of Political Science, University of Chicago
Roland Young, Department of Government, Northwestern University

INDEX

# INDEX

# INDEX

Cotton, 42, 51, 238

Councils of *notables*, French West Africa, 149

Cultural differences and government problems, 7, 122, 205

Cultural equivalent of racism, 290

Cultural self-determination, 9, 11

Culture, selective adoption of, 9, 11, 67, 208, 277-82

Culture bar, 7, 223, 283

Culture contact, problems of, 119, 177, 193, 223, 238, 244, 262, 273-74, 277-78

Customs, difficulty in adapting, 61, 67, 79-80, 205, 207

Cyrenaica, 205, 207

Dagomba, the, 118

Dahomey, 148

Dakar, 58, 143, 145, 155, 318

Dallo, M. Yacine, 174

Davison, R. B., 134 n.

Delamere, Lord, 199 n., 200 n.

Delavignette, Robert, 81 n., 143 n.

Deleeuw, E., 73 n.

Delinquency, juvenile, 80

Delval, J., 171

Deschamps, H., 157 n.

Detribalization, effects of, 76, 122

Deutsch, Karl, 155 n.

Development plans, 57, 110, 153, 206, 211, 213

Devize, M., 172 n.

Diagne, M. Blaise, 144, 145, 150

Diamonds, 35, 46, 247; industrial, 10, 43, 46, 151, 217, 318

Diouf, Galandou, 150

Discrimination in services, 224, 244, 283

Disorders, 175, 277-78, 306, 311; *see also* Mau Mau

Division of labor, 79, 83

Dodd, E. E., 182 n.

Doke, Clement M., 89 n.

Dollar earnings of colonies, 297, 308

Dutch settlement, 15

East Africa, 49-52, 182-203

East African High Commission, 195-96

East African Highlands; *see* "White Highlands"

*East African Standard*, 290

East African Union, 284

East-West conflict, 29, 296-97, 299, 317

Economic Co-operation Administration (ECA) aid, use of, 110

Economic development, 11, 12, 36, 44, 57, 98, 107, 110-11, 151-53, 216, 251; and cultural change, 55, 60, 66, 97-98, 134, 156, 262

Economic growth, 112; in Union of South Africa, 245, 249, 251-52, 255-56, 258-64

Education, 12, 58, 89 n., 100-102, 212, 241, 271, 288; barriers to, 58-59, 241, 288; in Belgian Congo, 220, 221, 224, 231, 233; culture conflicts in, 64, 68, 88-89, 93-95, 187, 271-76; drive for, 270-76; and elite, 57-59, 64; in French Africa, 58, 153-54, 156; in Gold Coast, 58-59, 154; higher, 59, 93, 305; issues in, 89, 101, 273-74, 275-76; in Portuguese Africa, 240, 242, 275-76, 288

Egypt, 4, 9, 16, 298, 311

Electric power, 33, 36, 152, 227, 249, 261

Elgon, Mount, 50

Eliot, Sir Charles, 199 n.

Elites: African, 57, 187; European, 62, 246

Emigration, European, 17, 24

Enstoolment, 117

Entente Cordiale; *see* Anglo-French Entente Cordiale

Entrepreneurship, 102, 104; by governments, 107, 249-50

Eritrea, 211-14, 310

*Essor du Congo*, 285

Ethiopia, 4, 50-51, 211-14, 215, 298

Eurafrica, 310

Europeans: 5, 192, 200, 246-47, 248-49, 269, 297, 299; attitudes of, 285-86, 290-94, 305; domination by, 95, 119, 125

*Évolués*, 223, 235

Ewe, the, 117 n.

Exchange economy, 60, 247

Exploration, 14, 19

Family, African, 71, 76-78, 81-83

Fang, the, 61, 64, 66, 68

Far Eastern trade, 14-16

Far West Rand, 262

Faris, Ellsworth, 90 n., 92 n.

Farmers and Planters Association, Kenya, 199

Federation of Colonists (Fédacol), 295

Federation of Ethiopia and Eritrea, 213-14

Federation of French West Africa, 157

Federation of Rhodesias and Nyasaland, 305

Fezzan, 205, 207

# INDEX

# INDEX

# INDEX

Toro, 186

Toynbee, Arnold J., 70

Trade-unions, 88, 256–57, 312

Trans-Volta Togoland, Territorial Council, 120 n.

Transportation, 52–53, 261

Tree crops, 41, 50

Treichville, 175

Tribalism, as adjustive mechanism, 138, 186, 198

Tripolitania, 205, 207

Tsetse fly, 32, 50

Tsonga, the, 234

Tubman, President W. V. S., 268, 310

Tungsten, 47

Tunisia, 28, 298, 300

Twi language, 276

U.D.S.R., in French West Africa, 175–76

Uganda: capital formation in, 111; cotton income of, 109; political development in, 184–89; race relations in, 284

Union pour la Défense des Intérêts de la Haute Volta, 178

Union of South Africa: Africans in, 8, 49, 74, 253, 268; and Arab-Asian bloc, 322; Asians in, 8; and British Commonwealth, 303–4; capital formation in, 111, 247; coal industry in, 261; communism in, 296, 312; delegation of, to United Nations, 301; economics of, 245–64; import financing in, 251; income-creating industry in, 250–51; and India and Pakistan, 302; industrialization of, 8, 249–50; labor in, 254–55; national income of, 251–53, 255–56; Nationalist party in, 303, 305; native reserves of, 48, 84–85, 254; output of, 249; political stability of, 318; population of, 246, 253–54; racial tensions in, 4, 8, 52, 284, 298; and the Rhodesias, 304; rural population of, 74, 248, 253; service industries in, 249; tariffs in, 249; transportation in, 261; uranium in, 35; urbanization of, 253–55; wage board in, 257; wages in, 253–58

United Nations, 28, 223, 298–301, 308; Ad Hoc Committee on South West Africa, 302; Ad Hoc Political Committee, 322; bloc politics of, 298–300; Charter, 27, 29, 96; Committee on Information from Non-self-governing Territories, 301, 308; ECOSOC, 207; General Assembly, 204, 295, 298–99, 301;

Information Center, 311; Soviet uses of, 312–13; technical aid, 204–6, 310–11; Trusteeship Council, 28, 210, 229, 291, 307; UNESCO, 311; and United States policy, 325

United States: aid by, 12, 110, 112, 206 n., 227–28, 310; and colonial rule, 319; dependence of, for metals, 26; interests of, 317; leadership of, 320, 325; and metropolitan governments, 319, 321, 322; military interests of, 206 n., 214, 310, 314, 317–18, 323; policy of, 313–25; policy dilemmas of, 318–19; policy internationalization of, 324–25; policy of nonintervention of, 322–24; and popular interest in Africa, 3, 10, 315–16; power relations of, 324; and race relations and foreign policy, 321, 323, 325; and South Africa, 320–21, 323; and United Nations bloc politics, 300

University education, 229, 271, 274, 276, 283

Upper Volta, territory of, 147 n.

Uranium, 10, 25, 35, 36, 43, 46, 217, 262, 318, 320

Urbanization, 56, 72–73, 79, 87, 155, 253–55, 281; and family, 75, 78, 254 n.; and race relations, 56, 75.

Values: and conflicts, 127; selection of, 270

VaMwila, the, 280

Van Royan, William, 34

Vanadium, 26, 35, 43

Vegetation, 33

Veld, 47

Vernacular issue in education, 89, 276

Villages, and labor drain, 74–75

Villard, André, 150

Violence, and frustration, 28

Volta River aluminum scheme, 134

Wages, 203, 253, 258, 283

Wallis, C. A. G., 186

Ward, W. F., 116 n.

Water power, potential of, 33, 36

Weber, M., 137 n.

Weller, A. L. H., 177 n.

Wenchi, 132

Wenchi Constituency, 132

Wenchihene, 132

West of Africa, 39–42

Westerman, Diedrich, 91

Western world: defense of, 10, 25–26, 29,

[ 341 ]